Furniture
Fix and Finish
Guide

THOMAS H. JONES

Reston Publishing Company, Inc.
A Prentice-Hall Company
Reston, Virginia

Library of Congress Cataloging in Publication Data

Jones, Thomas H
    Furniture fix and finish guide.

    Includes index.
    1. Furniture—Repairing. 2. Furniture finishing. I. Title.
TT199.J665   684.1'044   79–23642
ISBN 0–8359–2227–8

© 1980 by
Reston Publishing Company, Inc.
A Prentice-Hall Company
Reston, Virginia 22090

10 9 8 7 6 5 4 3 2 1

Printed in the United States of America.

To B. E. J.

Contents

Chapter 6:   Basic Upholstery   112

Chapter 7:   Other Repairs   133

Chapter 8:   The Original Finish—Rejuvenate or Remove?   157

Chapter 9:   Spot Surface Repairs and Spot Refinishing   176

Chapter 10:   Clear Finishes   193

Preface

In this book you will find the information you need to repair and refinish furniture in a competent and professional manner. The book has not been written for the professional refinisher, however, but for the home craftsman. Valuable information is also included on restoring collectible and antique furniture.

This book is not a compendium of all known professional methods and tricks, nor does it include shortcut refinishing and repair hints of the kind often found in magazines. The methods given in this book are straightforward and widely used. The materials and supplies described and used are readily available, mostly by mail order.

Special thanks are due to my wife Carolyn for her invaluable help in planning, illustrating and writing the book, and to William Roberts of Smith Supply, Inc., Ardmore, Pa. for his help in sorting out and illustrating period hardware.

T. H. J.

Getting Started

1

Why get involved in repairing, restoring, and refinishing furniture? There are as many reasons as there are people doing it. For some people, it is a very satisfying hobby providing a real sense of accomplishment and pride. For others, it's the challenge of restoring an antique to as near its original condition as is possible.

Sometimes it's sentiment—"That chair belonged to my great-aunt Minnie, or that desk was my grandfather's." You would not want to part with them, but if they are going to come down out of the attic, some work has to be done, and you are going to do it yourself!

It is not true that they don't make furniture the way they used to. They still do, but the "theys" are few and far between—a few companies and individual craftsmen. Prices for quality wood furniture are exorbitant. What you see in most stores is something else—plastic laminate tops, printed grain, injection molded plastic "carved wood" trim.

Furniture around the house loosens in the joints and breaks. Finishes become marred and scratched and upholstery fades and wears through. The costs of having the repairs and reupholstery done professionally are prohibitive. And it is almost impossible to find places where simple repairs can be done, let alone at a reasonable cost.

Auctions, second-hand and thrift stores, Salvation Army stores, farm sales, garage sales, country antique dealers are loaded with unusual collectible and antique furniture. The reasonably priced pieces require repair, restoration, and refinishing. If you are willing to

FIGURE
1-1

The furniture above was repaired or refinished using techniques described in this book.

FIGURE
1-2

Attics, flea markets, second-hand furniture shops, antique dealers, and garage sales are sources of furniture in need of restoration.

2

spend the time and effort, you can acquire some very fine furniture inexpensively, perhaps not valuable antiques, but fine furniture, nevertheless.

The best do-it-yourself reasons are to save money and get the job done.

Valuable Antiques

Should an amateur attempt to restore a valuable antique? That really depends on how much confidence you have in your own ability and what you mean by valuable. The methods shown in this book are used by professional restorers and refinishers. If you have stumbled on something really valuable while scrounging around flea markets, auctions, and garage sales, or think you have, get it appraised first.

Where do you go for honest appraisals? Your best bet is to look in the Yellow Pages under Antique Dealers and pick one who offers to do appraisals. He will charge you so be sure to find out the fee in advance. You should also get his appraisal in writing. This will make the appraisal more thoughtful. An appraisal, however, is only one man's opinion of worth, and no antique dealer can be expected to know everything about everything. For example, there are few antique dealers competent to appraise antique clocks.

The question of whether you should attempt a repair on something valuable hasn't really been answered yet. Did you gulp when hearing the value? Did the amount stimulate your greed? If so, let a professional do it, but first, get a second appraisal from another appraiser to make sure. Otherwise, if you are careful and cautious, why not do it yourself? But don't start out restoring and refinishing valuable antiques, practice first.

Fakes

One cannot talk about valuable antiques without getting into the subject of fakes. You have a better chance of finding a fake than the real thing. For example, how many pine dry sinks do you think could possibly have existed in colonial days? And how many of them could possibly have survived and not been converted to firewood when worn out or replaced? Yet you can find genuine Early American dry sinks all over. You figure it out. These same questions must be asked of more sophisticated furniture, American and imported. There just wasn't that much of it around originally for it to be turning up all the time.

A reproduction is a copy, and the maker admits it is a copy. It is sold as a reproduction. It might have been made in 1870, 100 years after the original was made in 1770. Today, many would consider such a piece a 100-year-old antique, even if it started out only as a copy. Today, it could be passing as a 200-year-old original. Someone cynically said "the first time a reproduction is sold it is a copy, the second time it changes hands it has become original."

If the price appears to be too good to be true, it probably is.

So, when you buy something to restore, pay what the piece is worth to you, be careful about paying a high price for something because it is claimed to be a valuable antique. If it were, the dealer would have it restored himself before offering it for sale. Of course, the dealer might not know!

Repair and Restore

These words don't mean the same thing. In furniture work, it is basically a question of approach and attitude. *Repair* is returning a piece of furniture to functional usefulness—gluing a broken rung, flattening a warped table top, patching a gouge, painting over a marred or unsightly varnish finish. *Restoring* is working over a piece of furniture to return it to its original appearance and function. Restoration can include all kinds of repairs but with more attention to correctness of materials and methods.

In the area of refinishing, finishes can be repaired, cleaned, or restored, without being removed. Sometimes a finish need only be partially removed, then repaired. Finally, a finish may be removed completely and replaced by the same or a different finish.

Tools

You cannot repair and refinish furniture with the contents of a tool drawer in the kitchen plus some string. On the other hand, you don't need a woodworking shop full of tools either. If you don't have a shop, buy tools as you need them. In each section of the book special tools required for the work are listed.

There are four hand power tools that you should have, a pad sander, belt sander, router, and variable-speed drill (see Fig. 1–3).

Pad Sander. Forget hand sanding except for sanding where you cannot use a power sander. Hand sanding on large surfaces is wasted time. All pad or orbital sanders are not alike. Those that have a large pad displacement leave scratches and must be used with the grain in finish sanding. The pad of a small displacement sander moves 1/10" or less, and the scratches are invisible. You can also move the sander in any direction without watching grain direction to minimize scratches. Buy a good sander.

Belt Sander. A portable belt sander will greatly speed your sanding operations. So much so, that once you have one, you will wonder how you ever got along without it. Buy one fitted with a dust collector bag.

**FIGURE
1-3**

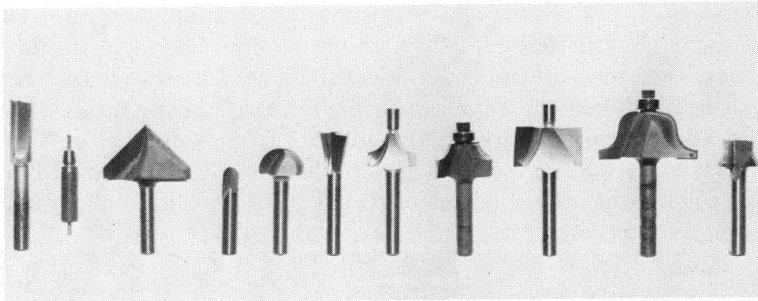

**Several indispensable power hand tools: pad sander, router, belt sander.
Shown below are some of the many router bits useful in furniture repair.**

Router.   A router is as close as you can come to a one-tool
furniture-making shop. With accessories, you can do almost anything
you can do with a table or radial arm saw, perhaps not as fast, but
with a lot less tool cost.

Variable-Speed Drill.   There are many occasions when you
want the control afforded by a slow turning drill (when reaming out
an old dowel hole to get rid of the glue, for example). Ability to run
in reverse is also nice, but not that useful, except for removing screws
when you have a lot of them.

Brushes

You can't do top-quality refinishing with poor-quality brushes. This
is standard advice, but as good-quality bristle brushes cost more and
more money, we are all tempted to get by with less than the best. To-

**FIGURE
1-4**

Foam brushes.

day, there is a cheap way out—"brushes" made of plastic foam (see Fig. 1-4). For varnishing and enameling, I have found them superior to the best bristle brushes. They are throwaways. Use them and toss them. The cost of a foam brush is just about equivalent to the solvent and brush cleaner cost for cleaning the same size bristle brush.

They are not usually recommended for lacquer and shellac. That is because lacquer solvent and alcohol dissolves the side seams. You can still use them for these materials but you will be discarding them faster.

Material and Supply Sources

Home centers, paint stores, hardware stores, and lumber yards do not carry all the materials and supplies you will need for furniture repairing, restoring, and refinishing. Fortunately, there are mail-order sources.

The first step is to get yourself some catalogs. Then you will really begin to get an idea of all that is available to you. See the Appendix for a listing of some recommended sources.

Work—and Results

There is a lot of hard work involved in repairing, restoring, and refinishing furniture, but if you go about it right, it can be well worth the effort. The furniture in Figure 1-2 was purchased at garage sales, thrift stores, and so forth for use as illustrations in this book. You can get the same results following the methods given.

Furniture Styles

2

There is no need to identify the historical style of a piece of furniture to make a simple one-for-one repair or to refinish it. You couldn't care less either if you were cutting the piece down or remodeling it to use for some purpose not originally intended, or to give it a contemporary style or finish. You can also greatly admire a piece of furniture without becoming an expert on the significance of its fine design points.

But when you pick up a piece of furniture at a flea market or garage sale and wonder what it originally looked like under all that paint, and what kind of hardware it might have had, and what the obviously missing parts looked like, then you have to know something about furniture periods and styles.

Furniture styles come and go, and come and go. An authentic American Colonial table might have been made in 1760, 1899, or 1977. The style lives on. An antique American Colonial table could only have been made during the years between 1650 and 1750 because that was roughly the American Colonial *period*. An American Colonial table made in 1870 may be an antique now, but it was merely a reproduction when new, just the same as any brand new American Colonial furniture today is. A Victorian table of 1880 is certainly an antique because it was made during its period. But let's not quibble about the definition of an antique.

Dates of furniture periods are indefinite. There was never a sudden change in the style of furniture. Then as now many people liked the old styles and were not impressed with the new—at least not until after the style-trenders pointed the way. Hardware—knobs, handles, and other brasses—particularly were used into a new period on *new period* furniture. Often the brasses were worth more than the wood and were salvaged to be used on the new replacement.

No furniture design developed on a desert island. What French furniture designers were doing influenced English and American designs, and vice versa. Designers copied (stole) from each other. Cabinetmakers could eyeball a piece and go back to the shop and fill an order for the same thing.

2-1 FURNITURE PERIODS

Seventeenth Century English (1603-1688)

The age of oak (see Fig. 2-1). There are three closely related styles here—Jacobean (James I and Charles I, 1603-1649), Cromwelian (1649-1660), and Restoration (Charles II and James II, 1660-1688); all are sometimes grouped together as Jacobean.

The straight-lined furniture has a stiff, ungainly, heavy, pretentious, uncomfortable look to it. The most attractive pieces have been tables—gate-leg tables, small tavern tables, and trestle tables. American Colonial furniture of the New England variety is based primarily on Jacobean furniture.

Furniture of this period was strongly built, with pinned mortise and tenon joints. Lines of furniture were straight and rectangular. Legs and stretchers were deeply turned, and some turnings were quite elaborate. Framed construction was used—rails and posts mortised and tenoned together. Large surfaces were generally paneled and panels were often decorated with low-relief carving.

Oak was the predominant wood, but pine, walnut, pear, chestnut were also used. Veneer was seldom used, and there was no marquetry. Inlay was used in floral panels; there were some intricate flowing patterns.

Turnings, pear, ball, bulb on legs, stretchers and spindles were very heavy and severe. Spiral turnings were used late in the period.

Applied ornament included rosettes, geometric mouldings, diamond panels.

Carving was done in well-moulded relief. Scratch carving with simple vigorous outlines was often used early in the period. Carving became plain, severe, and simple during Cromwellian years, then elaborately carved large areas became popular during the Restoration.

William and Mary (1688-1702)

The age of walnut (see Fig. 2-2). Pretentious furniture became comfortably Dutch, scaled more to a house than a palace, and elegantly

**FIGURE
2-1**

Twist-leg Table
Charles II Period

Gate-leg Table
Commonwealth Period

Typical Oak Chair
17th Century

Oak Draw Table
Ends draw out to almost double table length

Seventeenth Century English Furniture
(1603–1688):
• Straight lines
• Heavy, pretentious, uncomfortable-looking
• Principal wood—oak
• Heavy-handed turnings
• Principal decoration—carving

Seventeenth Century English Furniture (1603-1688).

**FIGURE
2-2**

Cabinet with
Double Hood

Cabinet on Stand
Top opens down

Secretary

Upholstered Chair

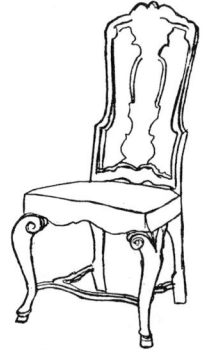

Side Chair

William and Mary Furniture
(1688-1702):
- Trumpet, spiral legs
- Single or double hoods
- Crossed stretchers
- Simple, clean lines
- Principal wood—walnut
- Extensive inlay and marquetry

Table with Flat Arches
and Pendant Drops

William and Mary Furniture (1688-1702).

designed, constructed, and finished. Lines were simple and clean. The overall shape remained rectangular. Predominant features were trumpet-turned legs with crossed stretchers under almost eveything.

Jacobean frame-and-panel construction was replaced with wide boards and solid unbroken surfaces. Cabinets began having single or double hoods rather than flat pedimented tops as before. Aprons were shaped with reverse curves or flat arches, or repeated the hood shape. Casework joints were pinned mortise and tenon, or dovetail. Trumpet-turned legs were doweled into the carcass frame; ball or bun feet were doweled up through the flat stretchers into the legs.

Walnut was the first and foremost wood; but many other woods were used if the piece or part of the piece was to be painted, gilded, or veneered. Veneers used included walnut, plain or oystered, on oak or pine core stock.

Both inlay and marquetry were used extensively. Inlay woods included sycamore, laburnum, box, holly, apple, and walnut. Marquetry was elaborate, mostly floral, with birds and animals worked into the designs. Turnings were limited for the most part to legs and feet. Applied ornament was seldom used. Carvings were elaborate, both high relief and in the round.

Queen Anne (1702-1745)

The style period extended beyond the 12-year reign of Queen Anne well into the reign of George II. Queen Anne furniture was comfortable and graceful, still very Dutch (see Fig. 2–3). The cabriole leg with pad or club foot, cyma curves on aprons and elsewhere, bonnet and broken-pediment tops predominated. Stretchers and underbracing were conspicuously absent. Seats on chairs were horseshoe shaped, backs were spooned.

Construction featured cabriole legs attached to frames with pinned mortise and tenon joints. Chair back top rails were mortise and tenoned to the tops of the posts, doweled if the posts were turned (rare). Splats were tenoned into top back rails and seat frames. Chairs were now upholstered—velvet, brocade, needlepoint. In casework, rails were often dovetailed into the end boards, which were now solid. Stiles were also dovetailed between rails.

Walnut continued to be the predominant wood, but there was some use of mahogany after 1720. Oak, pine, lime, chestnut, pear, beech, and elm were also used for pieces painted or gilded. Walnut veneer was sometimes used on lesser wood. Inlay and marquetry were not widely used.

Turnings were not much used except for side stretchers and Windsor chairs. Turnings, when used, were subdued, not ornate. Applied ornament was seldom used. Carving was extensive. Furniture forms were embellished and elaborated. The shell was the popular motif.

**FIGURE
2-3**

Queen Anne Furniture
(1702-1745):
- Cabriole legs
- No stretchers
- Principal wood—walnut
- Turnings used seldom

Early Queen Anne Highboy with Apron
in William and Mary Style

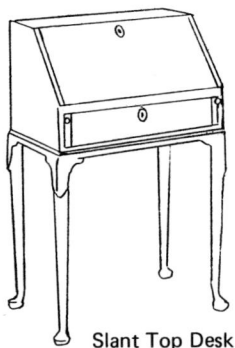

Slant Top Desk

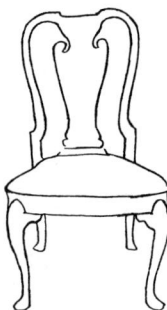

Side Chair

Wing Chair

Tea Table

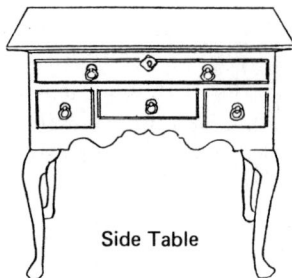

Side Table

Queen Anne Furniture (1702-1745).

The next four styles can be thought of as the Age of Mahogany.

Chippendale (1749-1779)

Previous styles were named after monarchs, but this one was named after a furniture designer, Thomas Chippendale. Chippendale adapted from Queen Anne, French, and Gothic styles, and developed a Chinese style. He was also a master woodcarver and cabinetmaker.

In Chippendale designs, cabriole legs—richly carved, with ball and claw feet—stayed, but it was back to straight lines otherwise (see Fig. 2-4). Late in the period, legs went straight, too, but were curved or moulded on outside faces.

Pieces were sturdy and ponderous. Proportions sometimes were odd. Cabriole legs had no stretchers, and straight legs had squared, fretsawed, or carved stretchers. Construction practices were not significantly changed from those followed during the Queen Anne period.

Mahogany was the primary wood, followed by rosewood, amboyna, and walnut. Pine was used for frames and pieces to be gilded. Veneers, inlay, marquetry, and applied ornament were seldom used.

Turnings were limited to bedposts and pedestal columns.

Carvings were a primary decorative feature. They ranged from delicate to ornate, plus pierced fretwork.

Hepplewhite (1770-1790)

Little is known about George Hepplewhite except that he was a cabinetmaker. He is recognized as one of the four greatest furniture designers. Characteristics of Hepplewhite furniture include slender tapered legs without feet, or slender straight legs with tapered spade feet (see Fig. 2-5). French bracket feet were used on cabinets and chests. Stretchers on chair legs were rectangular in cross section. Backs of chairs were shield and oval shaped. Many pieces were veneered and some painted ornament was used.

Mahogany was used for anything to be carved. Carving was elaborate and delicate. Satinwood, beech, pine, sycamore, and other woods were used if a piece were to be painted or gilded. Mahogany, amboyna, and many other veneers were used. Some carvings were applied.

Inlay was used extensively for decoration, using amboyna, thuya, sycamore, harewood, holly,, tulip, rosewood, and ebony.

Marquetry was confined principally to French-style pieces.

Turnings appeared on bed posts and pedestals, often fluted.

Adam Brothers (1762-1792)

There were four Adam brothers, all architects; Robert and James also designed furniture. They thought about furniture as interior

**FIGURE
2-4**

Bookcase

"Chinese" Chair

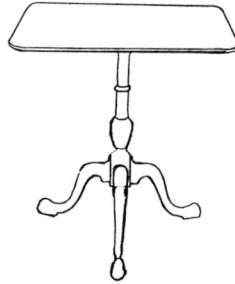

Square Tilt-top Table

Pierced Splat Chair

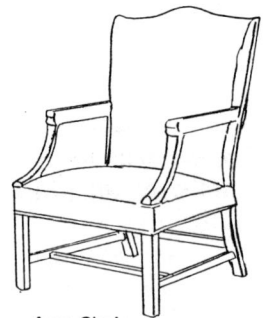

Ladder-back Chair

Chippendale Furniture
(1749-1779)
• Cabriole legs combined with straight legs
• Sturdy, ponderous construction
• Straight legs with stretchers late in period
• Principal wood—mahogany
• Chief decoration—carving

Arm Chair

Chippendale Furniture (1749-1779).

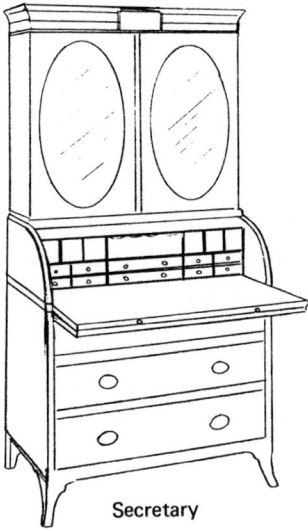

**FIGURE
2-5**

Hepplewhite Furniture
(1770-1790):
- Slender straight or tapered legs
- Copied French styles
- Shield or oval backs on chairs
- Principal wood—mahogany
- Extensive decoration

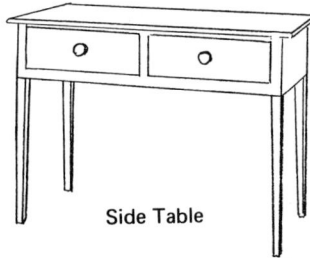

Secretary

Side Table

Oval Back Chair

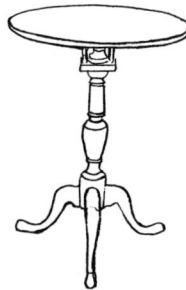

Tilting Table

Shield Back Chair

French Style
Ladies' Writing Cabinet

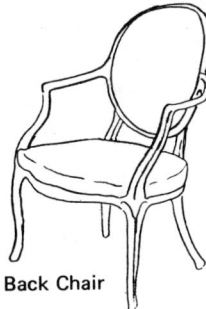

Oval Back Chair

Hepplewhite Furniture (1770-1790).

decorators would—furniture was just another architectural detail. Many of their designs were impractical and had to be modified by more practical and competent furniture makers.

They simplified the structure of their furniture by using straight lines instead of curved lines (see Fig. 2-6). Ornamentation reflected a classical influence. Furniture had a formal appearance with good proportions.

Mahogany was the wood most commonly used, followed in popularity by satinwood, sycamore, amboyna, and tulip (natural or stained). Pine and lime were used if the piece was to be gilded. Many varieties of veneers were employed, often in matched-grain panels; inlay and marquetry were done with ebony, holly, satinwood, and other woods. Turnings were seldom used. Applied ornament included plaster composition filigree work. Small oil paintings in mouldings were also used. Carving was extensively used for ornamentation.

**FIGURE
2-6**

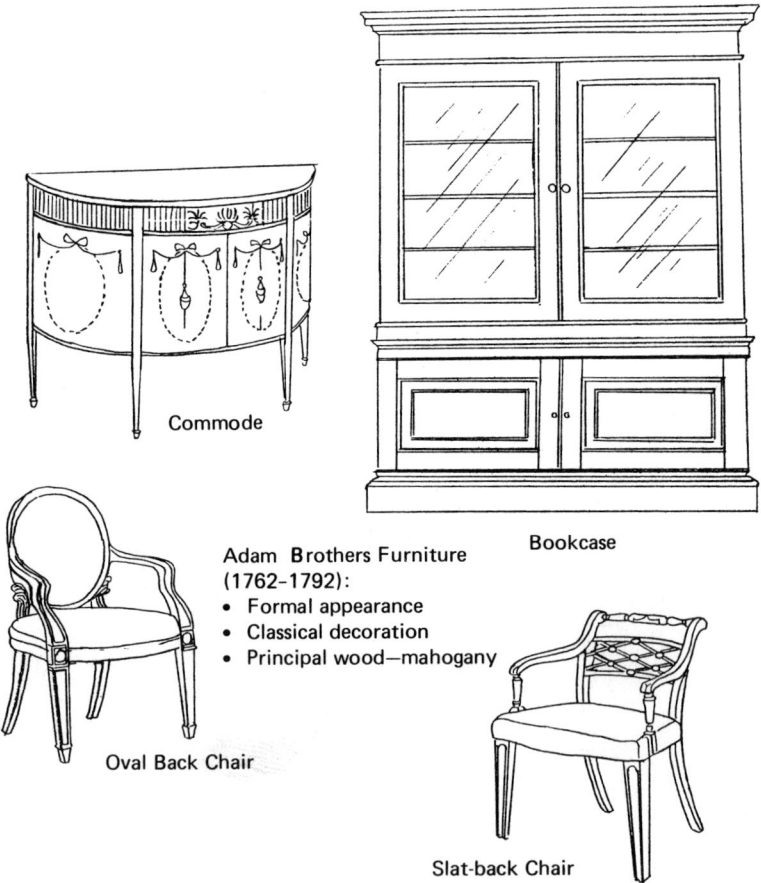

Commode

Bookcase

Adam Brothers Furniture
(1762-1792):
- Formal appearance
- Classical decoration
- Principal wood—mahogany

Oval Back Chair

Slat-back Chair

Adam Brothers Furniture (1762-1792).

Sheraton (1790-1806)

Thomas Sheraton was the last of the great English cabinetmakers and designers. He was born poor, lived poor, and died poor. The design and proportions of his furniture were superior to that of all his predecessors. Chairs had rectangular backs. Turned tapered legs were used on most furniture, but some chairs had tapered-squared legs. Turned chair legs when used were without stretchers. Straight lines were predominant features of his furniture (see Fig. 2-7).

Construction was very sturdy in spite of the light appearance of chairs and other legged pieces. Well-designed chair splats were a lot stronger than they looked because of adequate thickness.

Mahogany was used for all furniture to be carved. Other woods included beech and sycamore. Satinwood was used if the piece was to have painted decoration. Rosewood was used occasionally for mouldings.

Inlay and marquetry were both extensively used, and were the preferred decoration over painting. Woods used included tulip, ebony, holly, rosewood, and kingwood. Veneers often used were mahogany, thuya, satinwood, amboyna, and kingwood. Pine was often employed for core stock.

Legs, posts, and pedestals were elaborately turned, fluted, and reeded. Carvings were usually low relief, some carvings were applied.

Sheraton Furniture (1790-1806):
- Superior designs and proportions
- Predominantly straight lines
- Principal wood—mahogany
- Extensive inlay and marquetry

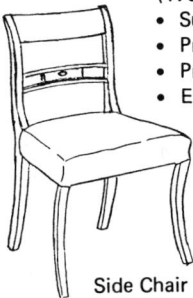

Side Chair

Sofa Table

Secretary Desk

Sheraton Furniture (1790-1806).

FIGURE 2-7

English Regency (1793-1820)

As it is becoming apparent, periods and styles overlap. By the early nineteenth century the influence of the four great cabinetmakers was in decline. Taste was turning to archaeological motifs and was influenced greatly by French Directoire and Empire styles running in the same direction. All influenced the American Federal style.

Bookcases resembled temple facades. Case furniture became very architectural in appearance. Applied and inlaid metal was the predominant ornamentation with Roman and Egyptian motifs (see Fig. 2-8).

Louis XIV (1643-1715)

Louis XIV, the Sun King, had a taste for grandeur. He was a patron of the arts and assembled an army of artisans in the Louvre—and kept them busy. Louis XIV furniture was solid, pompous, cumbersome, and formal (see Fig. 2-9). Shape was basically straight lined, but some curved lines were used. Ornament was applied overabundantly. Legs were at first square and heavily carved, then cabriole. Crossed stretchers were used.

**FIGURE
2-8**

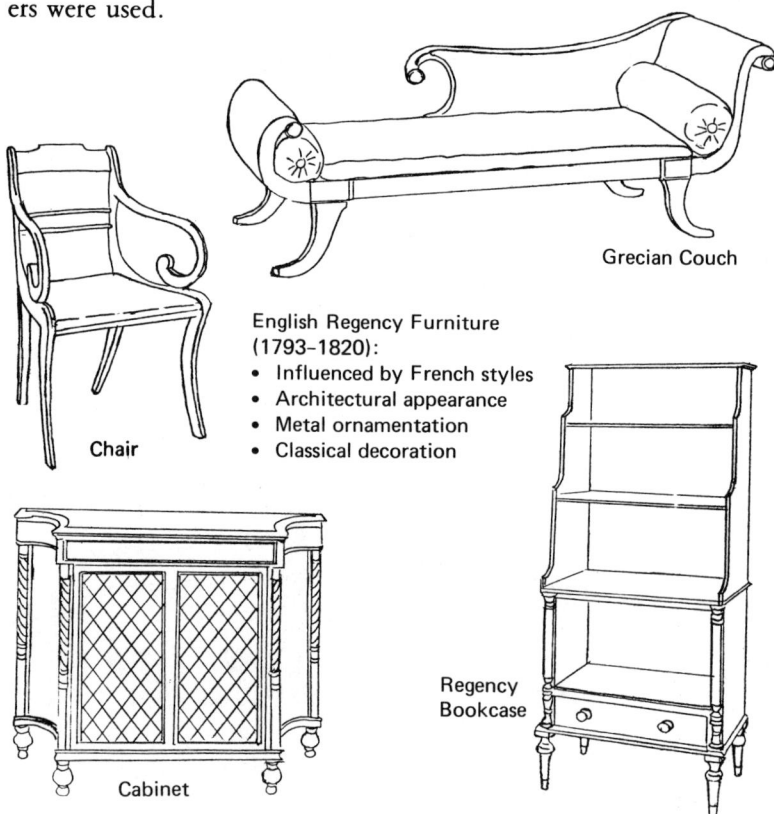

Grecian Couch

English Regency Furniture
(1793-1820):
• Influenced by French styles
• Architectural appearance
• Metal ornamentation
• Classical decoration

Chair

Regency
Bookcase

Cabinet

English Regency Furniture (1793-1820).

FIGURE
2-9

Louis XV Armoire
(Provincial)

Louis XVI
Cylinder Desk

FRENCH STYLED FURNITURE

Louis XIV (1643-1715):
- Solid, pompous
- Squared shape
- Overabundant ornamentation
- Principal decoration—carving
- Mostly painted or gilded

Louis XV (1715-1774):
- All curves, no straight lines
- Ultimate in decorated furniture
- Principal woods—walnut and mahogany

Louis XVI (1774-1793):
- Return to straight lines
- Simpler ornamentation
- Principal wood—mahogany

Louis XV Desk

Louis XVI Arm Chair

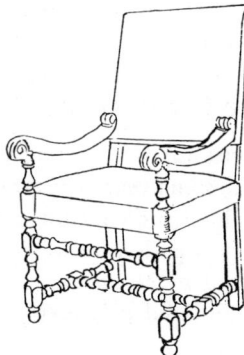

Louis XIV Arm Chair

Louis XV Chiffonnier

French Furniture: Louis XIV (1643-1715), Louis XV (1715-1774), and Louis XVI (1774-1793).

Woods included oak, walnut, and fruitwoods. Carving was the foremost method of decoration. Pieces were painted and gilded, often in combination. Colors used included dark green and blue, and crimson; later in the period, brighter colors became popular.

Louis XV (1715-1774)

Louis XV, the great-grandson of Louis XIV, also kept the artisans busy. Louis XV furniture was all curves—straight lines and right angles were avoided at all costs (see Fig. 2–9). It was the ultimate in decorated furniture. Lines flowed, and cabriole legs were almost always used. Underbracing was seldom used in this light and graceful style. Furniture was decorated with every type of ornament imaginable. Boulle work, inlay, carving, paintings, marquetry, veneering, precious and other metal, were all used in rococo and naturalistic motifs.

Walnut and mahogany were the most popular carcass and frame woods. Other woods were used under paint and gilding. Paint colors tended to be brighter, and all possible colors were used. Upholstery materials included brocades, silk, damask, tapestry, velours, and prints.

Louis XVI (1774-1793)

Louis XVI was the grandson of Louis XV. Furniture in this period changed abruptly in design—back to straight lines and rectangular forms (see Fig. 2–9). Legs were straight again, turned, fluted, reeded, or spiral. Ornament became more simple, with motifs of floral wreaths and ribbons, flowers, leaves, rosettes, diaper patterns, urns, vases, busts, and human figures.

Mahogany was the principal wood, but lesser woods were used under paint and gilding. Paint colors were light and dainty, in keeping with the overall furniture style.

French Directoire (1792-1804)

French furniture understandably became a lot simpler in design and execution in the troublesome years after the revolution. By and large, the artisans were left alone and continued working. Directoire can be thought of as a transition period between the style of Louis XVI and the Empire style decreed by Napoleon.

Solid mahogany replaced marquetry and Egyptian motifs took over (see Fig. 2–10).

French Empire (1804-1815)

The Empire style under Napoleon's rule by edict was based on what ancient furniture was supposed to have been like: symmetry at all costs, rectangular and geometric shapes, proportions ponderous and solid (see Fig. 2–10). Large surfaces were left without mouldings, paneling, or decoration to emphasize the figure and grain of the highly polished wood. Ornamentation consisted of tacked-on bronze or gilt metal. Motifs were military or ancient. Carving was used only on table legs and on the arms and posts of chairs.

The principal wood was mahogany, but rosewood and ebony were also used. Exotic veneers were used for decoration. Marble was widely used for table tops. After Waterloo, the style disappeared.

FRENCH STYLED FURNITURE

FIGURE
2-10

Directoire (1792–1804):
- Solid mahogany
- Egyptian decoration

Arm Chair

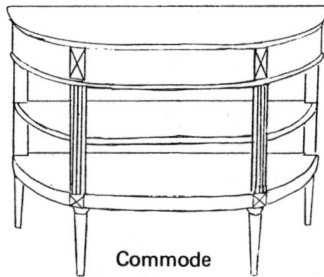
Commode

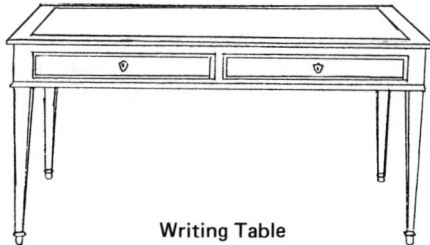
Writing Table

Empire (1804–1815):
- Symmetry
- Rectangular and geometric shapes
- Ponderous proportions
- Principal wood—mahogany
- Ancient or military decoration

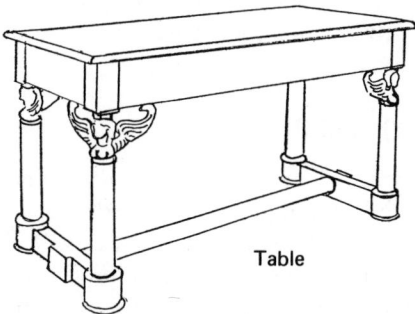
Table

Arm Chair

French Furniture: Directoire (1792-1804), Empire (1804-1815).

French Provincial (1600 to present)

While all these styles came and went in Paris, furniture style in the provinces, while affected to some extent by the Paris styles, didn't change very rapidly over the years. Living was simpler, and furniture was designed for family life. The simple lines of the Louis XIII period remained popular. The basic curved lines of the Louis XV style became fashionable in the provinces, but the elaborate ornamentation did not. French Provincial furniture as we know it today is based on this simple country furniture.

The woods most frequently used were those that were available locally, including oak, walnut, and of course, all the fruitwoods.

Early American or Colonial (1650-1750)

Furniture made in the American colonies up to 1750 or so is loosely called Colonial. It is a composite style, based primarily on English Jacobean and Queen Anne style, and to a lesser extent on Dutch, German, and other national styles in colonies populated by immigrants from those countries. In Colonial furniture, the ornateness and ponderous proportions of the original Old-World styles were considerably moderated and scaled down resulting in a style of furniture whose simplicity and clean lines have kept it always popular (see Fig. 2–11).

Construction was sturdy with well-made mortise and tenon joints, usually pinned. Glue was not always used in the earliest years. Dovetail joints were used in case construction and in drawer construction. Carcass framing was flush, not recessed. Legs, stretchers, and other structural members were both turned and plain. Proportions of parts of a piece of furniture followed no set rules. Surfaces were seldom ornamented; when they were, designs were simple, often crude. Chairs had slab, rush, or splint seats; upholstered chairs were rare.

Any wood that grew locally was used: walnut, oak, pine, cherry, pear, apple, elm, ash, maple, cedar, hickory, poplar, and gum. Woods were often mixed in a piece. Veneers were rarely used, then usually birds-eye maple, or curly maple. Some inlay and marquetry was done using woods of a contrasting color or ivory.

American Federal (1790-1830)

At the beginning of the period traditional English furniture styles lost some of their popularity in the new republic. The new style was classical with Greek and Roman motifs. Design influences still came from England, from Hepplewhite, Sheraton, the Adam brothers, and later the English Regency style. There was a growing French influence—Louis XVI, Directoire, and finally Empire.

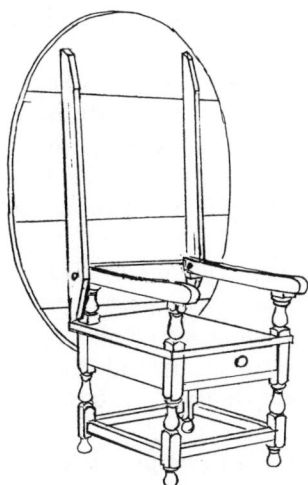

FIGURE
2-11

Chair Table

Corner Cupboard

Butterfly Table

Slant Top Desk

Windsor Chair

Tavern Table

Early American (Colonial) Furniture
(1650–1750):
• Composite of many styles
• Sturdy construction
• Surfaces seldom ornamented
• All available woods used

Early American (Colonial) Furniture (1650–1790).

The Federal period was the time of Duncan Phyfe, America's greatest cabinetmaker. His early work was based on English styles, his later, best work showed French influence. Predominant features in Duncan Phyfe furniture were the use of the lyre as a major ornamental and structural feature, pedestal bases with distinctive curved legs and animal feet (see Fig. 2–12).

Federal furniture was predominantly mahogany. Duncan Phyfe favored a rich red staining. Some curly maple was used as a substitute for the unobtainable satinwood used in England at the same time. Also used were cherry and other hardwoods. Rosewood became popular late in the period; high cost led to maple and pine being finished to resemble it.

Veneers of all kinds were used, including many highly figured varieties. Inlay was widely used for decoration. The most popular design motif was the American eagle. It was on almost everything.

Legs and feet, pedestals and posts were turned, reeded, fluted, and carved. Other motifs included the cornucopia, leaves, scrolls, and pineapples.

Toward the end of the period when the French Empire style was copied, furniture designs became gross and heavy.

Victorian (1837-1901)

Much has been said about Victorian furniture, most of it derogatory. There is no one Victorian style (see Fig. 2–13). At the start of the period, furniture in the style of Chippendale, Sheraton, and Duncan Phyfe was still new. Furniture making was in transition from a master-journeyman-apprentice craft, selling directly to the customer, to a big machine-powered industry, selling to the customers through shops.

Early Victorian furniture (up to about 1840) was made of mahogany and rosewood and in style was related to English Regency, French Empire, and American Federal. Then came the revivals, mass production, and walnut as the principal wood. Gothic, Greek, Turkish, Venetian, Egyptian, and French themes came and went.

Late Victorian furniture—what we think of as Victorian furniture—settled down to being bulky, ponderous, overstuffed, overornamented, and comfortable. Much of it was cheaply made with crude carvings and decorations. Marble tops were popular. Machine-made turnings abounded. The wood was walnut or mahogany, or finished to resemble one or the other.

Shaker (1789-1930)

Shaker furniture was functional, designed to be perfect for its purpose, without ornamentation and decoration that did not contribute to the basic use of the furniture. In other words, Shaker furniture

**FIGURE
2-12**

Bookcase

Tambour Desk

Work Table

Side Table

American Federal Furniture
(1790–1830):
- Influenced by English and French design
- Principal wood—mahogany
- Extensive use of veneer
- American eagle popular design motif

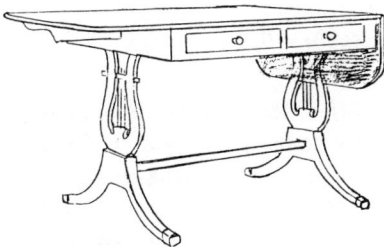

Lyre Pedestal Sofa Table

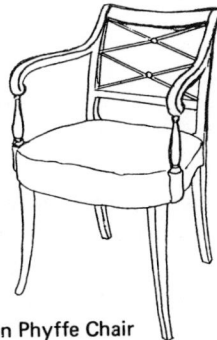

Duncan Phyffe Chair

American Federal Furniture (1790-1830).

**FIGURE
2-13**

Arm Chair

Dressing Table

Davenport Desk

Side Table

Victorian Furniture
(1837–1901):
• No one style
• Early furniture in many styles
• Later furniture was bulky, ponderous, overstuffed,
  over-decorated—but comfortable

Victorian Furniture (1837-1901).

design was exactly the opposite of Victorian design at its worst. Shaker designs were innovative in search of functional perfection, and when they arrived at such a design they let it alone, not making changes for the sake of change (see Fig. 2–14). Once the design of Shaker chairs was established, for example, there was little change for almost a century.

Pine was widely used, with hardwoods where required for added strength. Tables often had pine tops and hardwood bases. Hardwood was generally used for anything turned. Veneer for any purpose was

**FIGURE
2-14**

Shaker Furniture
(1789–1930):
• Very clean lines
• Functional design
• Little ornamentation or decoration

Chest of Drawers

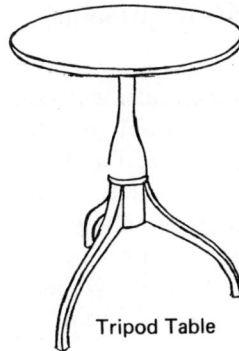

Desk

Tripod Table

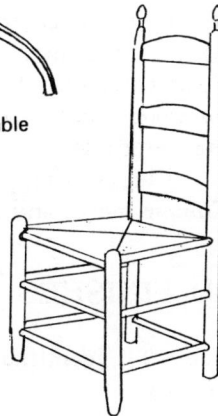

Sewing Desk

Rush Seat Chair

Shaker Furniture (1789–1930).

regarded as deceitful. Some mahogany was used in later years. The inherent figure and grain in wood was appreciated. Such surfaces were varnished. Other furniture was painted. The pious Shakers had nothing against the use of labor-saving machinery. The invention of the power circular saw blade is credited to a Shaker Sister in 1810.

Mission (1899-1914)

This style of furniture has nothing to do with the Spanish Missions of the Southwest, or any furniture therein. The style was invented by an American, Gustav Stickley, around the turn of the century as a revolt to all the excesses of Victorian furniture. His furniture was simple, functional, clean lined, with little ornamentation. It was furniture anyone could build with hand tools.

Oak was the principal wood used, followed by ash, elm, and chestnut. Table and desk drawers were lined with split calf. Chair and settle seats were rush, canvas, cow- and calf-hide. Hardware was wrought iron or hammered copper. By 1914 it was all over, smothered by cheap Grand Rapids products and a suddenly revived consumer interest in Colonial furniture.

Chinese (1366 to present)

The style did not change with every gifted cabinetmaker, whim of fashion, or enthroned ruler who came along. Designs were traditional and unchanging, with only discreet and subtle variation to suit the purpose of the piece (see Fig. 2–15).

The skilled joinery was unsurpassed anywhere, any time. Furniture went together without glue like the proverbial Chinese puzzle. Each complex joint reinforced the other. Finishes are polished hardwood or opaque lacquer. Woods used include narra, East Indian rosewood, sandlewood, shisham, camphor wood, cedar, and cypress, but never teak.

(Chinese Chippendale was an eighteenth century imitation of Chinese motifs and does not resemble Chinese furniture otherwise.)

2-2 PERIOD FINISHES

Table 2–1 identifies the finishes used on furniture in the different periods.

**FIGURE
2-15**

Cabinet or Bookshelf

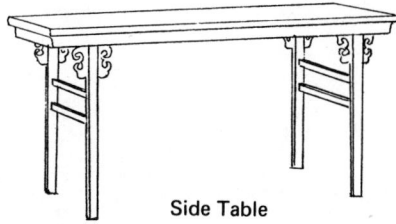

Side Table

Chinese Furniture
(1366 to present):
• Traditional designs
• Intricate joinery
• Many woods used

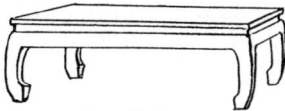

Low Table

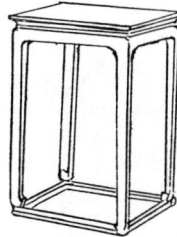

Stand

Chinese Furniture (1366 to present).

TABLE
2-1

Period Finish Summary

Period	Clear Finishes	Opaque Finishes
Seventeenth century English (1603–1688)	None, most pieces Oil and wax Varnish (rare)	Black Black with color decoration Black with gilt trim Some japan late in period
William and Mary (1688–1702)	Oil and wax, most pieces Shellac on veneer and mahogany	Black, red, green, blue Painted trim around marquetry Gilt trim Some overall gilding
Queen Anne (1702–1745)	Oil and wax Shellac	White paint White paint, gilt trim Lacquer, all colors in decoration
Chippendale (1749–1779)	Oil and wax, brick dust polish* Oil, brick dust polish* Wax only	Lacquer on Chinese style Gilding on mirror frames
Hepplewhite (1770–1790)	Same as Chippendale	Many colors used as grounds Paintings as decorations Gilding on small pieces
Adam Brothers (1762–1792)	Same as Chippendale	All colors used for grounds Polychrome on carvings Paintings as decorations Some pieces part clear, part opaque Gilding on small pieces
Sheraton (1790–1806)	Same as Chippendale	Lacquer
English Regency (1793–1820)	French polish	Seldom used

30

Style (Period)	Finish	Decoration
Louis XIV (1643–1715)	French polish	Lacquer, dark green, blue, crimson; Gilding
Louis XV (1715–1774)	French polish	Paint, all colors; Lacquer, all colors
Louis XVI (1774–1793)	French polish	Paint, lighter colors; Lacquer, lighter colors
French Directoire (1792–1804)	French polish	Seldom used
French Empire (1804–1815)	French polish	Seldom used
French Provincial (1600 to present)	French polish	Paint, all colors
Early American (1650–1750)	None, most pieces	Milk paint, natural pigment colors; Polychrome decoration
American Federal (1790–1830)	Stain and varnish; Oil and wax; French polish	Painted, black usual; Gilding rare
Victorian (1837–1901)	Stain and varnish; Varnish; French polish	Not regularly used
Shaker (1789–1930)	Varnish	Paint
Mission (1899–1914)	Varnish	Not used
Chinese (1366 to present)	Oil resin	Lacquer, usually red or black; Gilt or polychrome decoration

* No one is sure exactly what the brick dust was supposed to accomplish.

FIGURE 2-16

Queen Anne

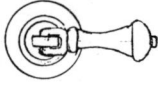

Chippendale

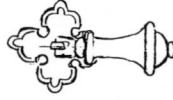

17th Century

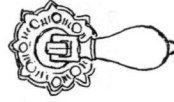

William and Mary

Chippendale

Queen Anne

Hepplewhite

Chippendale

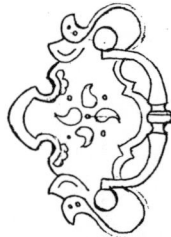

Queen Anne

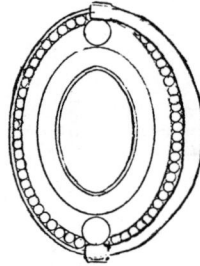

English Furniture Hardware Styles.

Chippendale

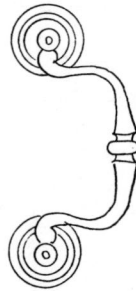

William and Mary

Hepplewhite

The design of handles and knobs changed as the styles of furniture changed. Although such hardware can be useful occasionally in determining the age of whatever they are attached to, very few pieces of really old furniture have their original knobs and handles. They break, they fall off, they get replaced. It has never been easy to get exact replacements unless they are handmade to order which was as expensive then as now. Whole sets would be replaced, with the major worry being that the replacements fit the same holes. Often hardware would be replaced with the then current style to make the piece look more contemporary.

Handle and knob designs did not change abruptly in design with each new style of furniture. Change was more gradual. For this reason the hardware shown in Figures 2–16 to 2–21 is not always grouped by exact period.

FIGURE 2-17

American Federal Hardware.
(Courtesy of Smith Supply Co.)

**FIGURE
2-18**

Louis XV and Louis XVI Hardware.
(Courtesy of Smith Supply Co.)

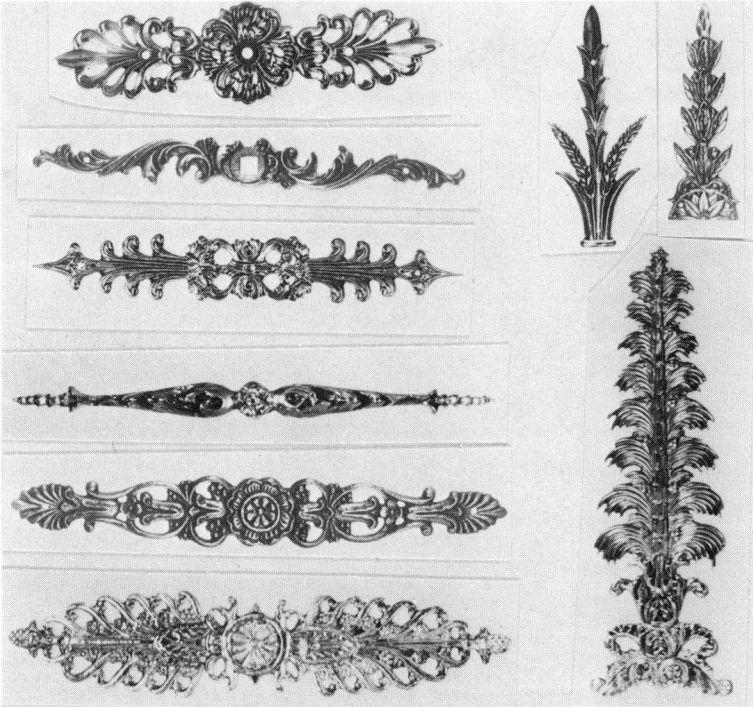

FIGURE
2-19

Directoire and Empire Hardware.
(Courtesy of Smith Supply Co.)

FIGURE
2-20

Victorian Hardware.
(Courtesy of Paxton Hardware Co.)

**FIGURE
2-21**

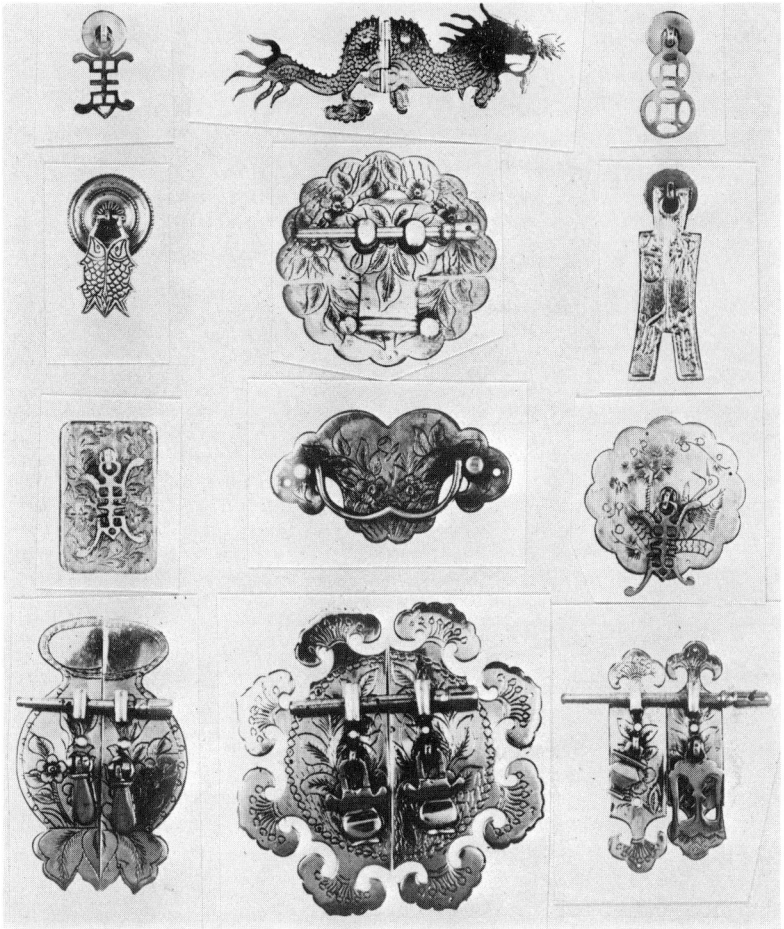

**Chinese Hardware.
(Courtesy of Smith Supply Co.)**

Adhesives and Gluing

3

3-1 ADHESIVES

Any substance that will hold two materials together by surface attachment is called an *adhesive*. If the two materials happen to be wood, the adhesive is usually called *glue*. If materials other than wood are involved, the adhesive is called *cement* (for example, contact cement and epoxy cement).

If you wonder why glue sticks at all you are in good company. For a long time glue was assumed to work by mechanical adhesion, with the hardened glue locking into the pores and roughened surface of the wood—hence the longstanding advice to rough up the surface before gluing. The current scientific theory gets it down to the molecular level with a chemical bond between the glue and the wood. The glue holds itself together by cohesion.

There is no one best glue to use for all furniture repair, and there are some glues you shouldn't bother to use at all, for one reason or another. The recommended glues are shown in Figure 3–1.

White Glue. (Elmer's Glue-All, Evertite.) Also called PVA, because the main ingredient is polyvinyl acetate. White glue sets by water absorption. Clamping time of one hour at 65° F or warmer is adequate if the joint is not under stress and the parts fit well together with a thin glue line. Normally, the glue is nonstaining and dries

FIGURE
3-1

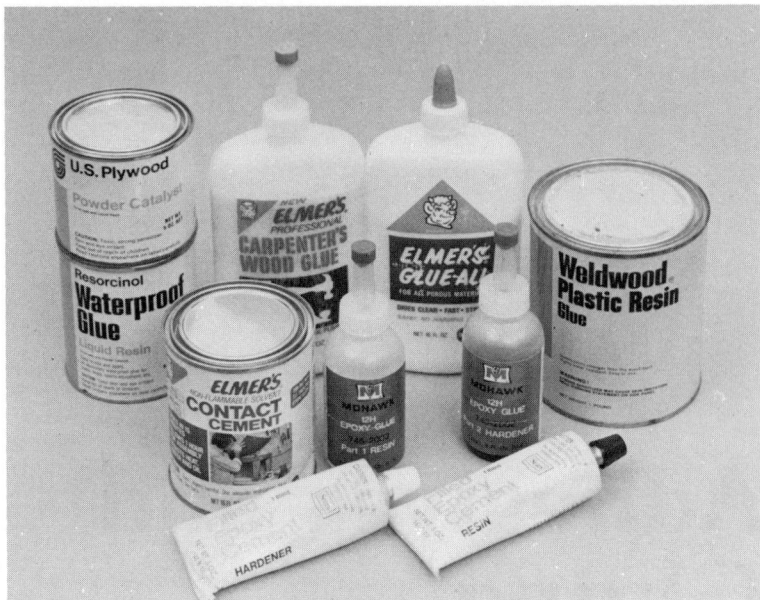

Glues recommended for use in furniture repair.

clear, but it turns brown next to iron or steel. You can scrape excess dried white glue from surfaces but do not attempt to sand it. The heat generated by the sanding process softens the glue, and the glue then clogs your sandpaper. White glue never dries rock hard; under stress it will cold flow. This means that if you put a continuous long-term load on the joint the glue will allow the parts to shift position. This can be an advantage in dowel or mortise and tenon joints where some differential expansion in the joined parts with changes in temperature and humidity is normal, but disastrous in an end-grain to cross-grain butt joint. White glue develops high strength, but has low moisture and heat resistance.

White glue dries clear and is therefore particularly good for veneering. Owing to its low viscosity it is also good for injecting into joints that cannot be disassembled. Because of the inherent sanding difficulty with white glue, it should not be too liberally applied under veneer and not used at all with porous veneers.

Aliphatic Resin Glue. (Elmer's Carpenter's Wood Glue, Titebond.) Also called yellow glue, this glue is a white glue modified to solve some of the inherent problems of straight white glue. Of minor importance is the fact that the glue has a higher viscosity which means it doesn't dribble as much. Its tackiness is also supposed to make joint assembly and clamping easier. But there are some real advantages of yellow glue over white glue. First, clamping time is reduced to 30 minutes for joints not under stress. Second, the glue dries harder and doesn't cold flow. Third, and best of all, yellow glue won't clog your sandpaper as badly as white glue does (see Fig. 3–2). If it had no other advantage, this alone would be worth the additional cost. Unless you have some specific reason to use some other glue in furniture repair, yellow glue should be your first choice.

Resorcinol-Formaldehyde Glue. If you need a waterproof glue, or a glue that will resist heat, this is it. It comes in two cans, one containing a dark reddish syrupy resin, and the other a tan powder hardener, paraformaldehyde. You mix what you immediately need in equal parts by weight; you must use what you mix in an hour or so, depending on the room temperature. Spread the glue on both surfaces, then assemble and clamp. Now the bad news. You have to leave the work clamped from three and a half to ten hours, depending on the room temperature (see Fig. 3–3). You can't use it at temperatures below 70° F because it just won't cure. The glue also leaves a dark red glue line that you can't make disappear. Use it for any glue joint that will periodically get wet.

Urea-Formaldehyde Glue. (Weldwood, Craftsman Plastic Resin Glue.) The glue comes in a tan powder combining resin and hardener which are activated by adding water. Pot life is about the same. The glue dries to a hardly visible tan line, and you must leave the joint clamped five to ten hours, depending on the room temperature. The glue joint is water-resistant, but not waterproof, and the joint weakens above 120° F.

Epoxy Cement. The preceding glues are for gluing wood to wood or wood to paper, cardboard, leather, or cloth. Epoxy will stick almost anything to anything, including wood, glass, bricks, metal,

**FIGURE
3-2**

Abrasive paper clogging: White glue vs. aliphatic resin (yellow) glue.

**FIGURE
3-3**

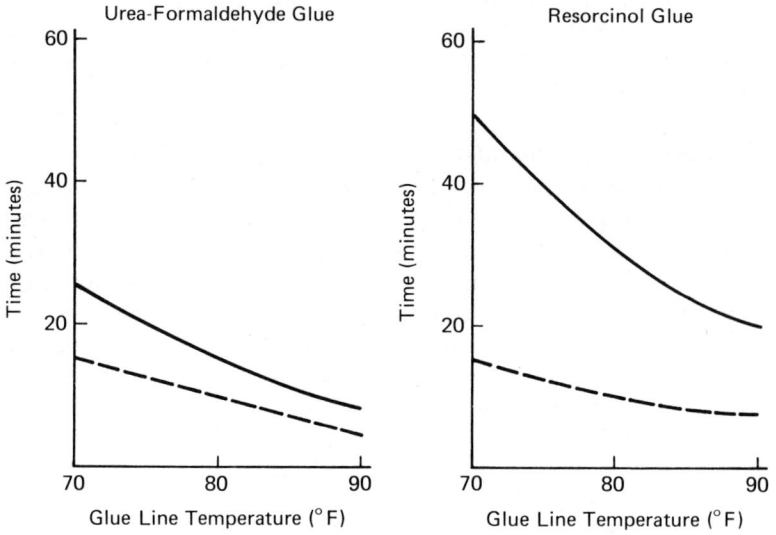

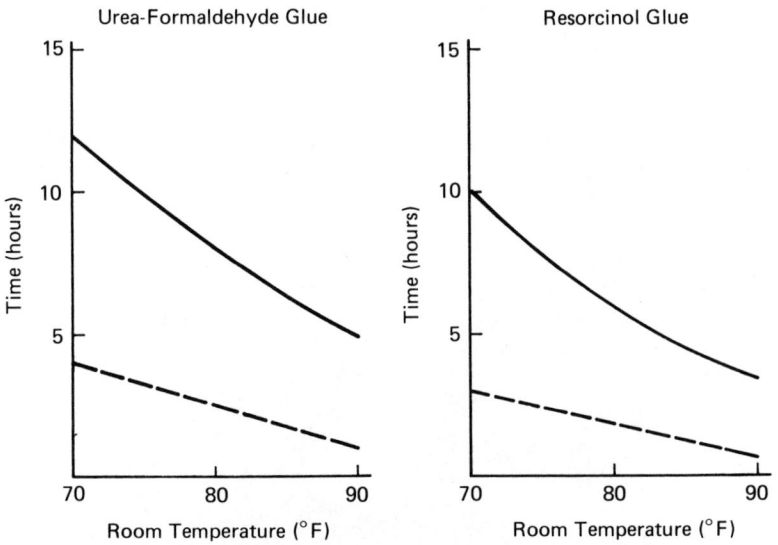

Urea-formaldehyde and resorcinol glues: Working, curing, and pot time vs. temperature.

and some plastics. Epoxy will not adhere to polyethylene, polypropylene, and Teflon, but then, practically nothing else will either.

The chemical compositions differ, but all epoxies come as two viscous liquids, a resin and a hardener, which are mixed in equal amounts as needed. They cure by chemical reaction. There are two different kinds available in small tubes—rapid-set and slow-set. The first hardens in about five minutes and is good for joints where you do the clamping with your hands only. The second hardens in twenty-four hours, but can be speeded up if you can heat the joint, for example, by using an electric heater or blow dryer.

Epoxy is waterproof and heat-resistant. The glue line is clear. As epoxy is an excellent gap filler, the glue is a good choice for poorly fitting joints, or joints where you can't apply enough clamping pressure to use one of the previously listed glues. Epoxy cement is normally sold in expensive one-ounce two-tube kits. It also comes in larger containers, considerably less expensive per ounce.

Filled Epoxy Cement.   (Sears No. 80605.) This is simply epoxy cement with an inert filler added, which gives the glue enough body to stay in a poorly fitting joint, at a cost low enough so you can afford to use it. The filler also leaves you with a gray glue line. This is the glue to pack into the hole in a chair leg so the rung that doesn't fit at all anymore will never come out again. You can also use it to build up damaged moldings if they are going to be painted or gilded.

Contact Cement.   For a long time, all used a flammable solvent and gave off noxious and dangerous fumes. No more. Now, most contact cements on the market are the nonflammable kind. Not all of them are safe and allow soap-and-water cleanup, however. Some contain 1,1,1 Trichloroethane as a solvent; this chemical, while not flammable, is harmful. Read the label before you buy.

To use these thermoplastic adhesives, you spread both surfaces, wait until the glue is dry and no longer tacky. Then you carefully align the two pieces and press them together. The glue grabs immediately, and you will have trouble repositioning the pieces if you have made a mistake or suddenly change your mind. How much trouble depends on what you are joining. If only part of the surface is joined, and one of the parts is flexible, you may be able to get them apart if you peel very slowly and slit the glue to encourage it to separate. But if you are working with two pieces of rigid wood—forget it.

Contact cement is the only glue to use for applying plastic laminates to wood. Some recommend it for veneering, but I do not use it for veneering except for curved surfaces because it doesn't have as strong a bond as white glue, and with all the rolling required to get good contact, I find it faster to clamp and walk away. Water-soluble types have low moisture resistance which can result in blistering when used for veneering, and they have a top temperature resistance of only 120° F. Table 3–1 lists recommended adhesives and compares their characteristics.

There are other glues available, but they are not recommended for furniture repair:

Mastic. These come in caulking cartridges and many are termed *construction adhesives.* There are many formulations. Some are moisture-resistant, most are not. Curing times vary and most remain somewhat flexible when dry. While they have good gap-filling capability, they do not have the strength necessary for furniture repair, and they leave a thick glue line that will be an eyesore in any furniture repair.

Hot Melts. These come as solid sticks of adhesive that are melted as required in an electrically heated glue gun. The big advantage is fast initial strength as the glue cools, but you also have to be very fast getting the joint together. The required fast assembly and the high cost of the glue and gun rule out hot melts for most furniture repairing.

Hide Glue. This glue is made from hides, tendons, and hoofs of horses, cattle, and sheep. You can buy it in granules that must be soaked in water, or you can buy it ready-mixed. Hide glue cures by evaporation and absortion of the water into the wood. It has high strength but low moisture resistance. With today's white and yellow glues, who needs it—unless you are faking an antique from scratch and want to use the glue grandpa used.

Casein Glue. This glue contains milk curd, lime, and other chemicals, and comes as a powder that must be mixed with water. There are no particular advantages to using casein glue except that some people claim that it works better than other common glues with oily woods such as teak, lemon, and yew. On the negative side it is very abrasive to cutting tools and cures slowly. It has an almost colorless glue line but may stain some woods. Strength is good, heat and moisture resistance, fair.

Household Cement. (Model Airplane Cement.) This glue does not sufficiently penetrate wood that is less porous than balsa. The result is an inadequate bond. Avoid.

3-2 CLAMPING AND CLAMPS _____

Clamping a glue joint does three things. First, clamping brings the pieces into accurate position. Second, clamping squeezes glue from

TABLE 3-1

Recommended Adhesives

	White Glue	Yellow Glue	Resorcinol-Formaldehyde	Urea-Formaldehyde	Epoxy	Filled Epoxy	Latex Contact Cement
Form	Liquid	Liquid	Liquid + powder	Powder	Two liquids	Two liquids	Liquid
Ready to use	Yes	Yes	Mix	Mix with water	Mix	Mix	Yes
Working temperature (minimum)	50° F	50° F	70° F	70° F	0° F	0° F	70° F
Minimum cure temperature	50° F	50° F	70° F	70° F	0° F	0° F	70° F
Clamping time (minimum)	1 hour	30 minutes	See Fig. 3–3	See Fig. 3–3	5 minutes to 24 hours	6 hours	0
Moisture resistance	Poor	Poor	Excellent	Good	Excellent	Excellent	Poor
Maximum temperature resistance	120° F	120° F	200° F	120° F	180° F	180° F	120° F
Glue line	Colorless	Pale yellow	Dark red	Tan	Colorless	Gray	Wide, Colorless to tan

the joint, leaving a thin, continuous film of glue between the wood surfaces which is necessary for all glues except the epoxies. Third, clamping holds the pieces together undisturbed until the glue cures.

Too much clamping pressure is worse than too little. Too much results in a too thin glue line with not enough glue left between the wood surfaces to produce a good bond. This is called a *starved joint*. Carried to extremes, too much pressure can compress the wood; when clamps are removed, the cells can spring back to weaken the glue line. Too little pressure results in a thicker and possibly unsightly glue line, but within reason, the glue line, although somewhat weaker, will still be stonger than the wood on either side. A thicker glue line, however, takes longer to cure with all adhesives except epoxies. Typically, this curing time could extend to several days with white glue, with the joint clamped by being weighted under a pile of books.

If you are going to be gluing furniture, you need clamps. Twisted string or a pile of books won't take the place of good clamps. For furniture repair, the clamps you will need are shown in Figure 3–4. If you are just getting started and don't already have a workshop, buy clamps as you need them. How many of each kind? Always buy at least two of a kind and size; invariably you will be using them in pairs.

Steel Spindle Handscrews. These clamps have hardwood jaws and around furniture can do everything C-clamps can do and many things C-clamps can't do. They are the basic woodworking clamp. The hardwood jaws can be set to apply pressure over a broad area, while the C-clamp applies pressure in a small spot and mars the work

FIGURE 3-4

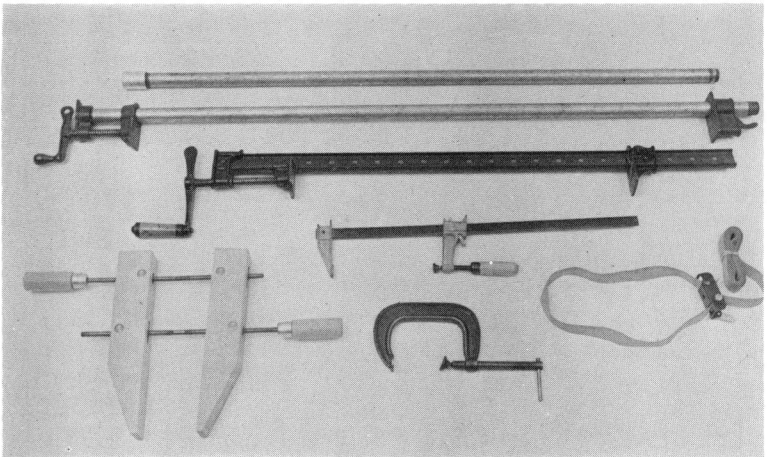

Clamps used in furniture repair: Pipe clamp with extension, heavy-duty bar clamp, light-duty bar clamp, steel spindle clamp, C-clamp, and band clamp.

unless a clamping block is used. The angle of the jaws of a handscrew can be adjusted to hold irregular shapes, and clamping pressure can be applied right out to their tips. They can clamp round work, and freshly glued work won't slide, crawl, or twist as you are closing the clamps. Keep them waxed and you won't have to worry about glue sticking to them either.

Pipe Clamps. You buy sets consisting of a tail stop and a sliding head, and mount them on 3/4'' iron pipe. You can make them up in any length you need. Always have extra pieces of pipe around for making longer or shorter clamps, and couple pipe extensions for really long clamps.

Heavy-Duty Bar Clamps. These clamps perform the same function as pipe clamps, cost more, are easier to set up, have larger jaws, and exert more pressure.

Light-Duty Steel Bar Clamps. These clamps have the sliding head casting riding on a 1/4'' by 3/4'' steel bar. These lightweight clamps can get into close quarters where you don't have room for any other style clamp, and they can be set with one hand. This is very handy when you are trying to hold something together and clamp it at the same time.

Band (Web) Clamps. Loop a 1'' wide by 15' long nylon web band around your work and draw it up tight. The band clamp is indispensable for gluing chair frames, veneering edges of a round table and other curved surfaces, clamping work over forms, and applying pressure to mitered picture frames. The clamps come with steel ''corners'' that get the band around sharp right angles without harm to the band or the work. The advantage of the band clamp in clamping chair frames, for example, over any other combination of pipe or bar clamps, is that the pressure is applied evenly everywhere at once, quickly, and without marring the work surface.

C-Clamps. These clamps are basically metal-working tools. They are readily available in a wide range of sizes and qualities. If you have them, use them. But if you have to buy clamps for your planned furniture repairing, put the money into steel spindle handscrews. When using C-clamps be careful to protect the work surface from the jaws with blocks of soft wood.

Rubber Bands. A multitude of rubber bands will sometimes save you hours of planning and jigging when assembling odd shapes. Rubber bands cut from an inner tube (in case you don't remember, they went inside your auto tires before we went tubeless) make useful clamps for chair work.

Clamping Pressure. If the mating surfaces of the pieces you are joining fit together smoothly without surface irregularities leaving gaps, you don't need much pressure to squeeze out excess glue and hold the pieces together in alignment until the glue takes hold.

In this less than perfect world, however, clamping pressure is often needed to pull irregular surfaces or warped wood into contact for gluing. The correct pressure in this case is that needed to close the joint, determined by watching the glue line. Some clamping problems and solutions are shown in Figure 3–5.

(a)

(b)

(c)

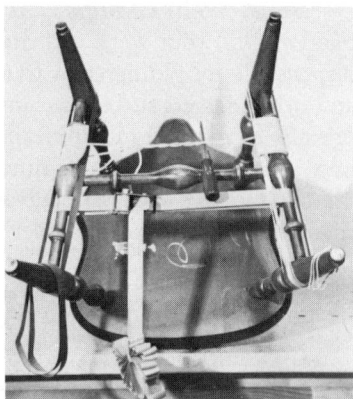
(d)

**FIGURE
3-5**

Some clamping problems and solutions: (a) The adjustable jaws of a steel spindle could not grip the chair back. One-inch upholstery foam gave needed grip; and a sack of lead shot on the seat keeps the chair from tipping over. (b) How to be sure the arms are not tilted when glued to the posts and back. (c) Gluing the leg tenon into the seat: Two bar clamps provide downward pressure localized with a beam and a sack of lead shot; a band clamp keeps the legs from spreading. (d) Several ways to clamp stretchers: Sections of inner tube, twisted string (with protective pads), band clamp, and multitude of rubber bands (office variety).

In board-edge joints, the species of the wood is more the problem than obtaining any particular clamping pressure, as shown in Table 3–2 and Table 3–3.

Joint Strength with White Glue

TABLE
3-2

Woods	Clamp PSI	Force to Break 3/4'' by 1 3/8'' Joint, LBS.	Test Result
Pine–pine	3–30	133	Joint stronger than wood
Poplar–poplar	10–30	210	Joint stronger than wood.
Mahogany–mahogany	30–100	200	Wood and joint equally strong.
Maple–maple	30–100	378	Wood and joint equally strong.
Oak–oak	30–100	294	Joint weaker than wood.

Furniture Wood Gluing Properties

TABLE
3-3

Excellent	Good	Fair	Poor
Alder	Aspen	Ash	Rosewood
Cottonwood	Basswood	Beech	Primavera
Maple, soft	Birch	Tupelo	Teak
Poplar	Buttonwood	Hickory	Yew
	Cherry	Lauan	
	Elm	Pine, yellow	
	Gum, sweet	Pine, ponderosa	
	Hackberry		
	Hemlock		
	Mahogany		
	Maple, hard		
	Oak		
	Pecan		
	Pine, white		
	Sycamore		
	Walnut		
	Willow		

When gluing large surfaces or long edges, evenly applied clamping pressure is more important than the amount of pressure each clamp exerts. Use clamping blocks (cauls) between the clamps and the work to speed the pressure. Table 3–4 shows the force exerted by typical clamps.

Clamp Force (Hand Tightening)

TABLE
3-4

Bar clamp (heavy-duty)	2,000 lbs.
Pipe clamp	1,300 lbs.
C-clamp, 4''	900 lbs.
10'' Handscrew (steel spindle)	450 lbs.
Bar clamp (light-duty)	350 lbs.
Band clamp (nylon)	200 lbs. (wrench)

You have to know two things about a joint to get it apart: the glue used, and how the joint was assembled.

Every wood glue has its weak points, such as solubility, heat sensitivity, brittleness, elasticity. The first step in getting a joint apart is to identify the glue used.

Table 3–5 lists all of the glues you are likely to encounter in furniture, the type of joints they are used in, and how to get them unglued.

If what you are trying to get apart is a piece of furniture more than 20 years old, you are on fairly safe grounds in assuming that it was put together with hide glue, or another animal glue with similar characteristics—unless someone has made a recent repair.

These older furniture joints are brittle and usually weaker than the wood and can be made to fail with shock stress such as a hammer blow. When you hammer a joint, use a block of wood to protect the furniture surface, or use a rubber mallet, but be sure to apply the blows in the direction that the joint can come apart.

Watch out for joints with locking pegs or dowels, or joints that someone has driven a nail or screw into. Look for signs of hole filling. These joints won't come apart without first having the locking device removed.

A little judiciously-applied joint deformation can also be used to part the glue line. Racking a joint is one good way to apply high stress to a joint with very good control (in other words, gently), so you crack the glue line and nothing else.

A scraper or putty knife tapped into the glue line is a method of last resort, because, unless the joint falls apart immediately, some deformation of the wood is inevitable.

Any joint put together in recent years can contain any of a great variety of glues, many of which routinely produce a joint stronger than the woods being joined. Attempts to force these joints apart without first weakening the glue risks breaking the wood on one or both sides of the joint instead of on the glue line.

Few of these glues, even the modern wonder adhesives, can withstand heat. Some hold up better than others, but all, except high-temperature silicones, which you are not likely to run across in furniture construction, will let go at or below 150° F. The one exception is resorcinol-formaldehyde, which is good to 200° F. Some glues fail completely, others lose strength. Heat usually works best in combination with mechanical stress.

Heat can be applied several ways to a joint. A blow dryer works nicely. If the piece you are trying to get apart is small enough, another alternative is to put it in the kitchen oven, with the temperature set below 200° F. Don't go away to do something else while it

TABLE 3-5

Glues and How to Unstick Them

Type of Glue	Glue Line	Top Temp °F	Water Resistance	Cured Condition	Where Used	Hot Water	Heat	Solvent	Shock Force	Slow Force
								To Get Apart—Try		
Animal hide	Tan to brown	100	Poor	Brittle	Everywhere	X	X	Water	X	X
Starch (vegetable)	White	100	Poor	Brittle	Veneering	X	X	Water	X	X
Casein	Neutral	100	Fair to poor	Brittle	Veneers, joints	X	X	Water	X	X
Resorcinol-formaldehyde	Dark red	200	Good	Brittle	Outdoor furniture	X	X	None	X	X
Urea-formaldehyde	Tan	120	Poor	Brittle	Everywhere	X	X	Water	X	X
White glue	Clear	120	Poor	Flexible	Everywhere	X	X	Water, acetone		X
Yellow glue	Yellow	120	Poor	Rigid	Everywhere	X	X	Water, acetone	X	X
Epoxy	Clear	180	Good	Rigid	Recent repairs			None	X	*
Filled epoxy	Gray	180	Good	Rigid	Recent repairs			None	*	*
Solvent contact cement	Wide	120	Good	Flexible	Laminates		X	Lacquer solvent		X
Latex contact cement	Wide	120	Fair	Flexible	Recent laminates	X	X	Water		X
Model airplane, China cement	Clear	100	Fair to poor	Rigid	Repairs			Acetone, lacquer thinner		
Mastic, solvent base	Tan	Varies	Good to fair	Flexible to rigid	Crude repairs		X	Acetone, lacquer thinner		X
Mastic, latex base	Tan	Varies	Good to poor	Flexible	Crude repairs		X	None		
Cyanoacrylates, (miracle one-drop glues)	Clear	Varies	Fair to poor	Brittle	Not used on wood or other porous materials	X	X	Hot water		X

* Forget it. If used, generally means poorly fitting joint, and a large mass of glue of unknown size and shape present.

bakes—the wood won't have to reach the selected temperature before the joint can be pulled apart. The reason for this, besides glue failure at the high temperature, is the difference in the coefficient of expansion between the wood pieces and the glue which puts a very high shear stress on the glue line. This technique works particularly well with white glued joints, which do not yield to shock treatments because of their flexibility.

For glues that are not waterproof, and you will seldom encounter waterproof glues in old furniture, getting the joint wet will help get it unstuck if physical persuasion doesn't work. Examine the furniture for traces of glue that were not cleaned off and moisten the exposed glue. If it becomes tacky you are on the right track.

Unless you are able to submerge the joint in a container of water, getting the glue in the joint wet will take some patience. The water will work better if it is hot—as close to boiling as you can apply it. A medicine dropper works well to dribble the water on the glue line. Add a wetting agent to the water, either a dish-washing detergent or a photographic photo-flow solution. These wetting agents reduce the water surface tension and help the water to penetrate into any started cracks.

Contact cements present a special problem. Contact cements are used to glue veneer and laminate. The technique for removing laminate is to get a knife blade into the joint at a corner, flood the crack with the appropriate solvent, and gently pry up the laminate. For most old work, the solvent is lacquer solvent (thinner). The solvent used for new work will be 1,1,1 Trichloroethane solvent or water, depending on the contact cement used.

If the adhesive is solvent based, it will let go fast. Results will not be as spectacular with water and a water-base adhesive, but the water will help. Keep the pressure on, keep squirting the appropriate solvent, and the laminate will usually slowly, very slowly peel off. This technique won't work with wood veneer.

Ungluing veneer without destroying the veneer is difficult, if not impossible, if it has been put down with latex-base contact cement. You would do it only if you wanted to transfer a spectacular piece of marquetry to some new piece of furniture. Old veneer put down with water soluble animal or casein glue can be coaxed up with water. Keep track of how the pieces go together.

Wood

4

A replacement for a broken or missing part of a piece of furniture should be made, ideally, from the same kind of wood used in the original. If you are working on an antique, especially a valuable antique, the replacement wood should also be as old as the antique you are restoring, in order to make the least detectable repair.

For most repairs, it is enough to replace mahogany with mahogany, maple with maple, and so on. There are occasions when the piece being repaired doesn't warrant such careful wood matching. Most of us don't get fanatic about that when replacing broken rungs on kitchen chairs. In such functional repairs, the wood will be selected on the basis of strength and appropriateness for the specific part, and from whatever stock is handy.

Identifying the wood used in fairly new furniture is usually not too much of a problem, but when you are dealing with furniture 50 years, 100 years, or 200 years old, the identification of the wood becomes more and more difficult.

4-1 WOOD IDENTIFICATION

Wood identification many times becomes a process of elimination. First, you establish what woods it cannot be. Is the grain open or closed; if open, how large are the pores? (See Fig. 4-2.) Is there a figure visible? The absence of a figure doesn't rule out a wood normally figured; you might just not be able to see it.

FIGURE
4-1

Black table (left), as acquired. After stripping layers of five different coats of paint and the traces of a clear finish, which had been mostly removed, two kinds of wood were revealed—neither is visually identifiable.

FIGURE
4-2

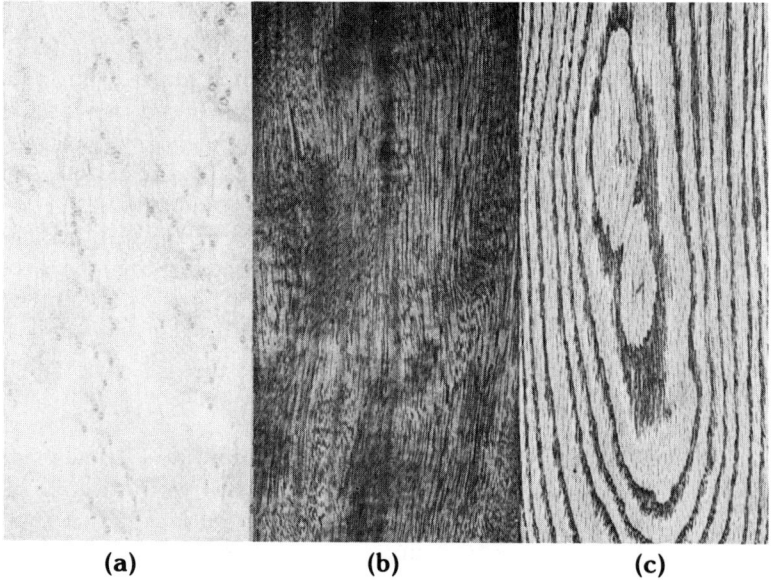

(a) (b) (c)

Closed and open-grain woods: (a) Closed grain (birds eye maple); (b) open grain with small pores (mahogany); and (c) open grain with large pores (red oak).

If the wood is finished, what is the color? In other words, what wood is the wood supposed to look like? There might actually be cherry under a reddish brown finish but there also might be lurking

**FIGURE
4-3**

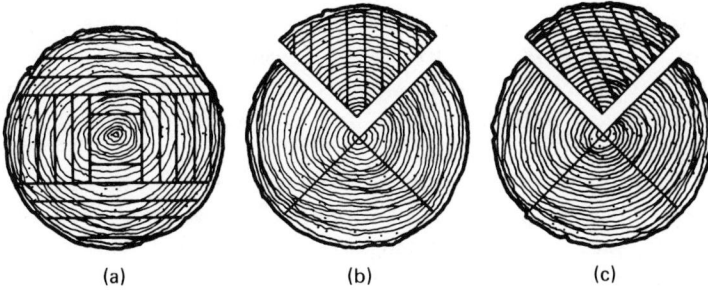

(a) (b) (c)

Methods of sawing lumber: (a) plain sawn; (b) quarter sawn; and (c) rift sawn.

beech, birch, maple, alder, poplar, or gum. You must investigate further.

The color of the wood after it has been stripped can be misleading too. Paint and varnish removers leave the stain to varying degrees, depending on wood, stain and remover. Age and years in sunlight darken many woods; sunlight fades some stains. Bleaching the wood after stripping many not remove all the stain color, and it will unnaturally lighten the wood.

Look at the period or style of the piece. Walnut was the most popular wood in some periods, mahogany in others, and so on. Modern reproductions and furniture copying the old style (in spirit even if not with fidelity) often use the same wood as the original to enhance the illusion of authenticity.

Wet the surface of the stripped wood with water for a fleeting look at how the wood will appear under a transparent finish. Grain and figure may suddenly appear.

The figure or grain in a piece of wood depends not only on the species, but also on how the log was sawed into boards. (See Fig. 4–3.) The simplest method of cutting up the log is to grab the log and saw off boards with repeated cuts through the log tangent to the rings. This method is fast, wastes the least amount of the wood, and produces a grain pattern of straight lines; any knots that occur have little weakening effect on the lumber. This cutting method is called *flat grained* in softwood, and *plain sawed* in hardwood. Both terms fairly well describe the grain pattern obtained.

If full advantage of the appearance of the grain is to be taken, the log must be cut another way, unfortunately more wasteful and requiring more time. This method is called *quarter sawing* in hardwood, *edge grained* or *vertical grained* in softwood. The log is first sawn into quarters, then each quarter is sawn into boards, with the saw cuts approximately perpendicular to the rings.

A third method of sawing is called *rift sawing*. The method is similar to quarter sawing, except that the boards are sawn from the quarter log at an off-perpendicular angle.

If you have taken the piece apart, weigh one of the parts to measure its volume and calculate the density of the wood. This test can be a clincher, because the wood is going to weigh what it is supposed to weigh with fair accuracy—say ± 3%. An example is shown in Figure 4-4.

Try a fingernail test underneath somewhere. You won't have any trouble indenting softwoods like pine, alder, basswood, butternut, chestnut, gum, Philippine mahogany, pine, or poplar. This is a good way—probably the only practical way—to tell chestnut from oak or ash and to identify a piece of poplar slipped in with the maple, birch, or cherry in an old table top.

Should you always replace solid wood with solid wood? Plywood many times will be a more practical choice. For example, a lot of Victorian furniture contains panels consisting of oak veneer on lumber corestock. If the veneer is shredding off and the lumber strips in the core are warped and coming unglued, would it not be better to replace the panel with plywood veneered with matching oak veneer rather than try to reassemble the core or build a new lumber core identical to the old?

Again, how far should we go in patching a chewed up and scarred table top or dresser top, before we decide to replace the top with plywood or overlay the top with veneer or plastic laminate?

And, what appears to be nicely figured wood in furniture may not be—it can also be laminated plastic, printed paper, a thin plastic overlay, or a skilled hand-painted imitation of grain. Finely carved chair arms and deeply moulded cabinet doors are today often nothing more than polyurethane—a foamed plastic with a thick skin that can be cast with beautiful detail. Even in older furniture, carving and trim is sometimes simulated with composition mouldings.

Of the 2,000 or so species of wood, most are of little interest in furniture making or repair. About 20 will be encountered as structural material in furniture, another 80 are used in the form of veneer.

Among the 20 structural woods, these seven are the most important—walnut, mahogany, oak, cherry, maple, birch, and pine.

Walnut

The outstanding grain, figuring, and coloring of walnut has made this wood the all-time favorite American furniture wood. Walnut has also been widely used in European furniture from the seventeenth century to the present. The wood was in common use long before mahogany became popular.

Most of the walnut you will encounter will be American black walnut (*Juglans nigra*), called black because of the color of the acorn shells. The color of the wood varies from light gray brown to dark purplish or chocolate brown. Walnut logs and lumber have been exported to European furniture makers for centuries, and so much of

FIGURE
4-4

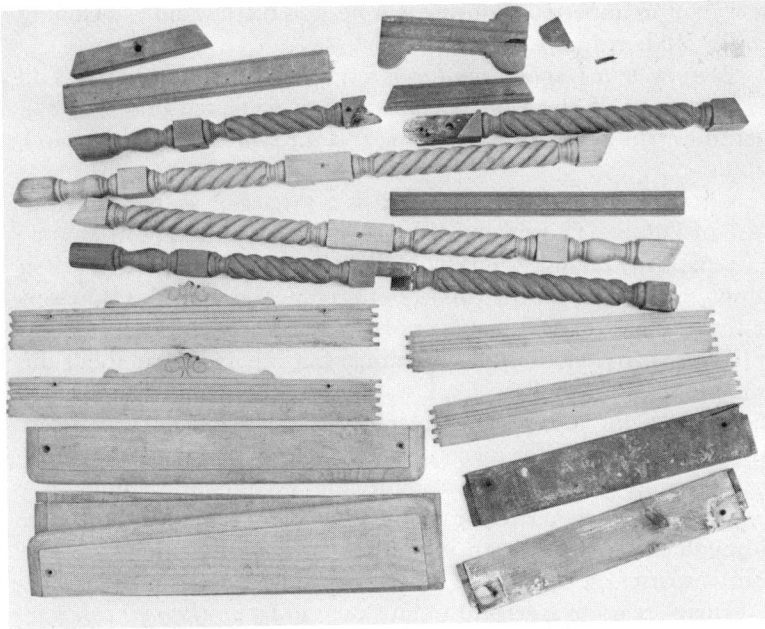

Identifying wood by density: Above, the parts of the table could not be identified visually. The lighter-colored wood looked like cherry; however, after the density of the reddish wood was calculated to be .44 (by measuring the volume of the stretcher and weighing it), cherry was ruled out. By weighing identical legs in the two woods, the density of the light-colored wood was found to be approximately .58, definitely eliminating cherry (.47) and making maple the likely candidate—considering, as well, color, hardness, closed grain, and the appearance of what figure is visible.

the walnut in imported furniture is American black walnut, including Danish Modern furniture.

Claro walnut (*Juglans hindsii*) is a species of walnut that grows on the west coast of the United States and is marketed only in small quantities. For all practical purposes, it is the same as American black walnut.

Circassian walnut (*Juglans regia*) is a species of walnut grown in much of Europe, Turkey, and Iran. It is also called European walnut, or Carpathian, English, French, Italian, Persian, Russian, or Turkish walnut, depending on the country of origin. The wood is tawny colored, with steaks of dark brown or black. In general, the color tends to be lighter than American black walnut, but otherwise has about the same properties. American black walnut can be substituted for European walnut for repair parts, keeping in mind the need to select lighter colored wood for a good color match.

Butternut (*Juglans cinerea*) sometimes called white walnut, is a wood species closely related to walnut, but is not a walnut substitute. Although the figure pattern is similar, the color is lighter, and the grain is coarser.

There are other species of walnut used in Japan (*Juglans cordiformis*), Argentina (*J. australis*), Peru (*J. neotropica*) and Manchuria (*J. mandshurica*), but these woods are not being imported in any commercial quantities. Some other woods, however, are being called walnut that are not walnut, including African walnut, Queensland walnut (Oriental Wood), and Rhodesian walnut. There is nothing wrong with these woods—they just aren't walnut.

Walnut is a strong wood, easily worked with both hand tools and machine tools. The figure of walnut varies greatly. Lumber is usually plain sawn. Veneers are plain sliced and quarter sliced. Figure patterns include plain, striped, figured, fiddleback, roll, mottled. Crotches, stumps, and burls produce valuable and highly figured veneers.

Figure 4–5 shows quarter-sawn and plain-sawn American black walnut, French (Circassian) walnut, and walnut crotch.

Mahogany

Mahogany was first introduced into European furniture making in the seventeenth century but did not begin to enjoy the great popularity it has currently until the middle of the eighteenth century. There are several not quite interchangeable varieties of mahogany, and some woods called mahogany that are not.

Cuban mahogany (*Swietenia mahogani*), also called West Indian mahogany, Jamaican mahogany, etc., is scarce today. Cuba was the principal source, but the wood has not been exported for three decades. This is the mahogany you will encounter in a lot of antique furniture, both domestic and European. The color of the wood is yellowish tan or light red when cut, but then darkens on exposure to a

FIGURE
4-5

(a)

(b)

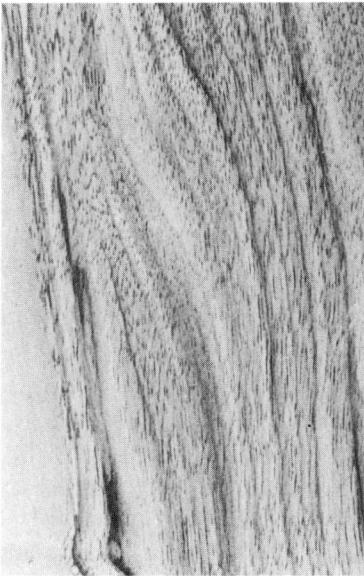

(c)

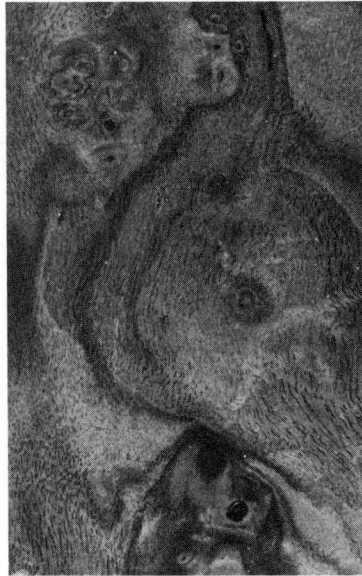

(d)

Walnut: (a) Quarter stripe, (b) plain stripe, (c) French, and (d) crotch.

deep rich red brown or golden brown. Patterns you will encounter include plain, striped, figured, mottled, fiddleback, and crotch.

Tropical American mahogany (*Swietenia macrophyllia*) comes
from Brazil, Guatemala, Honduras, Jamaica, Mexico, Nicaragua, and

**FIGURE
4-6**

(a)

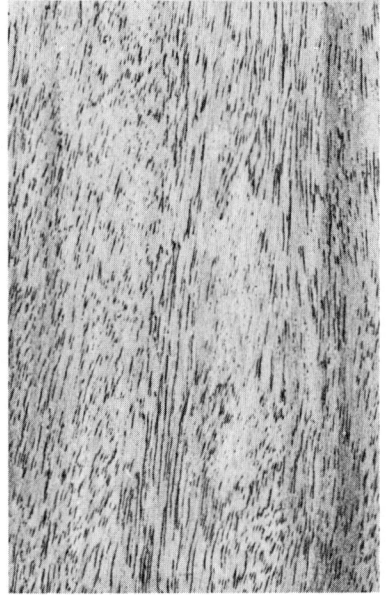

(b)

(c)

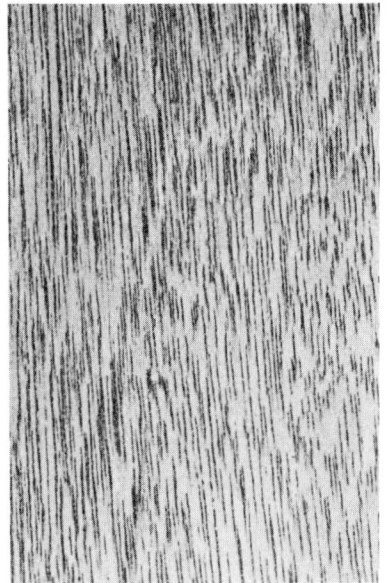

(d)

True mahoganies: (a) Tropical American mahogany and (b) African mahogany. Mahogany imitations: (c) Limba "blonde mahogany" and (d) Lauan "Philippine mahogany."

Peru. Most of this wood species used to come from Honduras and is also called Honduras mahogany. The color runs from light reddish brown or yellowish brown to a rich dark red, depending on the country of origin and the growing conditions of the particular tree. Most of the wood imported is light colored. On exposure after cutting, the wood color changes to a golden brown. The wood is lighter and softer than Cuban mahogany, and most lumber is plain figured.

African mahogany (*Khaya ivorensis*) is a true mahogany grown on the west coast of Africa. Large quantities are imported. The grain is coarser with larger and more widely spaced pores than other mahoganies, and the pattern is usually more figured than tropical American mahogany. The color is lighter, ranging from light pink to reddish brown and tannish brown. Lumber is available in great lengths and widths. Patterns available in veneer include plain, striped, mottled, fiddleback, burl, and crotch.

Philippine mahogany is a collective term applied to a great variety of Philippine hardwoods, also known as Lauan. None of these hardwoods are true mahoganies. These woods classed as Philippine mahogany include red Lauan (*Shorea negrosensis*), Tanguile (*S. polysperma*), Almon (*S. almon*), and white Lauan (*Pentacme contorta*). Compared to mahogany, these woods are coarse grained, coarse textured, stringy, and difficult to sand. Colors range from light pink to dark brown. Philippine mahogany should not be substituted for genuine mahogany in any furniture repair.

Mahogany is a strong wood, easily worked with both hand tools and machine tools. The figure of mahogany is more subdued than that of walnut. Lumber is usually plain sawn. Figure 4–6 shows tropical American mahogany, African mahogany, Limba "blond mahogany", and Lauan "Philippine mahogany", exact species unknown.

Oak

Oak has been used for furniture at least since Greek and early Roman times and has been a popular furniture wood ever since. The wood is hard and coarse textured.

American oak includes two major species—red oak (*Quercus rubra*) and white oak (*Q. alba*). Red oak is supposed to have a slightly more reddish tinge than white oak. White oak generally has a less coarse pattern than red oak, but less than tree-to-tree variations caused by growing conditions. For all practical purposes, the two woods can be used interchangeably. Plain-sawn oak has a prominant stripe and leaf figure produced by the large pores and the distinct layers of springwood. Quarter-sawn oak has a strong flake pattern produced by the very large and wide rays that have a high light reflectance. When rift cut, the oak figure is a fine pin stripe. Rotary cut oak veneer has a prominent watery pattern.

English oak, or English brown oak (*Quercus robur*) is distinctly different from American oak. The color varies from a light tan to deep brown. Available mainly as veneer, the pattern is very prominent with large wavy rays sometimes giving the wood an appearance of tortoise shell.

FIGURE 4-7

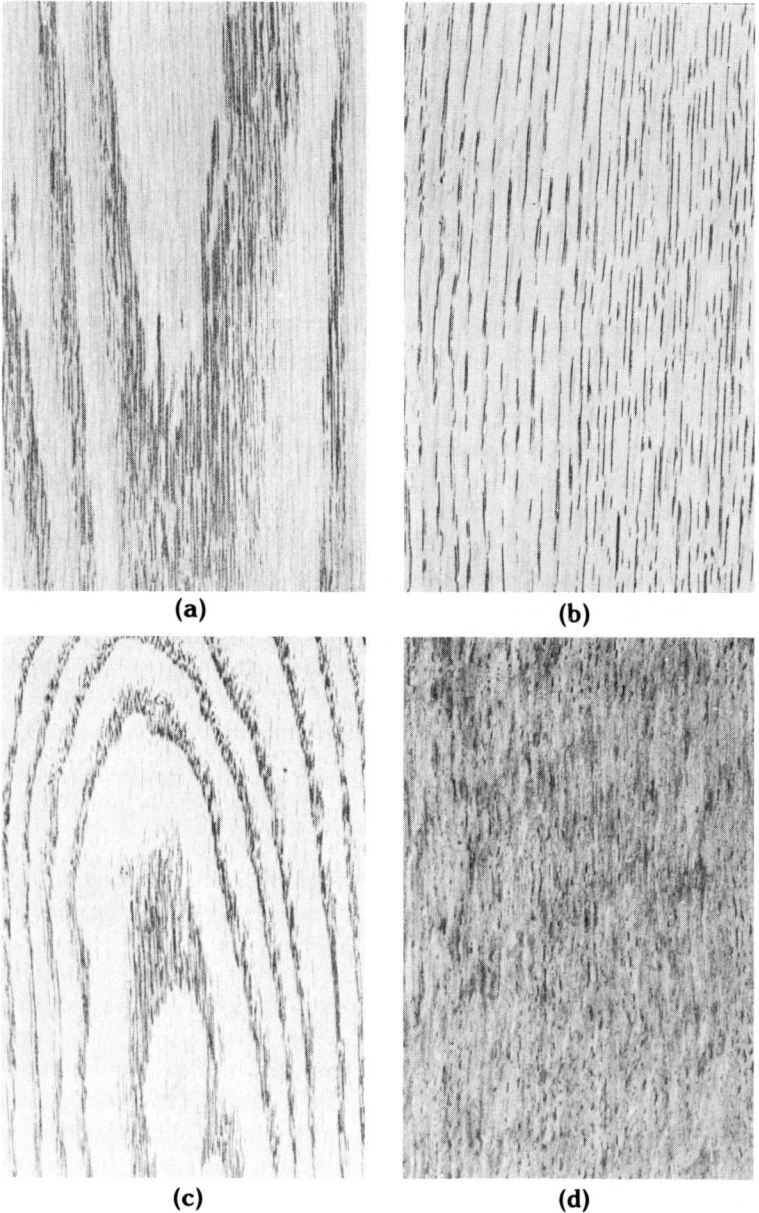

(a)

(b)

(c)

(d)

Oak: (a) Plain sawn white oak, (b) quarter sawn white oak, (c) plain sawn red oak, and (d) English oak.

Figure 4–7 shows varieties of oak. Several other woods closely resemble oak, and in old furniture it is almost impossible to tell them apart. These woods are shown in Figure 4–8: ash, chestnut, locust, and pecan.

**FIGURE
4-8**

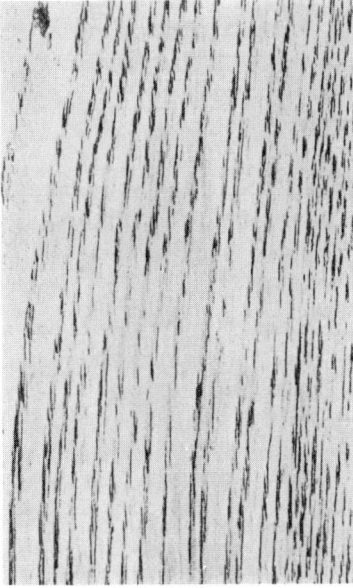
(a)

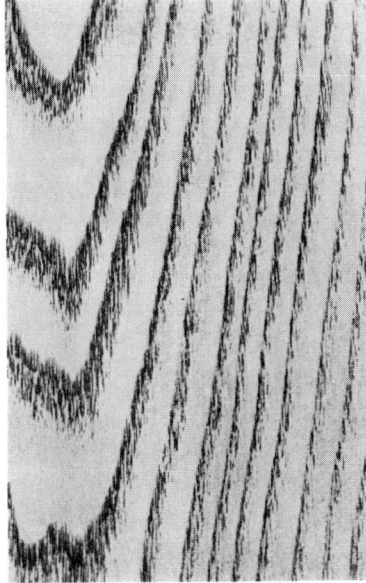
(b)

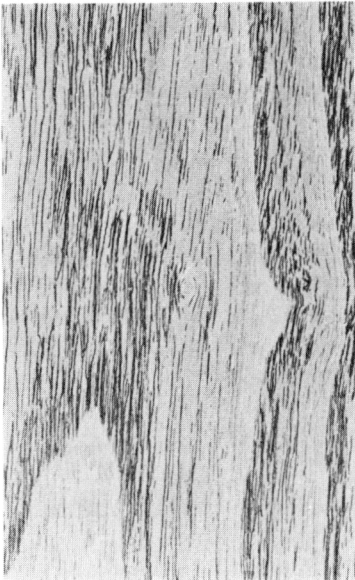
(c)

(d)

Oak look-alikes: (a) Ash, (b) chestnut, (c) locust, and (d) pecan.

Cherry

American black cherry (*Prunus serotina*) has been an important American furniture wood since colonial times. Cherry is another wood that has been used for furniture since early Greek and Roman times, but unlike oak that was steady in its popularity, cherry has had its ups and downs. European cherry (*P. avium*) is similar in color and figure, and in repair work, the two can be interchanged. The color of cherry is a light reddish brown that slowly darkens on exposure to a dark reddish brown. The grain is straight, sometimes wavy and figured. Small gum pockets are normal markings.

Cherry is a light and strong but hard wood. The wood is easily worked with machine tools, but hard to work with hand tools.

Maple

Maple is another American wood that has been popular since colonial days. There are two kinds of maple—hard maple and soft maple. Hard maple (*Acer saccharum*), also called birds-eye maple, sugar maple, fiddleback maple, northern maple, black maple, and rock maple is a heavy, hard, strong, close-grained wood with a uniform texture. The heartwood color ranges from a creamy white to light reddish brown. Sapwood is white. Soft maple (*Acer rubrum*) has the same characteristics as hard maple but is not as heavy, hard, or strong.

Both maples are easily worked with machine tools, but hard maple is difficult to work with hand tools.

Figure 4–9 shows light-colored woods: birds eye maple, curly maple, plain sawn maple, and poplar.

Birch

Yellow birch (*Betula alleghaniensis*) is the most important variety of the wood. While birch is widely used today with maple in Early American style furniture and reproductions, in colonial times it was seldom used as a furniture wood. Yellow birch heartwood is a cream or light brown tinged with red. Sapwood is white.

Sweet birch (*B.-lenta*) heartwood is brown, with light brown or yellow sapwood. European birch (*B. alba*) is a fine-grained, light-colored wood that is being extensively imported in the form of plywood.

Birch is a heavy hardwood, difficult to work with hand tools but easily worked with power tools.

Figure 4–10 shows characteristics of cherry birch, gum and pecan.

Fruitwood

There is no such wood as fruitwood. The term originated with clear-finished French Provincial furniture made of cherry, apple, pear, and other such fruitwoods. Today the term means a brown finish, usually distressed, on almost any close-grained hardwood, including cherry (rarely), maple, birch, alder, poplar, or anything else handy.

FIGURE 4-9

(a)

(b)

(c)

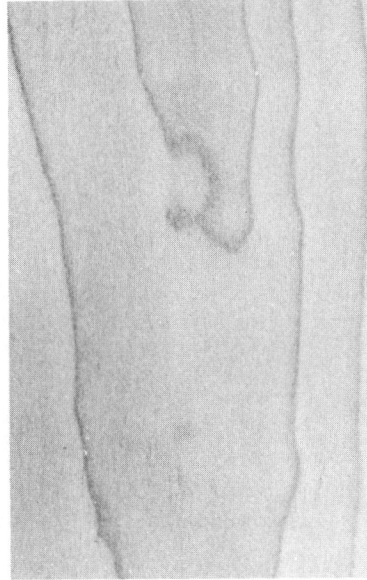

(d)

Light-colored woods: (a) Birds eye maple, (b) curly maple, (c) plain maple, and (d) poplar.

**FIGURE
4-10**

(a)

(b)

(c)

(d)

Hardwoods: (a) Cherry, (b) birch, (c) gum, and (d) pecan.

Poplar

Also called whitewood, tulipwood, cucumber. While classed as a
hardwood, yellow poplar (*Liriodendron tulipfera*) is comparatively
soft, but not nearly as soft as pine, Philippine mahogany, and red-

wood. American yellow poplar comes not from a poplar at all, but from the tulip tree, which belongs to the magnolia family. Poplar has been widely used in furniture since colonial times. Color is creamy to yellow brown with a greenish tinge, or greenish areas. Poplar can be finished to imitate most other common furniture woods—a practice which has been widely followed.

Poplar is easy to work with hand and machine tools. It can take any kind of finish.

Basswood

Sometimes called American whitewood (see "Poplar"). Basswood (*Tilia americana*) is a lightweight hardwood, uniform in texture and cream white to cream brown in color with little visible grain. It can be (and often is) finished to imitate walnut or mahogany. Basswood is easy to work with hand and machine tools.

Pine

White pine was one of the principle woods used in country Colonial furniture of all kinds and is used today in reproductions and adaptions in this perennially popular style. There is one difference, however. In today's knotty pine furniture, knots are far larger and more plenteous than would have been tolerated in colonial times.

Not all varieties of pine are suitable for use in Colonial style furniture. Sugar pine (*Pinus lambertina*), ponderosa (*P. ponderosa*) and western white pine (*P. monticola*) are three that are.

Pine is not just an American furniture wood. In England, Scotch pine (called redwood in Britain), and white pine (called yellow pine) have been used for furniture since 1600, and later used for pieces that would be painted or gilded.

Table 4-1 summarizes the characteristics of the woods that have been widely used structurally in furniture. In each case the listed wood is the American variety, as this is the species you will most often encounter.

4-2 PLYWOOD _____

Plywood, generally speaking, is wood panels made of thin layers of wood called *veneers* or *plies* that are glued together with the grain direction of alternate layers at right angles. This form of plywood is called *veneer core plywood*. Another form of plywood construction has a single core of thick wood strips in the center. This is called *lumber core plywood*. Particleboard is also used as a core material for a form of plywood. Figure 4-11 shows plywood construction.

The advantages of plywood over solid wood in furniture construction are worth considering. While solid wood is strong in the direction

Common Furniture Woods

TABLE 4-1

Species	Wood Color	Figure P-Plain Sawed Q-Quarter Sawed		Figure Pattern	Grain
Alder, red *Alnus rubra* Western cedar	Pale pinkish brown to white, darkens to golden or reddish tan with exposure	P	Faint	Plain	Closed
		Q	Scattered flakes		
Ash, white *Fraxinus americana*	Cream to very light brown heartwood, sapwood lighter	P	Conspicuous	Straight grain	Open
		Q	Distinct		
Basswood *Tilia americana* linden, American white-wood, lime	Creamy white	P	Faint	Practically none	Closed
		Q	None		
Beech *Fagus grandifolia*	Reddish brown heartwood, white sapwood	P	Faint	Straight grain, uniform texture	Closed
		Q	Numerous small flakes		
Birch *Betula alleghaniensis* Yellow birch	Cream, or light brown heartwood, white sapwood	P	Distinct	Fine, even texture, straight grain, times curly or wavy	Closed
		Q	Occasionally wavy		
Butternut *Juglans cinerea* white walnut	Light chestnut brown heartwood, white sapwood	P	Faint	Pattern resembles walnut, but pores larger	Open
		Q	None		
Cherry, American black *Prunus serotina*	Light reddish tan darkens to reddish brown on exposure	P	Faint, occasional burl	Satiny straight grain, some figured; small gum pockets normal	Closed
		Q	Occasional burl		

Wood	Color	Figure		Characteristics	Pores
Chestnut, sweet *Castanea sativa* Spanish, European chestnut	Light tan, some dark brown evenly or unevenly	P	Conspicuous	Resembles oak. Some worm holes occasionally, but this is not wormy chestnut	Open
		Q	Distinct		
Elm, American *Ulmus americana* Gray, white, water, soft elm	Gray brown, pinkish brown heartwood, lighter sapwood	P	Distinct	Fine wavy pattern within growth rings. Vessel lines appear as surface grooves and form irregular bands as growth rings	Open
		Q	Faint		
Gum, Red *Liquidambar styraciflua* sweet gum	Reddish brown heartwood, pinkish white sapwood	P	Distinct	No pattern except pigmentation	Closed
		Q	None		
Hackberry *Celtis occidentalis*	Yellowish, or greenish gray	P	Conspicuous	Straight open grain. Coarse, uneven texture. Pores show as distinct grooves. Resembles ash	Open
		Q	Distinct		
Hickory *Carya ovata*	Brown heartwood, cream to white sapwood	P	Distinct, not conspicuous	Pores visible, grade in size across growth wood rays small. Pores generally plugged.	Open
		Q	Faint stripe		
Mahogany, African *Khaya ivorensis*	Light pink when fresh cut, darkens to reddish tan	P	Faint	Grain texture coarser than tropical American mahogany. Normally stripe pattern; also mottle, crotch, swirl	Open
		Q	Faint		
Mahogany, troical American *Swietenia macrophylla*	Light reddish brown to dark red depending on where tree grew, fades to golden color	P	Faint	Fine texture. Striped, plain, mottled patterns	Open
		Q	Faint		
Mahogany, Philippine (Lauan) *Shorea negrosensis* red lauan	Red to brown	P	Faint	Coarse texture, large pores. Very subdued pattern	Open
		Q	Faint		
Maple, hard *Acer saccharum* rock maple, sugar maple	Cream to light reddish brown heartwood, sapwood lighter	P	Faint	Straight grain. Curly, fiddleback, burl, birds-eye	Closed
		Q	Faint		

(*Continued on page* 68)

67

Common Furniture Woods (Cont'd.)

Species	Wood Color		Figure P-Plain Sawed Q-Quarter Sawed	Figure Pattern	Grain
Maple, soft *Acer rubrum*, *A. saccharinum* silver maple, red maple	Cream to light reddish brown heartwood, sapwood lighter	P Q	Faint Faint	Softer and lighter than hard maple. Figure not as pronounced	Closed
Oak, English *Quercus petraea*, *Q. robur*	Light tan to deep brown, occasional black spots	P Q	Conspicuous Distinct	Prominent pattern, sometimes resembling tortoise shell	Open
Oak, red *Quercus rubra*	Light gray brown	P Q	Conspicuous Distinct	Pores open with distinct outlines. Wood rays 1/4" to 1" along grain. Flake figure less prominent than white oak	Open
Oak, white *Quercus alba*	Light gray brown	P Q	Conspicuous Distinct	Outline of large pores indistinct. Closer grained than red oak. Pores filled with tyloses	Open
Pecan *Carya illinoensis* pecky pecan	Reddish brown heartwood white sapwood	P Q	Distinct Distinct	Pores visible as grooves and lines. Rays invisible on plain sawn, distinct on quarter sawn	Open
Pine *Pinus spp.* sugar, western white pine	Cream to light reddish brown	P Q	Faint to distinct None	Knots need not be present	Closed
Poplar *Liriodendron tulipfera* white wood, yellow poplar	Light to dark yellowish brown with green or purple tinge occasionally	P Q	Faint Faint	When stained can look like cherry or maple	Closed
Walnut, black *Juglans nigra*	Light gray brown to dark chocolate brown heartwood, almost white sapwood	P Q	Distinct Distinct	Pores irregular, produce coarse but smooth texture. Dark vessel lines in all surfaces. Mottled, striped, plain figure	Open

FIGURE
4-11

Plywood construction: (Top, from left) Common A/C fir plywood, birch veneer plywood, veneered flakeboard, veneered particleboard, Baltic birch plywood (Finland, USSR); and (bottom) lumber core plywood construction.

of the grain, it is weak across the grain. Plywood is equally strong along and across the panel. Plywood has better dimensional stability than solid wood. What expanding and contracting is done with changes in humidity is done equally in both directions. Solid wood shrinks and expands far more across the grain than with it; this wood characteristic complicates furniture joint design and assembly. Plywood warps less than the best kiln-dried wood, and checking and splitting do not occur under normal conditions.

Plywood Construction

The outside plies are called *face plies*, or *face and back plies* if the backside is of a lower grade. The plies directly under the face plies are called *crossbands*. The crossbands and the plies under them are collectively called the *core plies*. The core may be veneer or lumber or a combination of the two. If the core is chipboard or fiberboard the crossbands are omitted. The different plies may vary as to thickness, number and kinds of wood. Wood for core plies is selected for low cost, strength, and stability; face veneers are selected for appearance.

The more plies used in a given thickness the more nearly equal will be the strength and shrinkage properties along and across the panel, and the greater the resistance to splitting. Warping is controlled by balanced construction. Plies are arranged in pairs about the core, so that for each ply except the core there is an opposite and parallel ply having the same thickness and kind of wood. This construction always uses an odd number of plies. This is to balance out any tendency to warpage.

There are other considerations besides strength in plywood selection, however. Plywood with veneers used for all core plies will have the best screw-holding power from the face or the back of the panel, but will have less screw-holding power from the edge than lumber core plywood. Core imperfections may "print" through the face veneer to disfigure the surface, particularly when a stain finish is used. Edges are difficult to rout, and exposed edges show core voids and imperfections and are difficult to stain. Figure 4–12 shows several methods of edging veneer core plywood.

**FIGURE
4-12**

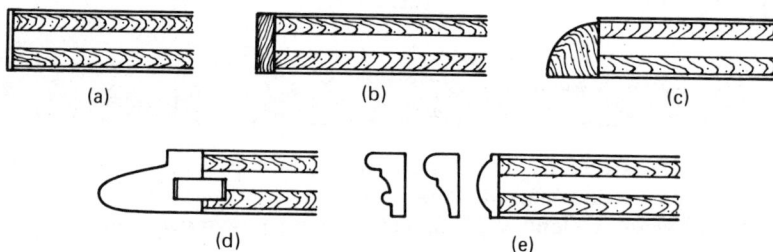

(a)   (b)   (c)

(d)   (e)

Edging plywood: (a) Veneer, (b) solid wood strip such as lattice, (c) stock quarter-round or other moulding, (d) solid wood splined to edge and moulded, and (e) stock hardwood decorative mouldings.

Lumber core plywood has a single thick core of narrow edge-glued strips of sawn lumber running lengthwise to the panel between veneer crossbands. Lumber core plywood is the most expensive, but provides an essentially solid-wood exposed edge that is easily shaped and finished. Screw-holding through the face and the edge is the same as for solid lumber. This is the plywood to use for anything that will have screws into the edges as for hinges.

Plywood made with a chipboard or flakeboard core instead of veneer or lumber core has many advantages including lower cost. It is the most dimensionally stable form of plywood construction, and there is no core ply print through. Moulded edges of chipboard are difficult to smooth and finish; edges of flakeboard plywood while easy to shape, must be covered with an opaque finish instead of stain. Screwholding power in the edges of either is poor, and both materials are heavy.

Figure 4–13 shows how the edge of flakeboard can be moulded.

FIGURE
4-13

Moulded veneered flakeboard edge.

Buying Plywood

Furniture-grade plywood is available from several sources. Lumberyards carry a limited selection in ¼'', ½'', and ¾'' thicknesses, but usually only in full 4 x 8 panels. Face veneers include pine, birch, maple, and cherry. Some yards will special order veneer plywood for you. Yards are your least expensive source, but as most furniture repair needs can be met with less than a full panel, you should look into other sources.

Check the Yellow Pages for cabinet and millwork shops in your area. They often have leftover pieces from jobs that they are more than willing to sell to you. You will be able to find most domestic woods one time or another.

You can also mail order plywood. Supply houses such as Constantine's and Craftsman and others sell furniture-grade plywood in a wide variety of woods, thicknesses, and panel sizes.

There is one, and only one, inexpensive plywood recommended for furniture repair work. This is Lauan underlayment-grade plywood imported from Korea, Japan, and other places in the Far East. It is also sometimes called Philippine mahogany plywood. In construction it has one thick core ply and quite thin face veneers, with no crossbanding. As it is an underlayment grade, there will be no voids in the core. It comes in a nominal ¼'' thickness. Lauan somewhat resembles mahogany in color and surface texture, but without enough of a grain figure to be used where it can be seen too clearly.

Fir plywood, the construction plywood sold in lumberyards in A-C Exterior and A-D Interior grades, is not suitable for furniture repair, even if it will be completely hidden. Knotholes and splits are permitted in core and back plies which result in voids that do not provide a solid backing for the face veneer, and edges that can be difficult to glue or finish. Another problem with these grades of fir plywood, especially when you are using them in small panels is ply delamination caused by glue failure or absence in patches.

71

Veneering is one of the oldest woodworking arts. The Egyptians used veneer in their finest furniture, as far back as 1500 BC. Veneer was used in most of the great styles of furniture—both English and French. Veneer was not used in American Colonial furniture, but it was used extensively in most later styles. Rare and exotic woods, too expensive or too fragile for structural members were, and are used to decorate furniture made of oak, mahogany, walnut, and other hardwoods, and pine. (See Fig. 4-14.)

There is nothing inherently cheap about this use of veneer in furniture. What has given veneer its bad name was late nineteenth century mass-produced "Grand Rapids" furniture, in which veneer was used—not as a decoration on otherwise visible frame wood, but as a means of making lesser woods appear to be what they were not. It is still being done, but today a lot of this kind of fakery is being done with plastics and printed overlays. This nineteenth century Victorian furniture is again popular, and undoubtedly some of the pieces you repair or restore will be made this way.

Veneer is a thin layer of wood that is sliced or sawn from a log, or a part of a log, called a *flitch*. Sawing is avoided whenever possible because of the amount of wood unavoidably turned into sawdust. The stack of cut-off veneer pieces is also called a *flitch*. As in lumber cutting, the way the veneer is cut from the flitch produces different grain patterns. (See Fig. 4-15.)

Prior to cutting on a slicer, the veneer flitch is prepared by steaming or soaking as required by the wood. Methods of cutting depend

FIGURE 4-14

A jewelry box is pictured. The visible structure is rosewood. The panels are thuja and avoidire veneer, trimmed with made-up holly and ebony inlay.

**FIGURE
4-15**

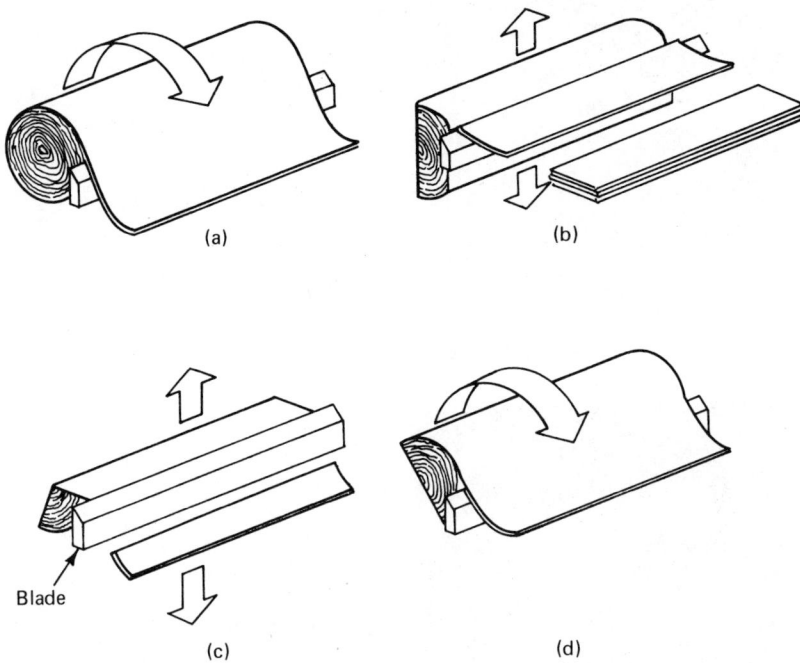

Slicing veneer from the log (called a *flitch*): (a) Rotary cut, (b) plain sliced, (c) half-round sliced, and (d) quarter sliced.

on the inherent grain of the wood and the characteristics of the particular log.

In rotary cutting the barked and trimmed log is lathe mounted and turned against a full-length blade. The veneer comes off like an unrolling paper towel. The grain pattern is big and bold. Rotary sliced veneer can be produced in big sheets, and there's practically no waste. Most softwood veneer is produced this way.

In plain slicing, a half-log flitch is mounted in a slicer and sheets of veneer are sliced off in a paper cutter–like operation, except that the flitch is moved against a stationary blade. Grain patterns are the same as would be obtained in plain-sawn lumber.

In quarter slicing, a quarter-log flitch is moved against the blade with the flitch turned so the growth rings in the wood are at an approximate right angle to the blade. This produces the same grain pattern as quarter-sawn lumber.

Half-round slicing produces the same grain pattern as is obtained with rotary cutting. The part-log flitch is mounted off-center and is rotated against the blade, producing a flitch of rotary-cut veneer.

Rift-cut veneer is similar to quarter slicing, with the slicing through growth rings, but at a significantly less than perpendicular angle.

FIGURE
4-16

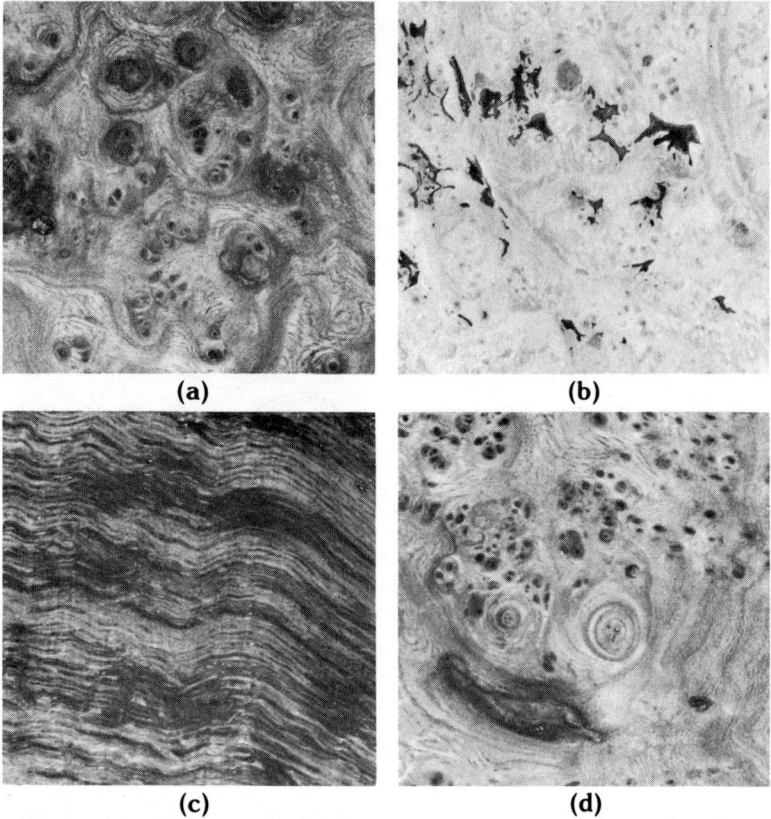

(a)　　　　　　　　　　　(b)

(c)　　　　　　　　　　　(d)

Fancy burl and crotch veneer: (a) Carpathian elm burl, (b) redwood burl, (c) walnut crotch, and (d) thuja burl.

Standard veneer thickness was until recently 1/28″, but veneer you buy today can be as thin as 1/40″; you won't know what you are getting until you open the package and put a micrometer on it. This can cause complications if you are using more than one kind of veneer on a panel.

Unlike board lumber that is cut only from the trunk of the tree, veneer—many with exotic grain patterns—are also cut from crotches, burls, butts, and stumps (See Fig. 4–16). These veneers lack mechanical strength and must be handled with great care when gluing and clamping.

After the flitch is cut into veneer, the flitch of veneers is kept together with all the veneers in the order they were cut—like the pages of a book. As the veneers are thin, the change in the grain pattern from one piece of veneer is slight, and these successive pieces of veneer can be matched in a variety of decorative ways.

In slip matching, the veneers, after trimming, are joined side by side to produce a repeating pattern. Quarter-sawn veneers are usually used for slip matching.

In book matching, alternate veneers are turned over, producing left and right symmetrical patterns, which in turn can produce a repeating pattern of pairs of pieces of veneer.

A diamond pattern is produced by diagonally cutting four pieces from the same, or successive, veneers in a flitch and joining them to form a diamond pattern. Veneers with a stripe pattern are usually used.

In a reverse diamond, the pieces are cut the same as for a diamond pattern, but reversed in layout position so the grain pattern produces an X.

A pair of book-matched veneers can be end book matched to produce a four-way symmetrical pattern that is often used on table tops. Actually, the way in which veneers can be attractively cut, matched, and contrasted is almost endless, particularly if you include checkerboard and diaper patterns. Figure 4–17 shows two of the ways veneer can be matched.

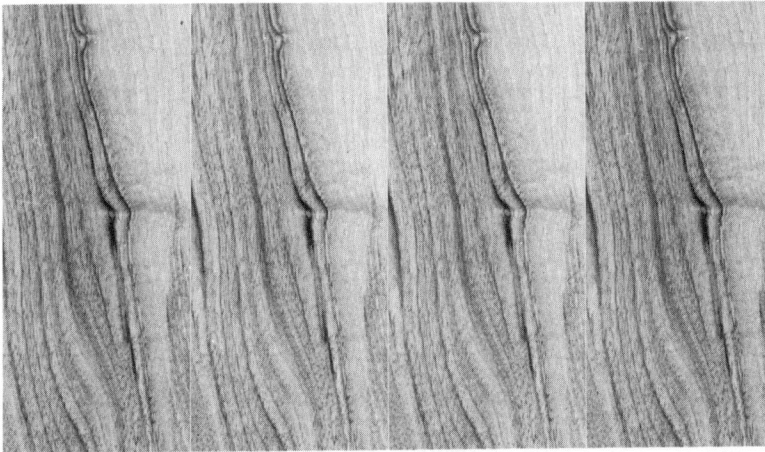

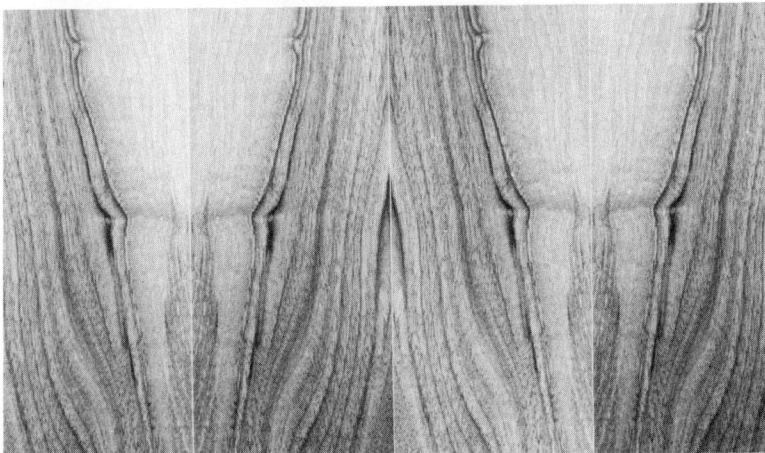

FIGURE 4-17

Veneer matching: (top) book matching and (bottom) slip matching.

More woods, particularly the more decorative and exotic woods, are available as veneer than as lumber or plywood. Table 4–2 lists the veneers generally available.

TABLE
4-2

American Woods and Historic Cabinet Woods Generally Available as Veneer

American	*Historic*
Ash	Amboyna burl
Aspen	Avodire
Beech	Carpathian elm burl
Birch	Ebony
Cherry	Faux satine
Elm	Harewood
Gum	Holly
Locust	Oak, English
Mahogany	Padouk
Mahogany burl and crotches	Pearwood
Maple	Rosewood, Brasil
Oak	Rosewood, East Indies
Pecan	Satinwood
Pine	Tulipwood
Redwood burl	Zebrano
Sycamore	
Walnut	
Walnut burls and crotches	

* Veneer is also available dyed in many colors for marquetry.

FIGURE
4-18

Veneer can be purchased in very large pieces, but it is normally available to craftsmen in pieces 36" long and from 3" to 12" wide, depending on the species. The samples shown are available as a set of 50. (See appendix.)

Veneer is usually sold 36″ long and in whatever width came off the flitch, which can be anything from 3″ to 12″, depending on log and species. Minimum orders for any one kind are 3 or 4 square feet and prices range, typically from $.20 per square foot for common woods like elm up to $1.50 per square foot for walnut burls. Burls, butts, and crotches come in odd-size pieces and you should expect to have some waste. Pieces of veneer are usually shipped in flitch, but if you plan to match panels, you should be sure to ask for the veneer in flitch.

You can also obtain some varieties of veneer in longer pieces.

**FIGURE
4-19**

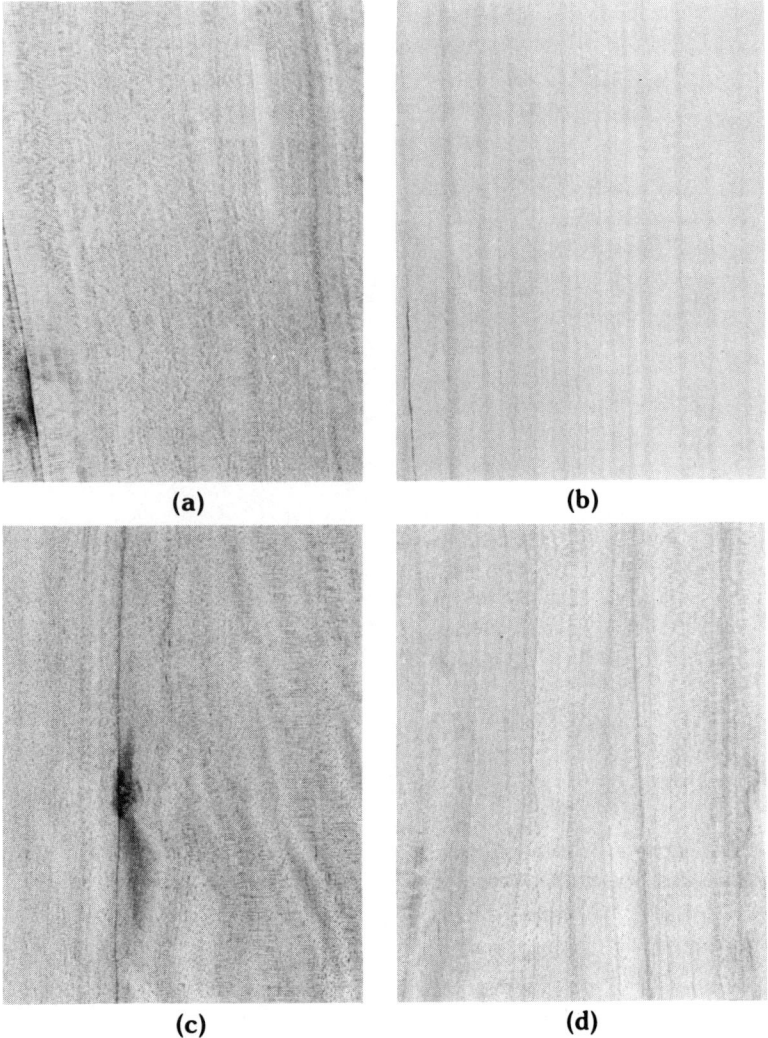

(a)

(b)

(c)

(d)

Light-colored veneers used extensively in period furniture: (a) Satinwood, (b) faux satine, (c) avoidire, and (d) prima vera.

FIGURE
4-20

(a)

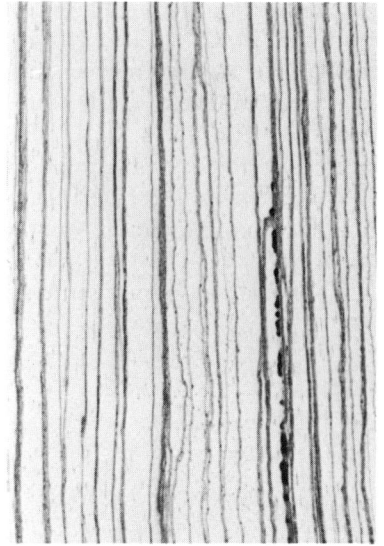

(b)

(c)

(d)

Exotic veneers: (a) Ebony, (b) zebrano (zebra wood), (c) teak, and (d)
East Indian rosewood.

Chair Repairs

5

Chairs take a beating even in normal use. They are subjected to greater stresses, strains, and shocks than any other kind of furniture. Over the life of any chair the need for frame repair is inevitable, and the repairs must be structurally sound—well-made, not just cosmetic.

5-1 CHAIR WOODS

Woods used in chair manufacture are chosen carefully. No one wood is best for all parts of a chair frame. Chair frame parts are identified in Figure 5–1. When replacing a broken part it is best to use the kind of wood used originally. If you cannot identify the original wood or are interested in a strictly functional repair, select one of the woods recommended below.

In general, hardwoods are used where the part will be subjected to shock and abrasion. Softwoods are used only in great thickness; usually they are confined to plank seats and to bulky backs on Captain's chairs. Softwood pieces are never joined to softwood pieces, only to hardwood pieces. A softwood-to-softwood joint cannot be made strong enough to be used in a chair construction.

- *Legs:* Maple is the first choice for legs, turned or plain. Other satisfactory woods include cherry, birch, beech, and walnut. Oak, ash, and hickory may also be used for legs if plain or with shallow turnings. Mahogany is not suitable for turned legs.

**FIGURE
5-1**

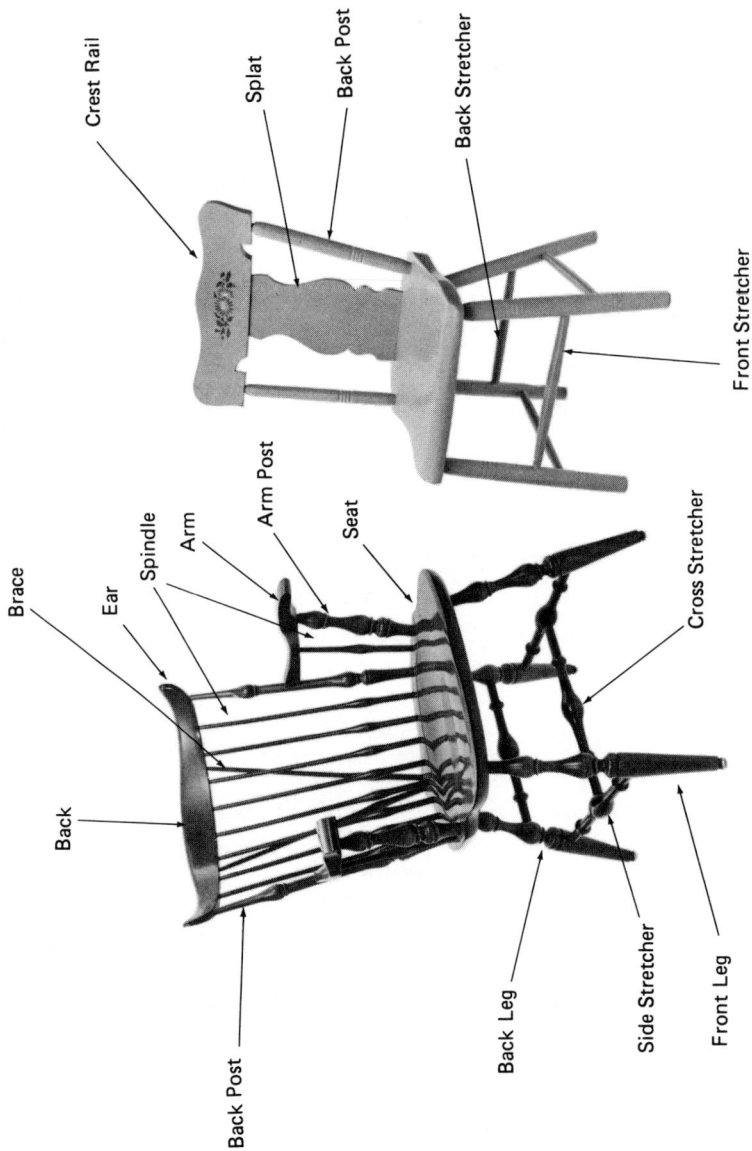

Crest Rail

Splat

Back Post

Back Stretcher

Front Stretcher

Brace

Ear

Spindle

Arm

Arm Post

Seat

Cross Stretcher

Back

Back Post

Back Leg

Side Stretcher

Front Leg

Parts of chair frames.

- *Stretchers:* Use maple, white oak, hickory, or match the wood used for the legs.

- *Seats:* Use maple, cherry, birch, beech, walnut, oak, sycamore, but not ash or hickory. Pine and poplar can be used for seats, if they are made two inches or so thick.

- *Spindles:* Wood for spindles should always be blanked by splitting rather than by sawing in order to assure the straightest possible grain, and the greatest strength. Maple, oak, ash, and hickory are good choices for spindles.

- *Bent Parts:* Use white oak, ash, and hickory.

- *Backs:* Almost any wood can be used for carved or shaped backs, but remember to use large sections of pine or poplar if you decide to use these woods.

  Note: Spruce, fir, cedar, and redwood are not used for any chair repair parts.

  Upholstered Chair Parts: Show wood—exposed finished wood—should be replaced with the same wood. Hidden frame wood can be replaced with any hardwood handy. No pine or other softwoods should ever be used. Upholstered chair frame parts are identified in Figure 5–2.

5-2 CHAIR FRAME REPAIRS

Minor chair frame repairs most of the time require solutions to isolated problems. Only when a chair has to be completely disassembled is there really any need for an organized start-to-finish procedure. Generally you look at the problem and decide on a course of action from many possibilities, then do what has to be done.

Cleaning up Tenons and Sockets

New glue, whether the same kind in the joint, or a different kind, will not stick to old glue. The old glue must be removed from the sides of the tenons and sockets. Encrusted glue should be removed also from the end of the tenon and the bottom of the socket but just enough to ensure these masses do not obstruct joint reassembly. The end and bottom have very little holding power.

Scrape, file, or sand the glue from the tenon and clean the sides of the socket by scraping, by drilling out with a 1/32″ oversize drill, or by a cylindrical burr in a hand grinder.

As there is no way you can clean the glue from a spindle tenon and a socket without removing some of the wood in the process, the joint is going to fit looser afterwards than before. This is not a

FIGURE
5-2

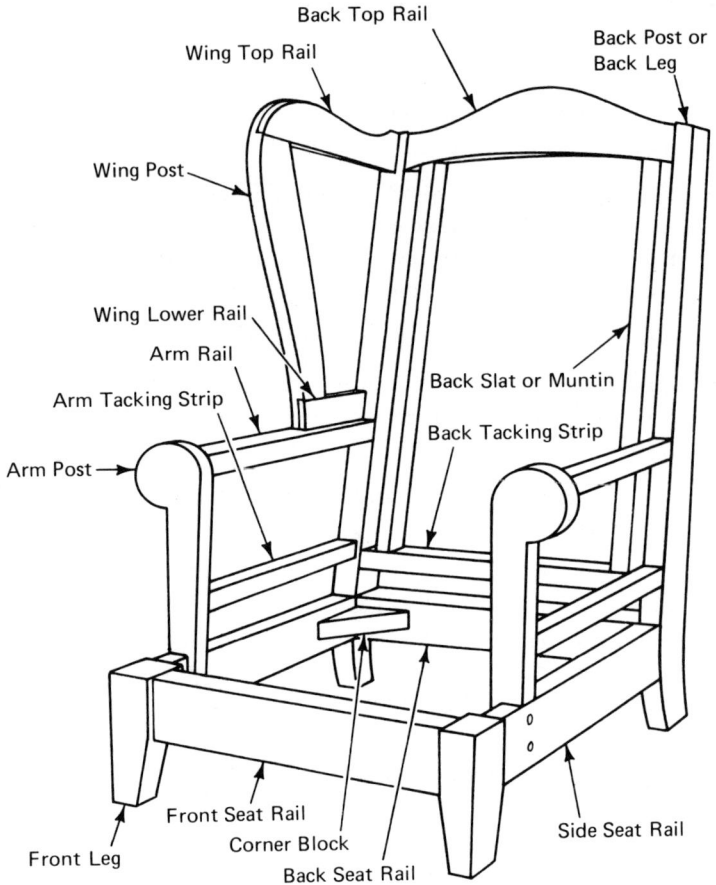

Back Top Rail

Wing Top Rail

Back Post or
Back Leg

Wing Post

Wing Lower Rail

Arm Rail

Arm Tacking Strip

Back Slat or Muntin

Back Tacking Strip

Arm Post

Front Seat Rail

Corner Block

Front Leg

Back Seat Rail

Side Seat Rail

Parts of an upholstered chair frame.

disaster, however. You simply have to choose a glue that will retain strength while bridging the gap. There are two choices for a permanent repair—epoxy cement for reasonably fitting joints and filled epoxy for those joints where the spindle rattles around in the socket. Not all repairs, however, should be considered to be permanent, and there are occasions when you should not use epoxy.

If you are regluing a single joint in a chair, it is not wise to use a glue so permanent as epoxy, without first carefully considering how and if the chair could at some future time be completely disassembled except for that joint. For example, in the chair in Figure 5-3 one end of a stretcher came loose from the leg socket. Examination showed that the glue line in the leg-to-seat joint had also failed, allowing slight leg movement; that is, just enough movement to allow for the stretcher end to be pulled clear of the socket in the leg. The leg was still tightly in the seat and there was no way it could be removed for regluing.

FIGURE
5-3

(a)   (b)

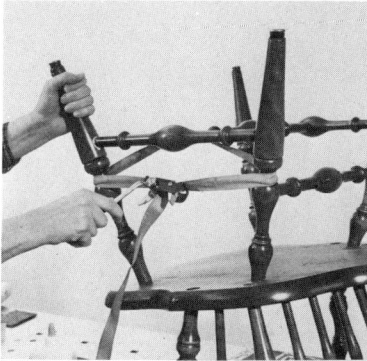

(c)

Regluing a loose stretcher: (a) Scrape glue from the tenon and the socket; (b) apply glue liberally; and (c) clamp the joint using a nylon band clamp.

The open joint was reglued with white glue, nothing was done about the seat joint. In the normal course of events, other stretcher joints will likely come loose and, hopefully, each can be repaired. At some point, failed glue and continuous minor movement will wear the seat joints to the point where the legs will begin popping out. Then, the whole underbody of the chair must be taken apart and every joint cleaned up and reglued. This is further evidence that if we make a practice of using epoxy cement each time we repair a single loose joint we will never be able to get the chair apart later when we have a bigger gluing job on our hands. Epoxy glue should be used only on joints that will never be taken apart.

Gluing Joints You Cannot Take Apart

As previously stated, you can't reglue a joint without cleaning the old glue from the mating surfaces. But by injecting glue into the joint to fill the spaces between the two parts, you can create a condition where the two parts cannot rattle about—you have already established they won't come apart. (See Fig. 5–4.)

In another situation, where you do not want to take the joint apart, for example to preserve an antique rush seat, the glue-injected joint can be immobilized with a peg or a metal pin.

To inject glue only, a hole is drilled from the least conspicuous side of the part containing the socket to reach the 1/16″ to 1/8″ void at the end of the tenon. If the joint is to be also pinned, the hole is drilled to pass through the tenon and into the other side of the socketed part.

FIGURE
5-4

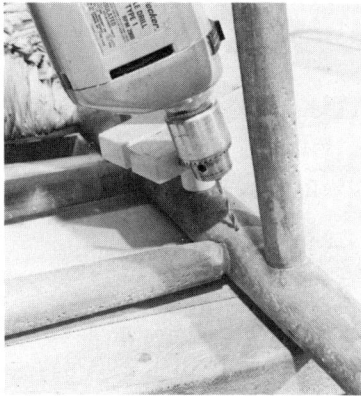
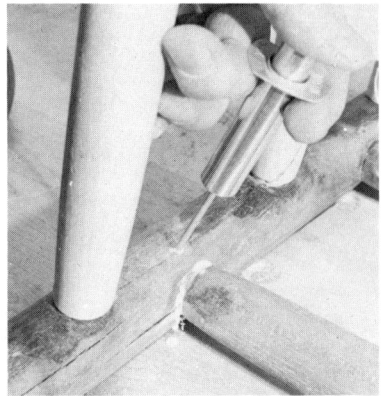

(a)   (b)

(c)   (d)

Regluing a joint that cannot be taken apart: (a) Drill a hole for glue injection and pin. (b) Inject glue; work the joint to help distribute glue; keep forcing in glue until it comes out everywhere. (c) Tap in pin, driving it below surface; cap with a wood plug. (d) Hole in seat rail joint is angled so one pin and glue injection would stabilize both front and side rails.

The next step is to blow out as much of the dust and powdered glue in the joint as possible. Work the joint as you are blowing it out to loosen the dirt.

Glue is pumped into the joint with a tool called a *glue injector*. (See Fig. 5-5.) The best glue to use is white glue. Its low viscosity lets it flow in confined spaces, and it can be easily cleaned out of the injector. As it does not dry brittle, it will not flake out of the joint. While injecting the glue move the parts to help spread the glue, and keep forcing glue in until it spouts out everywhere.

FIGURE 5-5

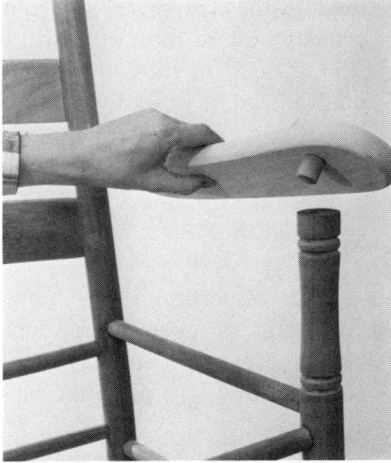

(a)

(b)

Attaching arm to post with pinned dowel: This chair had been repaired with an off-size arm from another chair, which was secured with a nail. (a) The new arm and post were drilled for the dowel. (b) The dowel is locked in each with 3/16" birch pins.

Pinning Chair Joints

If you use a metal pin, it should be at least 1/8″ in diameter. Use brass rod, brazing rod (wipe off the rosin with lacquer thinner), or steel drill rod. The steel rod is the least desirable because it will rust. Cut the rod so it can be driven 1/8″ below the surface, and chamfer one end for easier driving. After the pin is in, apply glue and tap in a wood peg. Trim when dry.

If you use a wood peg, have the minimum diameter 3/16″. Don't use birch dowels except for joints where there will be relatively little stress; for example, pegging the arm to the back or front leg. (See Fig. 5–6.) The birch in these dowels hasn't much strength. The ideal wood for pegs is locust, but as most of us will have a hard time finding locust, use hickory, hard maple, or ash. Trim the peg flush with the surface. The advantage of a peg over a pin is that it can be drilled out, but this is not particularly pertinent to a joint you can't get apart anyway.

Taking Chairs Apart

The first step is a careful inspection to see how the chair went together, and most important, to uncover any previous repairs that will make your work more difficult. Your biggest problem will be a loose joint that has been repaired by a nail pinning the tenon in the socket.

If the nail is thin—a 16 to 18 ga. finishing nail—try twisting the tenoned part to get it free of the nail. If the nail split the tenon when it was driven in, twisting plus a direct outward pull may work. This may work even with a heavier nail, particularly a rusted nail. But be careful when pulling; if you don't get some indication that the end of the tenon is split or that the nail is coming out of the tenon, you run the risk of splintering the wood at the side of the socket.

There are two other ways to get the nail out, both drastic. One is to dig away away enough of the wood at two sides of the head so you can get a hold of it with a pair of pliers. The other is to saw off the spindle close to the tenon, dig out the tenon, then put a new tenon on the spindle.

Look for joints locked with pegs through the tenon. Splats on chair backs are often fastened this way, many times without glue. The pegs have to be removed. The easiest way is to drill them out and replace them with new pegs.

Some very old spindle chairs may be constructed with tenons in the shape of bulbs, with sockets hollowed out to match. (See Fig. 5–7.) This was a form of glueless assembly. The tenoned parts were made from seasoned lumber, the members containing the sockets from green lumber. After snap-together assembly, the chair was put aside to allow the green lumber to dry—and shrink to produce tight

FIGURE
5-6

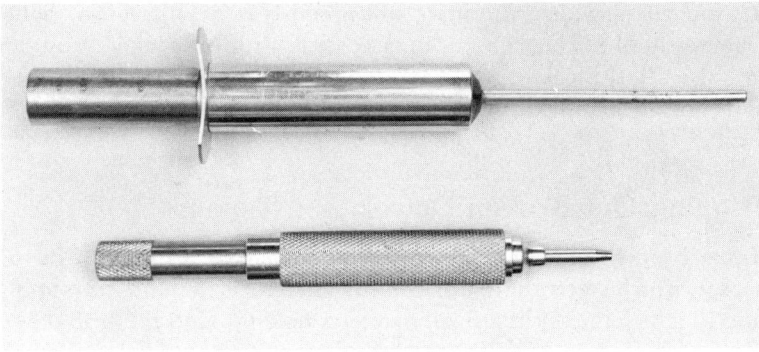

Glue injectors (both require 1/8" diameter hole).

FIGURE
5-7

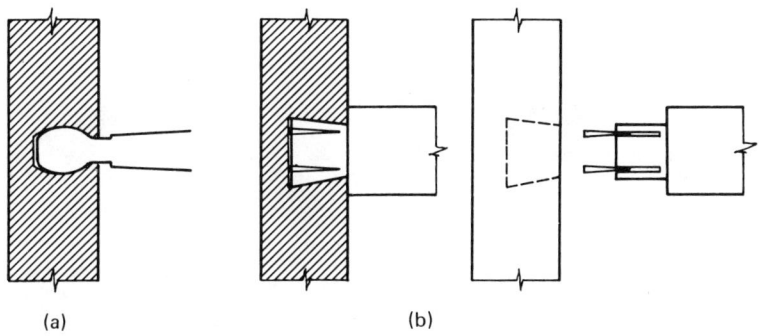

(a)   (b)

Joints difficult to get apart: (a) bulb socket joint and (b) wedged tenon joint.

joints in the process. The clue for this type of joint in an old chair is loose joints that won't come apart. These joints can be glued by injecting the glue into the joint, and, if required, pinning.

Another type of joint that may be loose but appears impossible to take apart is a wedged-tenon joint. In this joint, the round or rectangular tenon has a saw cut in the end into which a carefully dimensioned glue-covered wedge is inserted partway. With the socket and tenon covered with glue, the tenon is forced home. When the wedge comes against the bottom of the socket or mortise it is driven into the tenon, spreading the end of the tenon to make a very tight fit, particularly if the mortise or socket is slightly wider at the bottom.

Note: A wedged-tenon joint is often recommended as a means of tightening a loose joint when regluing, but it must be done absolutely right to work, and when you are repairing a chair, you have to do it right the first time.

Disassembly.   Mark the parts so you can get each one back in its proper place. The older the chair, the less likely it will be that parts are interchangeable. Also mark which end is front, up, left or right. The best tool for knocking a chair apart is a rubber mallet. You can also use a soft block of wood and a hammer, but then you will need someone to help you. For any chair with arms, try to get them off first.

Digging Out Broken Dowels and Tenons

There is only one way to do this without making a mess out of the socket, which you want to avoid in the interests of accurate reassembly and a tight joint. Drill a small diameter hole through the stub dowel close to the center. (See Fig. 5–8.) You have to go all the way through the dowel—you should know when you do because the drill will break through into the 1/8″ or so void in the bottom of the socket. Take it easy so you don't come out the other side of whatever you are drilling.

FIGURE
5-8

(a)

(b)

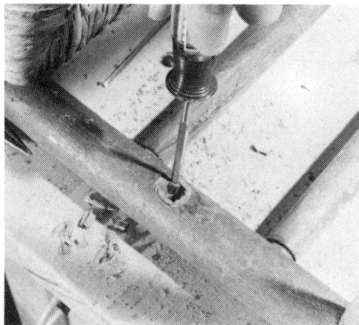

(c)

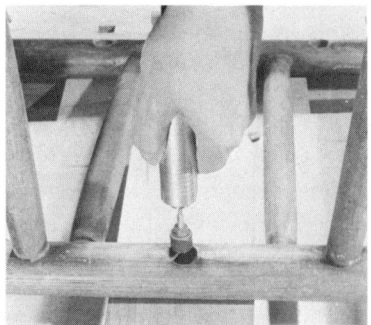

(d)

Digging out stretcher tenons: (a) Before (the hole at right remains from a previous attempt at stretcher repair or replacement). (b) A variable speed drill is preferred for cautious drilling. You should be able to sense the drill coming through the end of the tenon and going into the void at the bottom of the socket. Enlarge the hole with successive drillings. (c) With a chisel, splinter out the rest of the tenon. (d) Clean out the hole with a handgrinder and sanding drum.

Now remove as much of the dowel as you can by enlarging the hole with bigger drills. How much you can remove depends on how close to the center you started and on how well your drilling is aligned with the axis of the dowel. Now with a small straight chisel, remove a segment of the dowel from the thinnest side. Once this piece is out of the socket, the rest of the dowel will practically fall out, leaving a clean socket.

Removing Dowels

The best way to loosen a dowel is to try to hammer it further in (see Fig. 5–9). You can break the glue line far more easily this way than by grabbing the dowel in a vise and pulling, twisting, or tapping on the wood in which the dowel is imbedded. Hot water with or without a wetting agent, or heat, is alright if you have time to waste. You could be there annoying the dowel for an hour.

Broken Stretchers and Rungs

Breaks in stretchers and rungs should be reinforced with a dowel or dowels through the break if the break is clean and parts can go back together neatly. (See Fig. 5–10.) Blind dowels leave less visible evidence of a repair, but getting the holes aligned is a nasty problem, and it is important that dowel hole misalignment does not result in joint misalignment. The solution is oversize holes and gap-bridging epoxy cement.

If the rung or stretcher can be rotated, you can dowel from the underside which will make the dowels inconspicuous. Clamp the parts together and drill for the dowels before gluing.

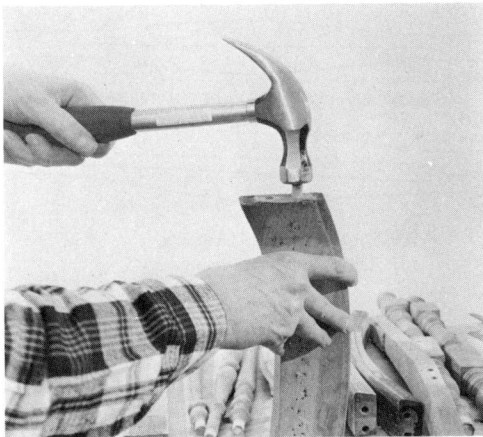

FIGURE 5-9

Removing a solid dowel: The best way to try to remove a solid dowel is to see if you can drive it in 1/16" into the void at the bottom of the socket in order to fracture the glue line. Then removal will be easy.

89

**FIGURE
5-10**

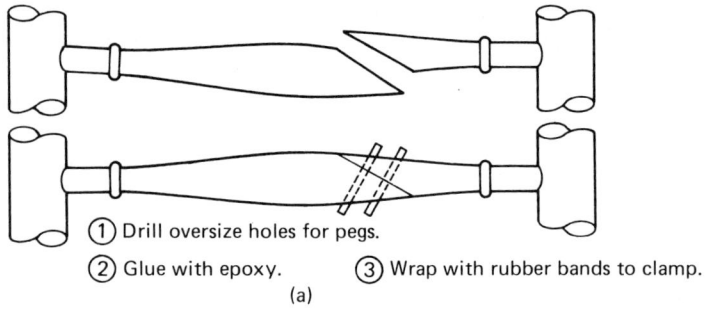

① Drill oversize holes for pegs.

② Glue with epoxy.   ③ Wrap with rubber bands to clamp.

(a)

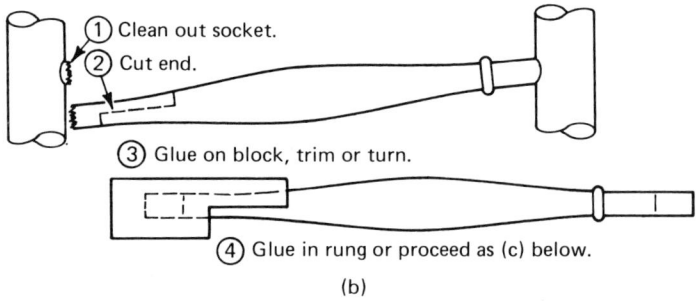

① Clean out socket.

② Cut end.

③ Glue on block, trim or turn.

④ Glue in rung or proceed as (c) below.

(b)

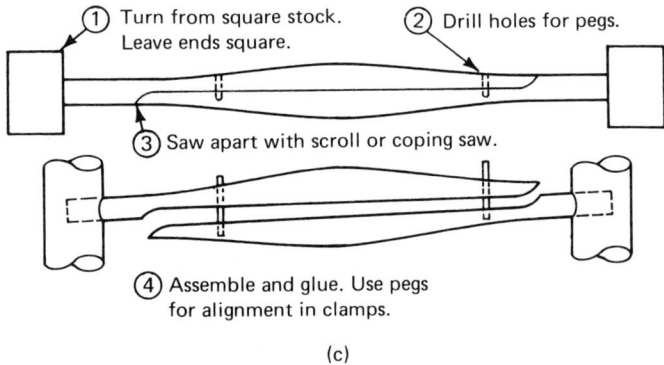

① Turn from square stock.
Leave ends square.   ② Drill holes for pegs.

③ Saw apart with scroll or coping saw.

④ Assemble and glue. Use pegs
for alignment in clamps.

(c)

Repairing broken stretchers: (a) A break where there is a decent amount of wood can be rejoined with dowels to reinforce the joint. (b) A stretcher broken at one end requires splicing on a new piece. (c) A similar technique is used to replace a missing stretcher when the legs cannot be spread apart.

A stretcher or rung broken at one end is not difficult to repair. First remove the stretcher and then remove the stub tenon from the socket. Trim the end of the stretcher and glue on a block of wood from which you will shape a new end for the stretcher. When shaped, drill holes for two dowel pins and cut the block from the stretcher, leaving some of the block attached. (Gluing the block to the stretcher interleaved with paper so they can be pried apart after shaping is not recommended as it will be difficult to get a strong glue line afterwards.) Clean glue from the good tenon and the sockets, and insert the ends of the replacement stretcher in the sockets, then glue the two parts together, using dowel pins to get them into alignment. Rotate the stretcher (if round) so the glue lines and dowel pins show least. When the glue is dry, resand and finish.

This same procedure will work replacing a missing stretcher when the legs can not be moved (see Fig. 5–11). On a dowel stretcher, the glue lines are least visible and the stretcher strongest when the cut is made as shown. When making the saw cuts, use a saw with a thin blade. A coping saw can be used if you don't have a scroll saw. The cut doesn't have to be straight so long as it is a smooth cut without sudden changes in direction.

For well-turned stretchers, make the joint where there is a decent amount of wood, even at the center if necessary, and make the joint several inches long for strength.

Thin spindles, such as those in the back of a Windsor chair, can most of the time be replaced by springing the new part into the sockets. To make a spindle you must start with straight-grained stock. The strongest spindles are made from blanks split rather than sawn from large stock to ensure that the grain runs straight. The spindle can be either lathe-turned (a steady rest to prevent the thin piece from whipping will be needed), or carved by hand with rasp, plane, and spokeshave.

Broken Legs

Repairing a broken chair leg is a risky business because of the high stresses put on chair legs in normal chair use. Making the problem worse is the fact that legs usually break where they are joined to a stretcher. Repairs of breaks at stretchers are never very strong because the ends of the stretchers do not leave any room for the reinforcing dowel required. Replace the leg.

A break below the stretchers or rungs can be fixed with glue and reinforcing dowels. Do not attempt blind dowels. Clamp the leg together dry and drill the holes for the dowels. Now, glue, dowel, and clamp the leg. When dry, trim the dowels.

If there is a break where a leg tenons into a seat, you can usually fix it by removing the leg, removing the tenon from the seat, drilling

FIGURE
5-11

(a)   **(b)**

(c)   **(d)**

(e)   **(f)**

Replacing a stretcher without spreading the legs: (a) This chair is miss-ing four side stretchers and cannot be disassembled without destroying its antique rush seat. (b) Measure the remaining stretchers, taking an average for the replacements. (c) Turn the tenons individually to fit each of the socket holes, which are not all the same size. (d) With the square ends of the turning clamped between boards, the stretcher is sawed into two pieces, as shown in Fig. 5-10c. (e) Stretcher parts in place. (f) Chair assembly. All stretchers are clamped as shown, band clamps hold chair together and square. One by one, stretchers are glued, with everything else acting as an alignment jig.

out the end of the leg the same diameter as the old tenon, and gluing a dowel into the top of the leg to form a new tenon. The same procedure would be used for a backpost–crest rail joint, as shown in Figure 5–12.

Broken Backs

A high stress point for the back of a chair is the area where the seat frame is tenoned or doweled. A break here often takes the form of a partial break and split as shown in Figure 5–13. This can be repaired by mortising the back two inches or so above and below the break and inserting a mending plate which will be secured by a combination of pin and epoxy cement.

In the example, the first step was to decide on the location for the plate and the size of the plate, taking into account the configuration of the chair framing in the break area. Some cutting into the spindles was unavoidable. The mortise was located slightly to the outside of the backpost centerline. Part of the side rail tenon was removed as was the very end of the back seat rail. The lower pin hole in the plate was located in line with the back seat rail so when the pin was installed it would also reinforce the rail.

Holes were drilled into the back for the pin, the plate was then marked and drilled, and then the back was drilled further but not through.

**FIGURE
5-12**

Replacing a broken leg or backpost dowel is simply a matter of drilling out the member for a replacement dowel.

FIGURE
5-13

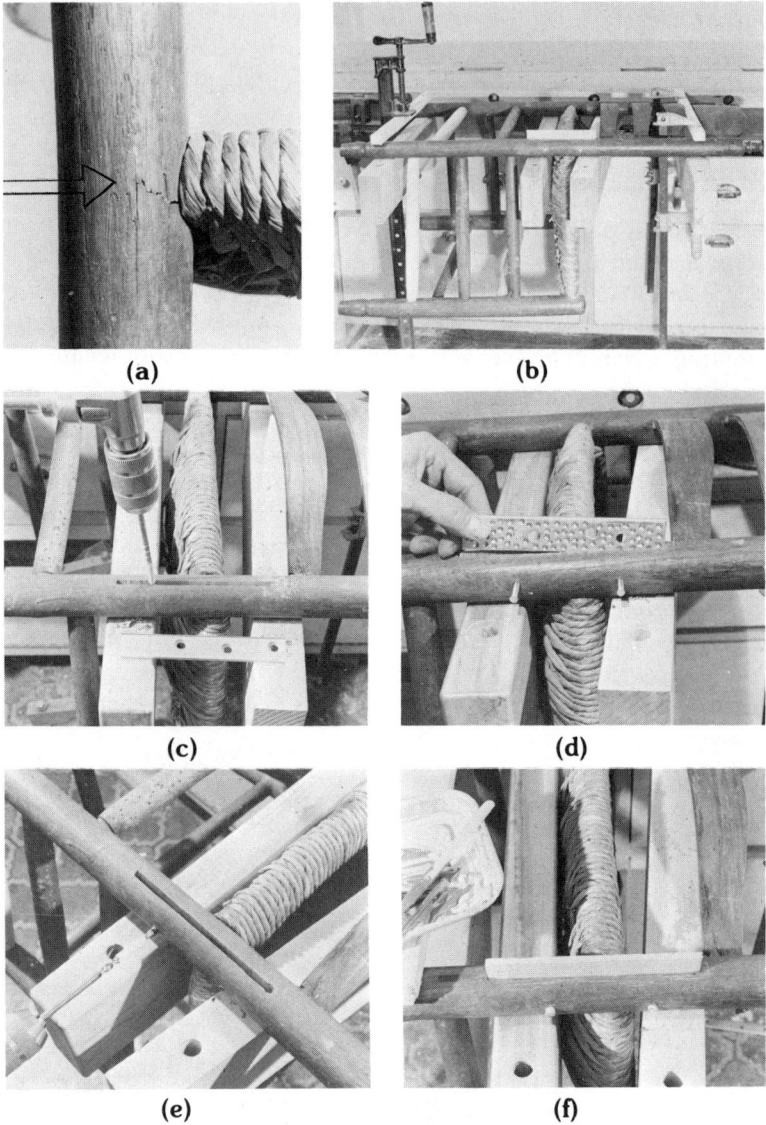

(a)

(b)

(c)

(d)

(e)

(f)

Repairing a cracked chair back: This is difficult because stresses at the join' are very high and the seat-rail joints do not leave a lot of wood in the post. (a) The cracked joint. (b) The chair is clamped for the repair (the maple 2-by-4s slide out from under the bench top). (c) First, drill and chisel out a mortise for the steel mending plate. (d) The mending plate is fitted. Existing holes in the plate are not used; holes are drilled to align with pins in back post. The surface of the plate was dimpled with a drill tip to provide good mechanical locking surface for epoxy cement. (e) After fitting, the plate is removed and the holes are extended into the second side of the post, but not through it. (f) The plate is bedded in filled epoxy, the mortise is covered with wood, and the holes for the pins are plugged.

The plate was made from a standard 6″ straight mending plate cut to 4″. The surfaces of both sides were cratered with a drill bit to provide a good mechanical locking surface for the filled epoxy cement.

When installing a plate it is important that it be well bedded in the epoxy with no voids. The pins also must be sealed in epoxy so there can be no movement. After the plate is in, cover with a wood plug and trim to the leg contour.

Putting a Chair Back Together

After all the joints are cleaned, broken parts fixed or replaced, finish removed, surfaces sanded, the next step is a trial assembly with all the parts. (Hopefully, you have continued to mark the parts through all this, and they can be reassembled correctly. If not, it is better to find out now, rather than when the chair is partly glued up.)

You can glue the whole chair in one shot if you have the clamps for it and can get the joints closed as fast as is required for the glue you are using. It is usually more convenient (and less nerve wracking) to glue up the chair in major assemblies—back, front, all. (See Fig. 5-14.) If you are having alignment problems, start with as few joints as you can, and use the rest of the chair assembled without glue as a

FIGURE
5-14

Clamping the back frame of a chair. (Don't try to clamp all the joints in one shot.)

FIGURE
5-15

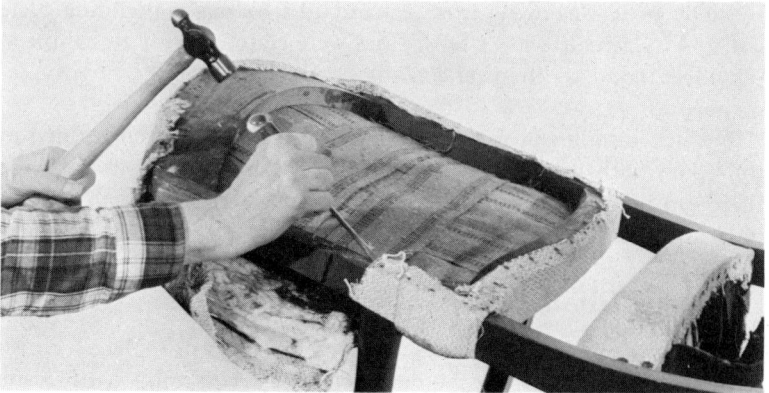

(a)

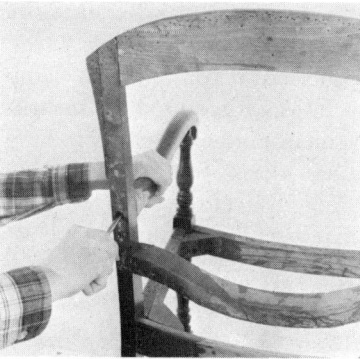

(b)

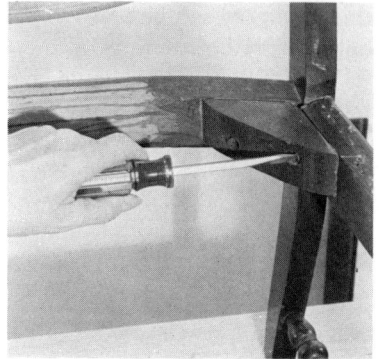

(c)

(d)

(e)

Stripping a chair: (a) Ball pein hammer and sharpened screwdriver pry up tacks as fast as any special tool. (b) If chair has arms, first remove screws holding the arms into the backposts. (c) Glue blocks should have two screws into each rail (unless tongue-and-grooved to rails). (d) The thick mass of glue in the joint suggests that the glue never contributed much to chair strength. (e) After the glue blocks are removed, the frame is easily knocked apart.

fixture to obtain the proper alignment. This was the procedure used in replacing the stretchers in the chair shown in Figure 5–11. All of the split stretchers were assembled and clamped dry. The chair legs were held together with band clamps. One by one the stretchers were glued.

When gluing the whole chair, it is important that it is standing on a level surface with all feet on the surface. The angle of clamps can be altered to accomplish this.

Upholstered Chair Frames

We will discuss frame repairs in this chapter; but springs, webbing, and other topics associated with upholstery itself are covered in Chapter 6.

Frame repair is not the same for upholstered chairs as for other chairs. First, the construction is different, with glue blocks and other joint reinforcement, making joints more rigid to begin with. Construction can be appallingly crude and the hidden wood rough. But there is the advantage that your repairs for the most part won't show.

Once the cover and padding is removed from the chair, the state of the frame can be determined. If any of the joints are loose, it is prudent to assume that all are loose. The only long-term cure is disassembly, joint cleaning, and reassembly. (See Fig. 5–15.) Procedures have been previously described.

Nails are not used in any furniture frame construction except to position parts for gluing. Nails do not reliably hold frame parts together. Wood screws, nuts, and bolts can be used for installing metal parts or braces, or for attaching parts that must be removed—arms, dress panels, wings, seats, and decorative pieces—but cannot be relied upon for seat, leg, and back frame assembly. The only assembly methods that work for chair frames are glued dowel, and glued mortise and tenon joints.

Use aliphatic resin, urea-formaldehyde, or resorcinol glue, or epoxy cement for regluing upholstered chair frames. Be especially careful when sanding glue from the frames and glue blocks so that the blocks still fit flush against the frames. It will be necessary to reposition the blocks up or down and drill new screw holes in the frames as the old holes will no longer line up with the holes in the blocks. (See Fig. 5–16.)

Steel mending plates and angles are often useful in reinforcing reglued joints in these chair frames, but they are useless in reinforcing loose joints as an alternative to regluing (see Fig. 5–17).

It is a good idea to give the hidden framing a quick sanding while you have the cover off to eliminate rough areas that can tear burlap, muslin, or cover fabric.

Filling the old tack holes is a decision that should be based on whether you think there is enough solid wood between the holes to

FIGURE
5-16

Reassembled chair frame.

FIGURE
5-17

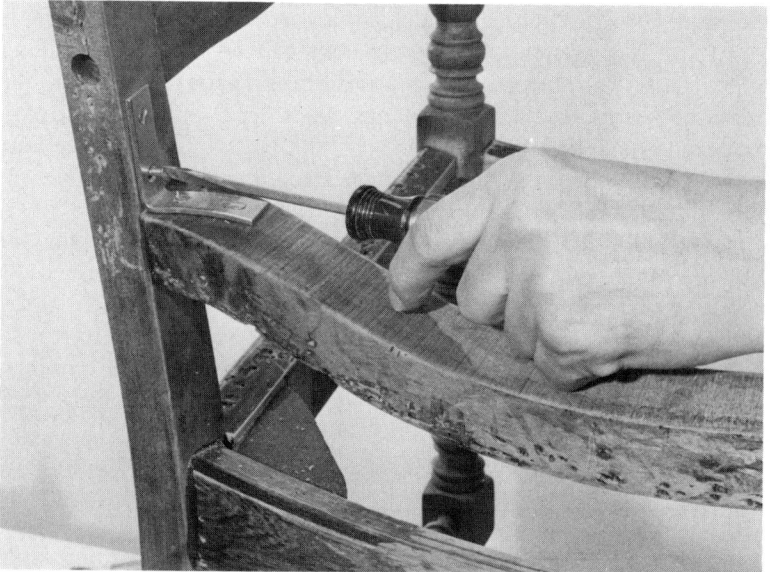

Steel mending angle is used to keep single-doweled lower back rail from
turning.

**FIGURE
5-18**

Plugging old tack holes with round tooth picks which are cut in half and hammered into the glued holes.

get your new tacks into. If this is the first time the chair has been recovered, there are probably not so many tack holes that you won't be able to find solid wood for most of your tacks the first time you drive them. Using any of the puttylike wood fillers will not contribute anything to the strength or tack-holding capability of the frame wood, so don't waste time using these products to fill the holes. You will only get the top of the hole filled, and as you drive tacks through these shallow plugs you will get a false sense of tack security. Better you should know the tack is going into a hole.

The best way to fill the tack holes is with pegs cut from round tooth picks smeared in white glue and hammered into the holes. (See Fig. 5–18.) After the glue is dry, snip the protruding pegs with diagonal cutters and sand smooth. You now have a solid-wood surface for your tacks.

Woods for replacement hidden framing, while not requiring much in attractive appearance, must be straight grained and free of knots; it is difficult to get tacks to go into even the smallest knots or into the hard and unpredictably grained wood around the knots without curling over.

Appropriate hidden-frame repair woods include oak, ash, birch, and maple.

If you don't find glue blocks (see Fig. 5–19) when you remove a seat cover, by all means install blocks. These blocks should have large gluing surfaces, not the small surfaces you would get from narrow diagonally spanning stock. Narrow diagonal blocks do work, however, if they have been finger-jointed into the frames.

Do any refinishing required on the frame before starting any upholstery.

FIGURE
5-19

Glue blocks will have to be positioned up or down when replaced, because the old holes will no longer line up after glue is sanded off the surfaces.

FIGURE
5-20

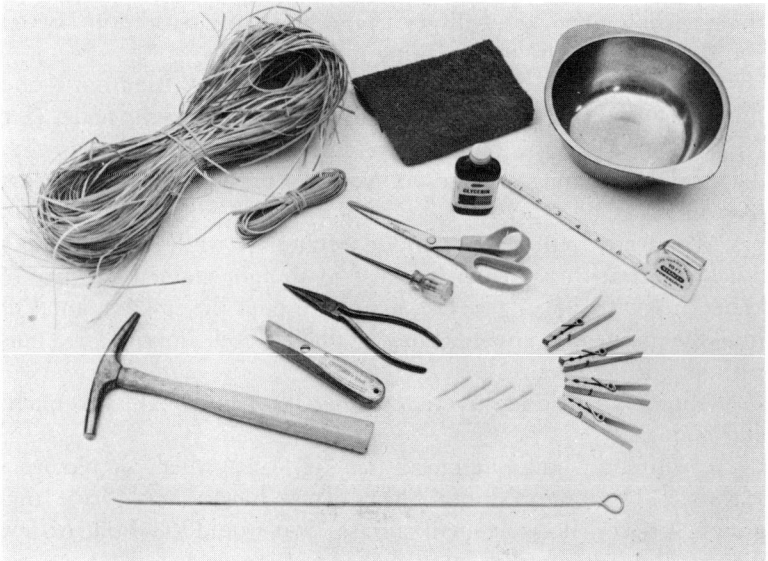

Caning tools and materials: (from top left) bundle of cane, binder cane, damp cloth, bottle of glycerine, pot for dampening cane, steel tape, hammer, utility knife, longnose pliers, awl, scissors, pegs (make your own), clothespins, and bodkin.

Cane was first used in open weaving for chair seats and backs during the Restoration period in England. It is also generally used in Queen Anne, William and Mary, Adam, Louis XV, Louis XVI, and Chinese Chippendale styles. A well-caned chair seat or back is strong, and will wear for years if not cut.

Cane is flexible rattan made from the stem of a palm growing in Indonesia, Sri Lanka, Malasia, and Sumatra. The stem is stripped of bark, then split to width. The cane is put up in 1,000-ft. hanks with pieces running 4 ft. to 15 ft. Plastic cane is also available.

Cane widths and how to select the correct size are given in Table 5–1.

Cane Sizes Available

TABLE
5-1

Cane Width*	Diameter of Holes	Distance Between Holes
Carriage	1/8 inch	3/8 inch
Superfine	1/8 inch	3/8 inch
Fine fine	3/16 inch	1/2 inch
Fine	3/16 inch	5/8 inch
Medium	1/4 inch	3/4 inch
Common	5/16 inch	7/8 inch

* For round seats you may want to use cane one size finer because of the doubling of cane in the holes.

Machine-woven cane can also be purchased by the running foot in several widths and patterns. This pre-woven cane cannot be installed in a chair frame drilled out for cane weaving. It can only be used on furniture where it can be wedged into slots provided in the frame for the purpose.

When you do caning, carry the job through until it is finished. This doesn't mean you have to work straight through until done, without breaks, but don't put it aside for a few weeks partially finished and expect to finish some other time. The cane will loosen and become too brittle and, if you are critical of your own work, you will end up cutting the old cane out and starting over from scratch. Tools needed for weaving cane are shown in Figure 5–20.

After setting up your work at a comfortable height, the first step in recaning is to carefully cut away the old cane. Try to get the cane off in one piece so you can use it as a pattern. Except for a rectangular panel, there are always decisions to make on skipping holes.

All dirt must be out of the holes including paint and varnish dribbles. If necessary, ream the holes with a twist drill to clean them. The sides of the holes should be smooth.

Preparation

Pull strands of cane from the hank one by one. Do it carefully because the cane is brittle.

Cane is smooth and glossy on the outside, rough on the inside. Eyes, or spots, where the stems of leaves grew out should be unbroken and smooth. Discard strands of cane that are rough and splitting.

Before weaving, rattan cane must be soaked in a mixture of glycerin and water for 20 minutes. Use 1 part glycerin to 20 parts water. The glycerin makes the cane more pliable than water alone, and lubricates the cane somewhat.

Coil one strand of cane, smooth side out to fit your container. Keep several strands soaking. It is important to keep the cane moist while you work. After work interruptions, dampen the cane by laying a wet cloth over what has been woven.

Cane Weaving

Cane weaving is done in seven steps. You weave front to back twice, side to side twice, diagonally twice, and bind the edge once. The following steps describe the weaving of a seat. Weaving any other panel would be done in the same way. The steps are illustrated in Figure 5–21.

●*Step 1.*   Count the holes on the back seat rail. If an odd number, put a peg in the center hole. For an even number of holes put a peg in either hole nearest the center. Locate and peg the equivalent hole in the front (see Fig. 5–21a).

Blot a strand of soaked cane and uncoil it. In all cane weaving, the smooth side is up.

Start at the pegged hole in the middle of the back. Poke five inches of cane through the hole, hold it with a peg. Bring the cane, smooth side up, forward and down through the corresponding pegged front hole, then up through the adjacent hole. Hold with pegs and repeat back and forth until you run out of strand. Be sure the cane is not twisted in the holes or underneath the chair.

Don't weave the cane too tightly. It should sag very slightly below the seat level when you press it down at this stage with your fist. Tie off the ends of the cane as soon as possible by weaving it under a strand beneath the work and finish with a half-hitch. Ends must be moist before tying or they will break.

Be careful not to block holes when carrying cane across the underside of the frame. For chair seats that are wider at the front than at the back, short pieces of cane should be woven front and back along the side edge—using only those holes that allow the correct cane spacing.

At the end of this step make sure all cane ends are tied off. You cannot hold the cane down with pegs for long periods to tie later. It won't work.

FIGURE
5-21

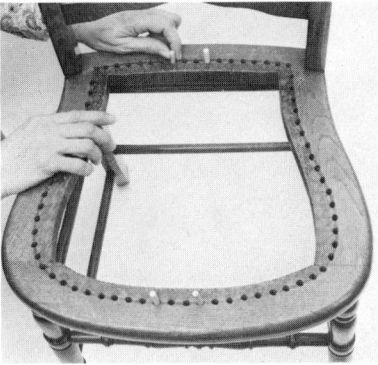

(a)

(b)

(c)

(d)

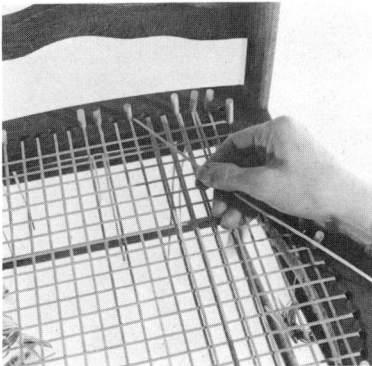

(e)

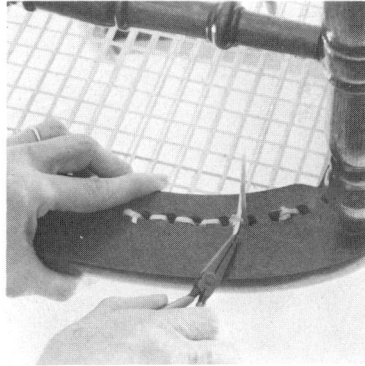

(f)

Steps in weaving a cane seat: (a) Locate front and back rail center holes. (b) First, place a strand of cane front-to-back. (c) skip the holes at the sides to keep cane straight. (d) Next, place a strand of cane side-to-side. (e) Third, place another strand of cane front-to-back, on top of the strands in position. (f) Tie the ends of the cane as you go along.

(continued)

FIGURE
5-21
(Cont'd)

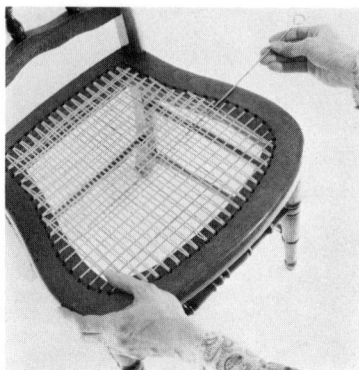

(g)

(h)

(i)

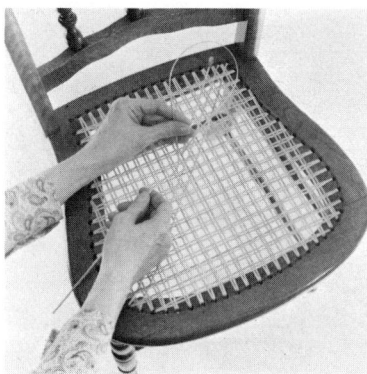

(j)

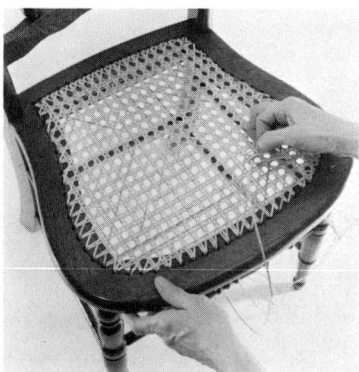

(k)

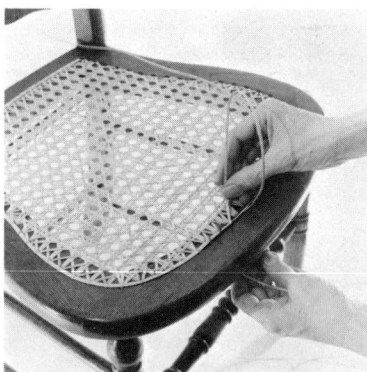

(l)

(g) Fourth, weave another strand of cane side-to-side. (h) The bent end of a bodkin helps weaving. (i) With pegs, align the strands of cane before going further. (j) Fifth, weave two strands of cane from back-right to front-left. (k) Sixth, weave two strands of cane in the opposite diagonal direction. (l) Last, finish off seat weaving with binder cane.

● **Step 2.**   Starting at the back of one side, weave cane side to side just as you did front to back in the last step. This layer of cane goes on *top* of the previous layer. (See Fig. 5–21d.)

● **Step 3.**   Repeat Step 1, keeping the strands slightly slack as in Steps 1 and 2. This layer of cane goes on top of the first and second layers. Locate each strand to the right of the cane woven in Step 1. Be sure all cane ends are tied off. (See Figs. 5–21e and 5–21f.)

● **Step 4.**   In this step you finally get to do some weaving. Use the bodkin—the weaving will go faster.

Start at the side hole next to a corner. Weave across in front of the Step 2 row. Weave *over* the canes on top and *under* the canes underneath (that is, over the Step 3 canes and under the Step 1 canes). (See Fig. 5–21g.) While working, straighten the canes that were woven in Step 2; this helps to get the Step 4 cane correctly in place. About a third of the way across, pull the full length of the cane through carefully. While pulling keep your hand level with the caning–to avoid lifting and sawing the cane with the cane.

Keep the cane moist. If it gets too dry, wrap the cane in a wet cloth for about 10 minutes. (But, if the cane squeaks when pulling, it is too wet.)

Continue weaving across the row. At the opposite side, put the end of the cane down through the hole and peg it until you weave the next row. Pull the cane up through the next hole and weave it back across the seat so the cane passes over and under the same canes as it did the first time across. Continue until all rows are done.

Before going on with Step 5, moisten the woven cane seat by dampening it with a wet cloth for 20 minutes. Then, using two pegs, straighten the rows and dress them together in pairs (see Fig. 5–21i). Tie everything off.

● **Step 5.**   The diagonal weaving is started now. Begin at a back corner hole and weave the first row toward the opposite front corner. You might or might not end in a front corner hole, depending on the geometry of the panel. The cane is woven diagonally *over* the pairs from front to back and *under* those from side to side. Dress the cane to run straight from the corner hole (see Fig. 5–21j).

Weave a second strand from the same corner hole, passing on the opposite side of the crossed side-to-side and front-to-back-canes, going over the front-to-back pairs and under the side-to-side pairs in exactly the same way as the first strand. Continue diagonal weaving until all the diagonals that appear to be necessary to the design are in. Use your judgment; be guided by the old cane if you have it.

Unless the panel is square or rectangular, you will not have a diagonal cane in each hole. Skip and double up as appropriate. As a last part of this step dress the canes straight, using pegs and a straightedge as a guide.

●*Step 6.* Now weave diagonals in the opposite direction. Start at the opposite back corner hole.

In this step weave *under* the pairs from front to back and *over* the pairs from side to side (see Fig. 5–21k). When weaving in this step, use holes exactly opposite the holes you used in the last step to maintain symmetry. Finally, dress the cane.

●*Step 7.* This step using binder cane and weaving cane will cover the holes and give a finished edge to the seat. Binder cane is the next size wider than that used for weaving. For a rounded panel use one piece of binder to go all the way around. For a square panel, use four pieces.

It is important to keep the weaving cane and the binder cane moist and pliable while working. Insert four inches of the binder cane in a back corner hole and dress the binder. Place the binder flat over the center of the holes.

Secure the binder cane in the corner hole with a peg. Pass the end of a piece of weaving cane as long as you can manage down the first hole along the binder and tie off. Now pass the free end of the weaving cane over the binding cane and down through the same hole (see Fig. 5–21l). You may need an awl to ease an opening for the weaving

FIGURE 5-22

Round Seat Rails

Chair requiring rush seat.

cane. Then weave up through the next hole over the binding cane and down again. Repeat until the binder is fastened all around the edge. Now secure the ends of the binder in the starting hole with a short peg hammered in flush. You will have to make a special peg to get the right fit.

5-4 RUSH SEATS

Rush has been used for chair and stool seats as least as far back as the ancient Egyptians. If a chair frame has round rungs at the seat level, it requires a rush seat (see Fig. 5–22). The side rungs will usually be slightly higher than the front and back rungs to ensure the frame's structural strength.

Most rushing is done today with fiber rush rather than natural rush. Fiber rush is made from kraft paper twisted into a strand resembling natural rush. It is easier to weave, inexpensive, and comes in very long pieces. Two sizes are generally available—1/8" and 3/16" diameter. You can also ''rush'' with macramé cord, raffia, rope, or plastic clothesline. The tools and supplies required for seat rushing are shown in Figure 5–23.

Preparation

Before you rush the seat, have all frame repairs and finishing completed.

FIGURE 5-23

Tools and material used in rushing: Coil of fiber rush, upholstery tacks, hammers and mallet, stick for packing stuffing, paper clamp, tape, and formed block for packing rush.

Corner Weaving

Is the front seat rail longer than the back seat rail? If it is you will have to begin rushing in the front corners of the seat to square off the area to be woven. Corner rushing is shown in Figure 5–24.

Cut a piece of fiber rush about 3 1/2 times the length of the front rail. Coil it and dunk it in water for 20 seconds. Do not leave it in the water longer than 20 seconds as the paper will start coming apart.

Fold the fiber rush in half and tack it on the right rail about two inches back from the front post. Now take one end of the fiber rush and bring it over the front rail, wrap it around the front and up over itself and then over the right rail. Keep the fiber rush close to the corner of the chair seat and keep a steady tension on it.

Next wrap the fiber rush around the right rail and bring it along the front rail and over and around the left rail. Bring the fiber up and over the front rail close to the left front post.

Now wrap the rush around the front rail, dress it along the inside left rail and tack it to the rail about two inches back. Cut off any excess.

It is important that a steady tension be kept on the rush all through the weaving. Now repeat these steps with the other half of the cut rush.

Continue filling the corners this way until the open area of the seat has been squared off, which will be when the open length of the front rail equals the length of the back rail. For each new piece of fiber rush add six inches to the length to allow for the added length along the side rails. Locate tacks so both start and finish ends of the rush dress straight back (i.e., at right angles to the front of the chair).

It is very important to keep right angles while weaving. Use a hammer or mallet and a block of wood to tap the fiber rush into

**FIGURE
5-24**

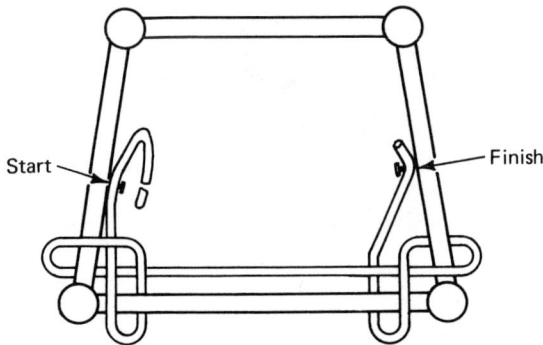

Corner rushing diagram.

place. The hammering will compact the fiber rush. Do this after every two courses of rush.

Now you are ready for straight rush weaving. If the chair seat is square this is where you start.

Weaving

Cut off as long a piece of fiber rush as you think you will be comfortable fishing through the chair frame. For a starter, try 12 yards. Coil the rush and soak it for 20 seconds in water. The steps in weaving a rush seat are shown in Figures 5–25 and 5–26.

Tack the fiber rush on the inside of the right side rail towards the back. Bring the rush over, then around the front rail. Now bring the rush up over itself and make a right angle over the right side rail then across the front of the chair and over and around the left side rail. Bring the rush up and over itself and make a right angle toward the front.

Come up over and around the front rail then bring the fiber rush back and over and around the back rail.

Next make a right angle toward the left rail, over and around the rail, and then bring the rush across the back to the right side rail.

Bring the rush over and around the right side rail and make a right angle toward the back rail. Go over and around the back rail and bring the rush forward and over the front rail.

Got the idea? Now you just keep going round and round the seat.

When you come to the end of the rush, dampen the end and tie on another piece with a square knot. Locate the knot along one of the rails where it will be out of sight. Cut off any excess.

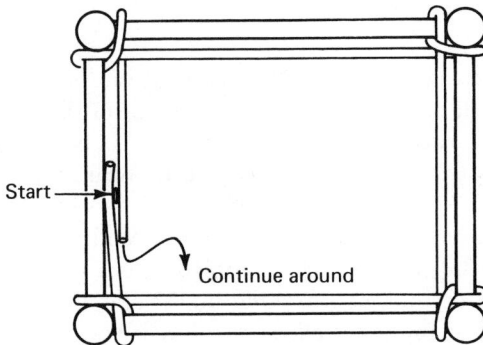

FIGURE
5-25

Seat rushing diagram.

FIGURE
5-26

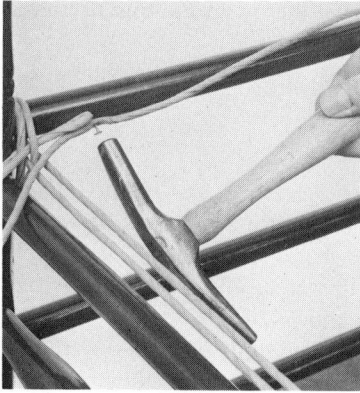

(a) (b)

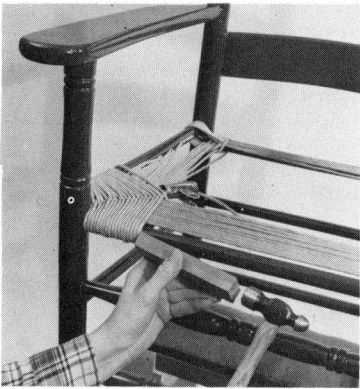

(c) (d)

Seat rushing procedure: (a) Tack the end of the rush to the inside of the side rail. (B) Begin corner rushing. (c) Pack the rush tight with the block. (d) Nearly completed seat reveals corrugated inserts to help maintain its shape.

Stuffing

If you insert triangular pieces of corrugated cardboard between the rush layers it will help maintain the basic shape of the fiber rush seat. Insert the cardboard in the sides when there is about four inches of side rail left open. Cut the cardboard to the seat shape but slightly smaller.

As the weaving progresses, the area between the upper and lower strands should be stuffed. Use crumpled brown paper for stuffing. Packing should be thorough to build up the seat and prevent it from breaking down at the inner edges of the rails and sagging with continued use.

How much stuffing you put in is a matter of judgment. Chairs differ in the amount of stuffing needed. The seat should not be overly stuffed and lumpy—just firm and solid.

A ruler is a good tool to push the stuffing into place. Or use a dowel—3/4'' diameter tapered to 1/2'' flat at the other end.

Continue to weave until about four inches remain on the back and front rails. Now insert the cardboard pieces cut for the front and back sections. The points of the cardboard inserts that extend into the center opening should be trimmed off where they overlap leaving a gap 1/2'' wide. Weave until the side rails are completely covered. Unless the seat is square there will be open space remaining on the front and back rails. This open space is filled by bridging.

Bridging

Bridging is figure-eight weaving. Bring the fiber rush up through the center opening and bring it over the front rail. Weave it around the front rail back up through the center opening again. Now take it back and over the back rail, then forward up through the center gap again. Repeat this procedure until the front and back rails are filled.

When the bridging has been completed the end of the fiber rush should be tacked to the underside of the back rail.

Allow the seat to dry—wait at least a week—then give the rush two coats of varnish.

6 Basic Upholstery

It is not possible to describe reupholstery completely in a few pages. Here are the basics—the tools and materials you will need, upholstery terms, rewebbing, spring retying, stuffing, and recovering without restyling.

Repair to upholstered furniture begins with an assessment of the possible scope of the job. You can generally get a better handle on the problem by turning the chair over and removing part of the black cambric covering the bottom of the chair. This will expose the webbing and springs. You don't have to strip every chair to the bare frame. A faded, threadbare, stained, torn, or wrong-color finish fabric can be replaced without disturbing the rest of the chair upholstery. A lumpy seat or back might mean packed-down or shifted padding, but it's more likely that a spring is loose and has shifted its position or is beginning to work its way through the padding. This in turn usually means failure of the webbing, as does a sagging seat in a pad-upholstered chair. Curing these problems requires stripping.

If the chair is the slightest bit loose in the joints or creaks when you sit in it (not spring noise), the condition can only be cured by stripping to the frame, then taking the frame apart and regluing. Spring noise usually means springs are out of position or loose. Short-cut frame repairs with screweyes and twisted wire, steel mending angles, table corner braces, screws, and nails are a complete waste of your time and effort. You must reglue.

Trestles.   It is a lot easier on your back to put furniture up on benches for reupholstery. The benches or trestles shown in Figure 6–2 are different from the usual upholstery trestle design in that the padded tops are removable making the trestles more useful in your home shop for other purposes. You can build the trestles in conventional upholstery style with a bead of fox edge around the rim of the top to

**FIGURE
6-1**

Upholstered chair—before and after.

**FIGURE
6-2**

Trestles are used to raise the piece of furniture to a convenient working height. Those shown have removable top pads.

keep your work from rolling or sliding off plus a top padding of carpet. Or you can build it as shown in Figure 6-3.

Sewing Machine.   Most types of upholstery work require competent machine sewing. Make sure you have someone available.

You need a variety of hand tools for upholstery work. Some are common shop tools, some are more specialized (see Fig. 6-4).

FIGURE
6-3

Brace 4 not shown this side.

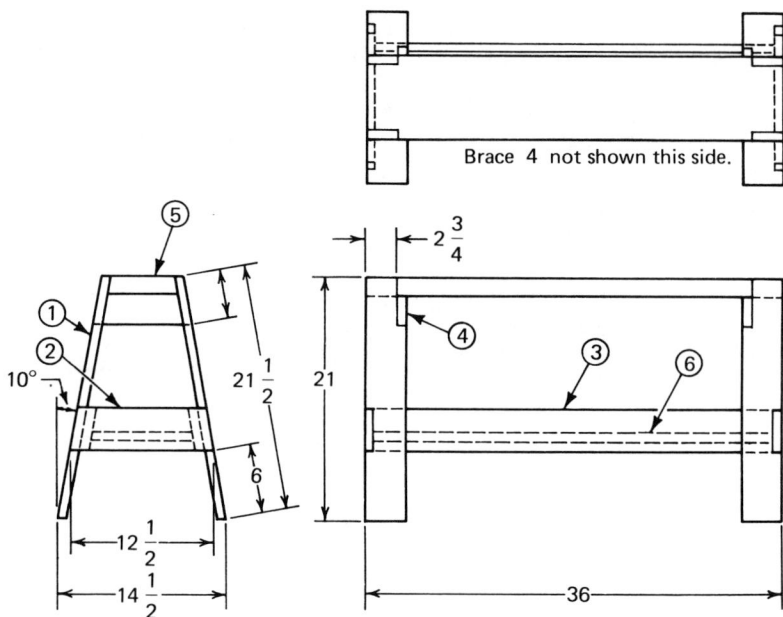

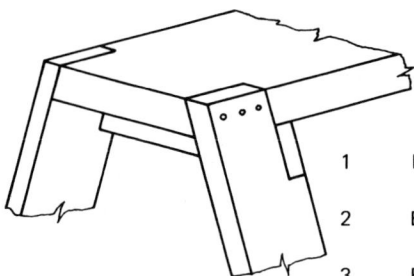

1	Legs	8	1 X 4 X $21\frac{1}{2}$	Pine
2	Brace	4	1 X 4 X $12\frac{1}{2}$	Pine
3	Brace	4	1 X 4 X $34\frac{1}{2}$	Pine
4	Support	4	1 X 3 X $8\frac{3}{4}$	Pine
5	Top	2	2 X 8 X 36	Pine
6	Shelf	2	$\frac{3}{4}$ X 9 X $34\frac{1}{2}$	Plywood

Plans for trestles.

Tack Hammer. There are two kinds of magnetized tack hammers. Use the upholsterer's model that has a solid head and magnetized tip rather than the claw model with a magnetized head.

Webbing Stretcher. This tool is used to draw jute webbing tight when you are nailing it to the frame. The tines are inserted into the webbing, and the other end of the wood handle (which should be rubber covered to protect the framing) is wedged against the frame.

Webbing Pliers. This tool does the same thing as a webbing stretcher, costs more, is more likely to damage the wood framing, but can grab short ends of webbing.

Ripping Tool. These are used to drive out tacks when you are stripping off old upholstery. There are several kinds. A chisel-end ripping tool is driven with a mallet; it works better if you grind a sharper bevel on the end. Ripping claws are worked by muscle power and do best removing tacks holding heavyweight finish cover.

The least expensive ripping tool is a 1/4″ sharpened plastic-handled screwdriver no longer used for driving screws. Drive it with a ball pein hammer for least fatigue and fastest tack removal.

Shears. You should have two pairs. One pair should be heavy duty for cutting webbing and rubberized hair stuffing. For all other fabric cutting, get an 8″ pair of inexpensive Fiskars® scissors.

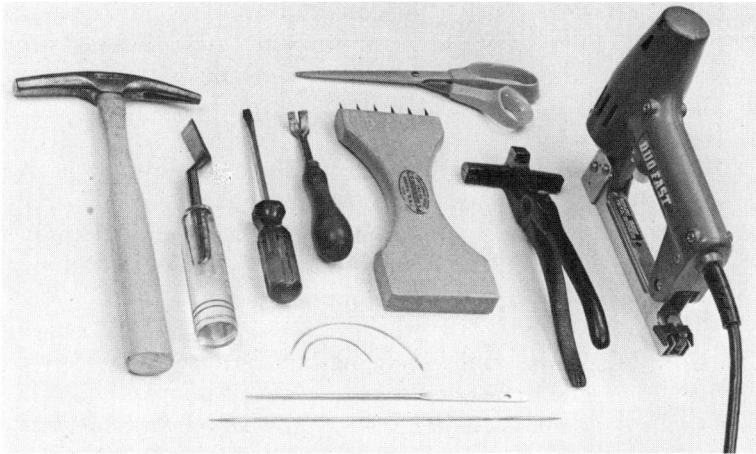

FIGURE 6-4

Upholstery tools: (From left) magnetic hammer, ripping chisel, screwdriver (for ripping), ripping tool, webbing stretchers, webbing pliers, and electric stapler; (below) curved needles, regulator, and two-pointed needle.

Needles. Curved needles work a lot better in upholstery than conventional straight ones. They come in sizes from 2″ to 7″. Get a small one and a medium-sized one. Straight upholstery needles come in 8″, 12″, and 16″ sizes. Get an 8″ one.

Regulator. Stuffing regulators look like 8″ and 12″ needles flattened at the eye. They are used for moving stuffing around and adding bits of stuffing under muslin covers to smooth things out.

Electric Stapler. You don't have to hold everything down with tacks. Hand staplers do not have the power to drive staples into hardwood frames, but an electric stapler does. You won't be able to use an electric stapler everywhere or all the time, but staples are a lot faster than tacks. Check driven staples for good penetration into the wood.

6-2 MATERIALS

Materials used in reupholstery are shown in Figure 6–5.

Webbing. Webbing is used to support springs (or padding if springs are not used) in open-frame construction. The most widely used webbing is 3 1/2″ wide jute webbing which you can buy by the yard or in 72-yd. rolls. Jute webbing is tan in color. The best grade has red stripes woven in. The weave should be tight with no evidence of sizing. As the webbing supports everything else in upholstered furniture, buy the best. If a piece you have stripped has chintzy-looking webbing or if the webbing is threadbare, torn, or sagging, replace it.
Steel webbing is made in plain, perforated and corrugated strips. It is made in narrower widths than jute webbing—5/8″, 3/4″, and 1″. It is used in low-cost furniture and as a quick backup for sagging jute webbing.
Rubber webbing is used in some modern style furniture in place of jute webbing. Attachment is simpler (metal clips) but the webbing doesn't last as long as jute webbing, as the clip wears the rubber. Some rubber webbing is attached to frames by being passed through slots and tacked or stapled on the opposite side.

Springs. Three kinds of springs are used in upholstery—coil springs, innerspring units, and no-sag (zigzag) springs.
Coil springs are made in several heights and in three degrees of firmness—hard, medium, and soft. Finding an exact replacement for a broken spring can be a problem.
Innerspring units, also called Marshall units, are custom-made for furniture manufacturers for use in seats, backs, and cushions of overstuffed furniture. The springs are sewn into muslin or burlap

FIGURE
6-5

Upholstery materials: Roll-edge, rubberized horsehair slab stock, cotton padding, foam cushion, burlap, webbing, muslin, and black cambric.

FIGURE
6-6

Zigger springs. (Small coil springs keep zigger springs in alignment.)

pockets. For repairs, they are sold in strips already pocketed. Innerspring cushions are usually replaced with foam cushions when repairs to the springs are needed.

No-sag wire springs are the easiest to install as no webbing is required. They are attached directly to the frame with clips. The serpentine springs are rolled into coils. When cut to length for use, the arcing from being coiled remains; springs are attached to front and rear frames, with the coiled curvature upward (see Fig. 6–6). Small coil springs or steel bands attached the no-sag springs side by side and to the side frames.

117

Spring Twine. This strong heavy cord is used to tie springs to webbing and to restrain and maintain the location of the free ends of the coil springs. This cord is made of six-ply hemp and put up in one-pound balls.

Burlap. Burlap is a coarse strong heavy tan-colored cloth woven from jute. It is used to cover webbing if springs are not used, and to cover springs, providing a base for the stuffing. Burlap is used in several weights; 10-ounce is a good weight to have on hand for repairs, although 12-ounce is better over seat springs.

Stuffing. In upholstery, stuffing is any of several resilient materials used to provide padding over springs, webbing, and frame edges. As padding, it must eliminate any feeling of springs in the seats and backs, provide the chair with the desired shape, and return the seat or back to its original appearance when the load is removed. Many materials have been and are used for stuffing. Expect to have to substitute for many of them.

Animal hair is one of the better stuffings. Of these the best is horse hair, followed by cattle hair and hog hair. The hair is processed to give it a long-lasting curl which provides the resiliency. Hair stuffing is sold by the bag and should be moth-proofed before using.

Rubberized hair is produced by coating individual hairs with rubber. It is made up in one inch thick slab stock and is a good choice for seat and back stuffing.

Other stuffings include sisal, tow (made from stems of flax plants), Spanish moss, palm and coconut shell fiber, excelsior, kapok, and even grass. All of these stuffings do not retain their resiliency as well as hair stuffings. They pack down and also disintegrate. The best of these is Spanish moss.

Cotton is used as a stuffing, but cotton should be used only for arms and other areas not so subject to packing down. Cotton is also used as a protective layer between other stuffings and the finish fabric. It is purchased in felted rolls. Cotton has a tendency to go lumpy.

Roll Edge (or Edge Roll). These are rolls of stuffed burlap fastened along frame edges to soften and contour the edge both for appearance and to lessen finish cover wear. They also prevent stuffing from working its way down over the edge of the frame. Roll edge is not always used. Ready-made roll edge is not often available at retail, and then only in a few of the many sizes made, but you can make your own if needed.

Foam. Foam stuffing and padding is widely used in upholstered furniture and is often used to replace other stuffings in repair work. Once made from natural rubber, foam is now made from

FIGURE
6-7

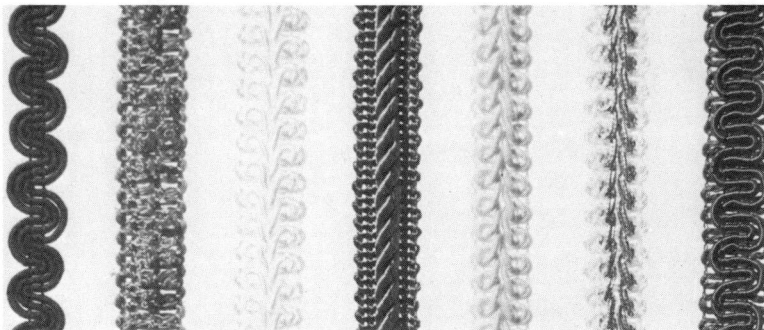

Decorative gimp.

polyurethane. Polyfoam—as it is called today—comes as slab stock, cored stock, molded cushions and pillows, and shredded. It is also made in four densities—firm, medium, soft, and very soft.

Advantages of foam over other padding and stuffing materials include ready availability, superior resiliency, comfortable and uniform seat and back support. Foam also is nonallergenic, won't mildew and is washable.

Muslin.   Unbleached muslin is used as an undercover for the finish fabric. Many chairs do not have it, but using an undercover of cheap material simplifies reupholstery; it lets you get everything into the proper shape before you tackle the job of putting on the expensive finish cover. You can also reposition stuffing with a regulator poked through the muslin without worrying about leaving visible holes.

Black Cambric.   This thin, glazed cotton fabric is tacked to the bottom of upholstered seats to prevent dust and loose stuffing from falling to the floor and to finish off the upholstery job.

Tacks.   Upholstery tacks have large smooth flat heads and shanks tapering to a very sharp point. When pressed into the frame wood they will stay in place while you pick up the tack hammer to drive them. You can also pick up a tack with the magnetized tip of the tack hammer and start them with a well-aimed first blow. These tacks are made in lengths from $3/16''$ to $15/16''$ (see Table 6–1).

Webbing tacks are similar to upholstery tacks except that they have barbs on one side of the shank for greater holding power. Gimp tacks have small round heads and are used in areas where the tacks must unavoidably show.

Gimp.   This is a finishing tape used along upholstery fabric edges to cover tacks. The $1/2''$ wide tape is available in a wide variety of colors and patterns. Gimp is glued down or attached with gimp tacks (see Fig. 6–7).

119

TABLE
6-1

Tacks

Upholstery Tacks

Size (oz.)	1	1½	2	2½	3	4	6	8	10	12	14
Length (in.)	3/16	7/32	1/4	5/16	3/8	7/16	1/2	9/16	5/8	11/16	3/4
Post panel covers	X										
Post panel welts		X	X								
Light and heavy fabric, muslin, cambric			X	X	X						
Heavy fabric, burlap, leather welts, many fabric layers						X	X	X			
Tacking strip, blind tacking						X	X	X	X	X	X
Webbing, spring twine, edging											
Gimp and fringe											
Covers, back											
Covers, around arms and legs											
Overlay panels											

	Upholstery Tacks (cont'd)			Webbing Tacks		Gimp Tacks					
Size (oz.)	16	18	20	12	14	2	2½	3	4	6	8
Length (in.)	13/16	7/8	15/16	11/16	3/4	5/16	3/8	7/16	1/2	9/16	5/8
Post panel covers											
Post panel welts											
Light and heavy fabric, muslin, cambric											
Heavy fabric, burlap, leather welts, many fabric layers											
Tacking strip, blind tacking		X	X								
Webbing, spring twine, edging				X	X						
Gimp and fringe						X	X	X			
Covers, back									X		
Covers, around arms and legs										X	
Overlay panels											X

121

Tacking Strip. Tacking strip is 1/2″ wide cardboard stripping put up in rolls. It is used for blind-tacking finish covers to wood framing. Ordinary chipboard cut into 1/2″ strips can also be used.

Decorative Nails. These are used along the edge of the final cover either strictly for decoration or as an alternative to trying to hide tacking under trim.

6-3 DEFINITIONS

- *Band:* A fabric strip used around the edge of spring edge wire and platform spring constructions. The top of the band is hand sewn to the spring edge wire and the bottom is tacked to the frame.
- *Blind Tacking:* Tacking the final cover so that the tacks do not show.
- *Border:* A fabric strip blind-tacked at the top edge and tacked at the bottom to the frame.
- *Boxing:* Fabric forming the thin edge of a cushion.
- *Buttoning:* Geometrically located buttons are used to hold the final cover and stuffing in place and to provide a low-relief decorative effect. If the buttons are pulled down tight it is called *tufting*.
- *Channeling:* Stuffing enclosed in fabric tubes—channels—to provide a decoration in the form of rounded ridges with deep pleated depressions between.
- *Decking:* Any fabric, but usually denim, used in place of expensive cover fabrics on cushion-supporting platforms or decks that will be hidden by cushions.
- *Felted Stuffing:* Generally cotton batting, but sometimes coarser fibers. Cotton batting is used directly under the muslin cover. Also polyester batting.
- *French Seam:* A simulated welt on the right side of upholstery fabric. The upholsterers' version is the reverse of the seamstress' French seam.
- *Panel:* A stuffed overlay of cover material used to cover exposed frame, tacks, or bulky pleats as on the front of stuffed arms. It can be blind-nailed, but screws and nuts are more secure—if physically possible.
- *Railroad:* To run fabric with its length parallel to the floor instead of vertically as normal. Often used for economy and to avoid vertical seams in the back of sofas.
- *Show Wood:* The parts of the wood frame of an upholstered chair that will be visible and must be finished.
- *Slip-Tack:* The technique of driving a tack only partway into a surface to provide a temporary fastening that can be either removed or driven tight later.

- *Stretcher:* Inexpensive fabric, usually denim, attached to the edge of a piece of cover fabric to provide a tacking extension in an area that will be invisible when the chair is assembled.
- *Undercasing:* A fabric cover, usually burlap, used to enclose stuffing materials to build up special shapes.
- *Welt:* A final-cover fabric-covered cord sewn into a cover seam or made up separately. Welting is used to trim the upholstery fabric and emphasize the shape of the piece of furniture.

6-4 UPHOLSTERY PROCEDURES

Stripping

The first rule in stripping is to remember the order in which the pieces of the cover came off so you can get their replacements on in the correct reverse order. List the pieces as you take them off.

The second rule is save everything. The old cover can then be the pattern for the new. Also, you can lay it out and accurately determine how many yards you need for the new cover.

If you are reupholstering your own furniture, or you know who owned the furniture previously, then it is not necessary to replace muslin, padding, stuffing, burlap, and webbing just because you are putting on a new cover. Even if you have to strip the piece all the way to replace sagging webbing, the old springs, stuffing, and padding can go back on. In most areas, all secondhand furniture is supposed to be fumigated before being offered for sale. If you buy at a garage sale the odds are that there was no fumigating, and you might rather replace everything.

Before removing the springs, twine, burlap, and webbing check the precautions under ''Retying Springs.''

Installing Webbing

Webbing for pad seats is tacked to the top surface of the seat frame (see Fig. 6-8). Webbing that will support coil springs is tacked to the bottom surface. New webbing should be tacked into the same locations as the old webbing. When tacking replacement webbing, it is more important to get the tacks into solid wood than to arrange them in neat staggered rows or to use the correct number of tacks. If in doubt, use extra tacks, but keep them away from the edges of the wood to avoid splitting.

Install webbing directly from the roll without cutting pieces to length, otherwise you will have difficulty stretching it. Fold the free end of the webbing over 1 1/2" and tack it to the front rail using at least seven tacks spread the width of the webbing but not in a straight

FIGURE
6-8

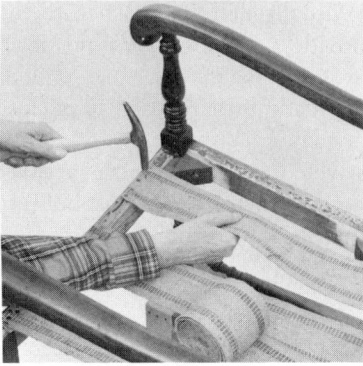

(a)

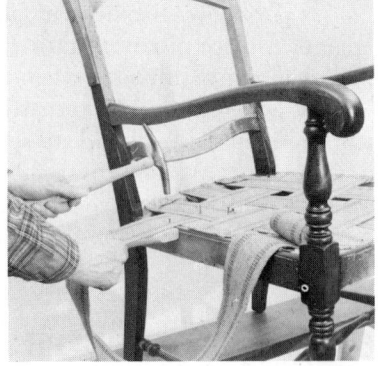

(b)

(c)

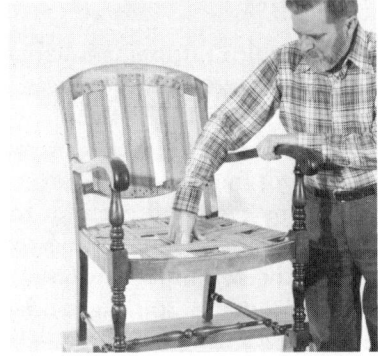

(d)

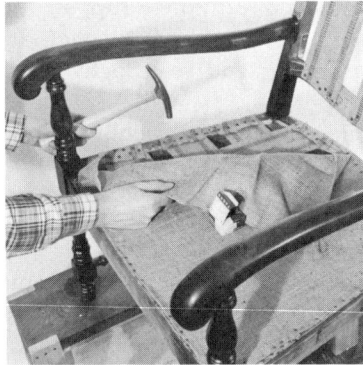

(e)

(f)

Installing webbing: If chair has pad seat without springs, webbing is tacked to the top of the seat frames. (a) Tack folded-over first end of burlap webbing to the chair rail. (b) Draw webbing tight with webbing stretcher before tacking second end to chair rail. (c) Webbing pliers can grip short webbing ends; use of electric stapler speeds work. (d) Interlaced webbing should give just a little when pressed by fist. (e) Tack burlap over webbing (burlap keeps stuffing from falling through webbing). (f) Webbing on back is usually installed only between top and bottom back frames.

line. Stretch the webbing across the back frame and tack it down with four spaced tacks. Now fold over the webbing and retack.

How tight should the webbing be pulled? If you lean heavily on the center of the webbing with your hand it should give slightly. After installing the front-to-back webbing, do the cross webbing. Be sure to interweave the webbing for stronger support.

Webbing for pad backs is installed on the front of the frame and usually only between the top and the bottom frames. Webbing for coil-spring backs is installed on the back of the frame and includes up-and-down webbing and cross webbing.

Retying Springs

The objective in retying coil springs is to get them tied down in exactly the way they were originally positioned. Springs can be tied for either a flat or round seat, as shown in Figure 6–9. If you do not have any frame repairs to make that require removing the springs, don't remove them for a fresh start or any other reason. The existing cords whether in position, frayed, or broken will tell you exactly how the springs are to be tied. Start replacing the twine, tying in the new twine before you cut out the old. (See Fig. 6–10.)

If the springs must be removed for frame repairs, try to remove the springs, webbing, spring twine, and covering burlap as a unit. Start by untacking the burlap around the frame, then pull the tacks or nails anchoring the spring twine to the frame. Finally, untack the webbing.

If you can't get it out in one piece because it is too far gone, remove the burlap. Then, sketch the position of all of the twine ties and record the length of twine between knots, and the tied height and exact positions of the springs. If you can, take pictures, from several angles.

There is an important advantage to taking out the springs as a unit; that is, the appearance of the springs will be fresher in your memory when you start taking them apart after you complete the frame repair and refinishing than if the pieces were stored in a supermarket bag while you did the other work.

Some General Notes on Springs

● The height of tied springs should extend as far above the top of the rail as the rail is high so that there is no stress put on the spring-tying twine and the burlap spring cover when the springs bottom when sat upon.

● Springs are tied with clove hitches. If you have trouble getting the knots right so the springs are in the correct place, tie the springs first with simple loops. Then when everything is where

FIGURE
6-9

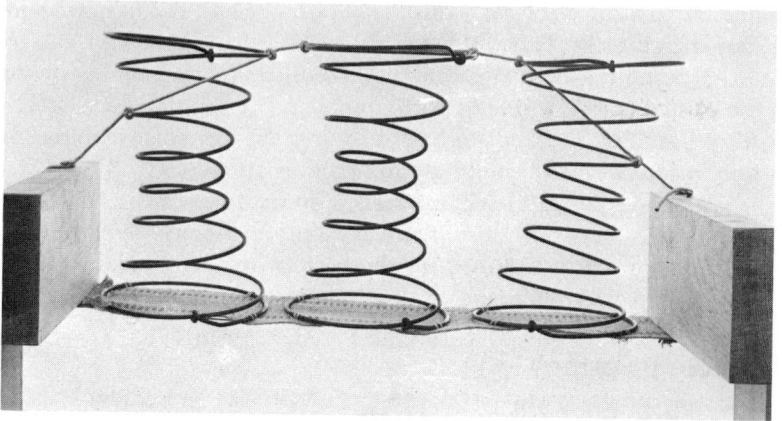

(a)

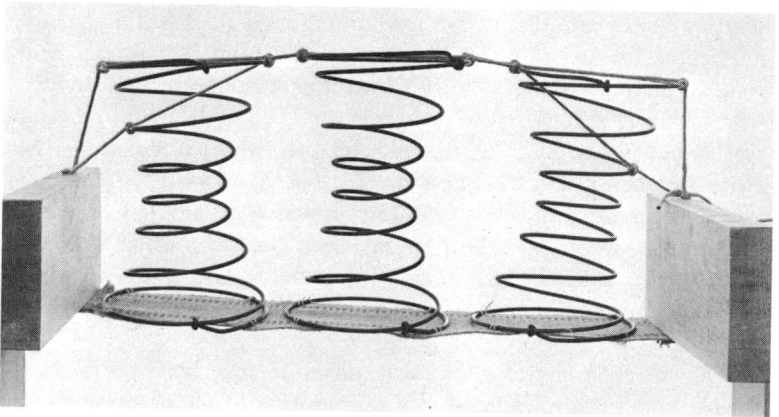

(b)

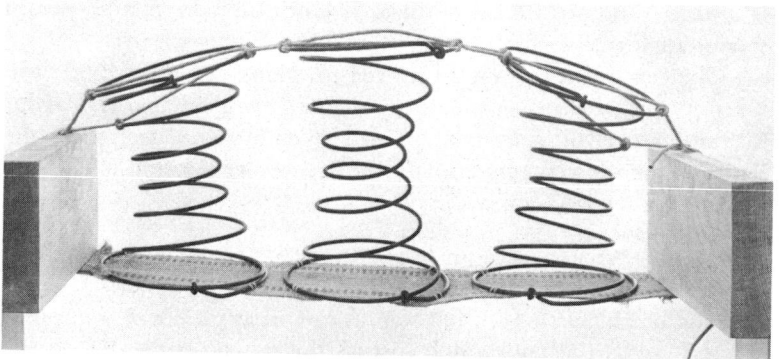

(c)

Tying springs for flat or round seat: (a) When tied, springs should be compressed to not less than twice the height of the chair rail. Start twine at one rail, tie the springs with clove hitches in the order shown. (b) For flat seat, continue as shown. (c) For round seat, pull outer spring top coils down as shown.

FIGURE
6-10

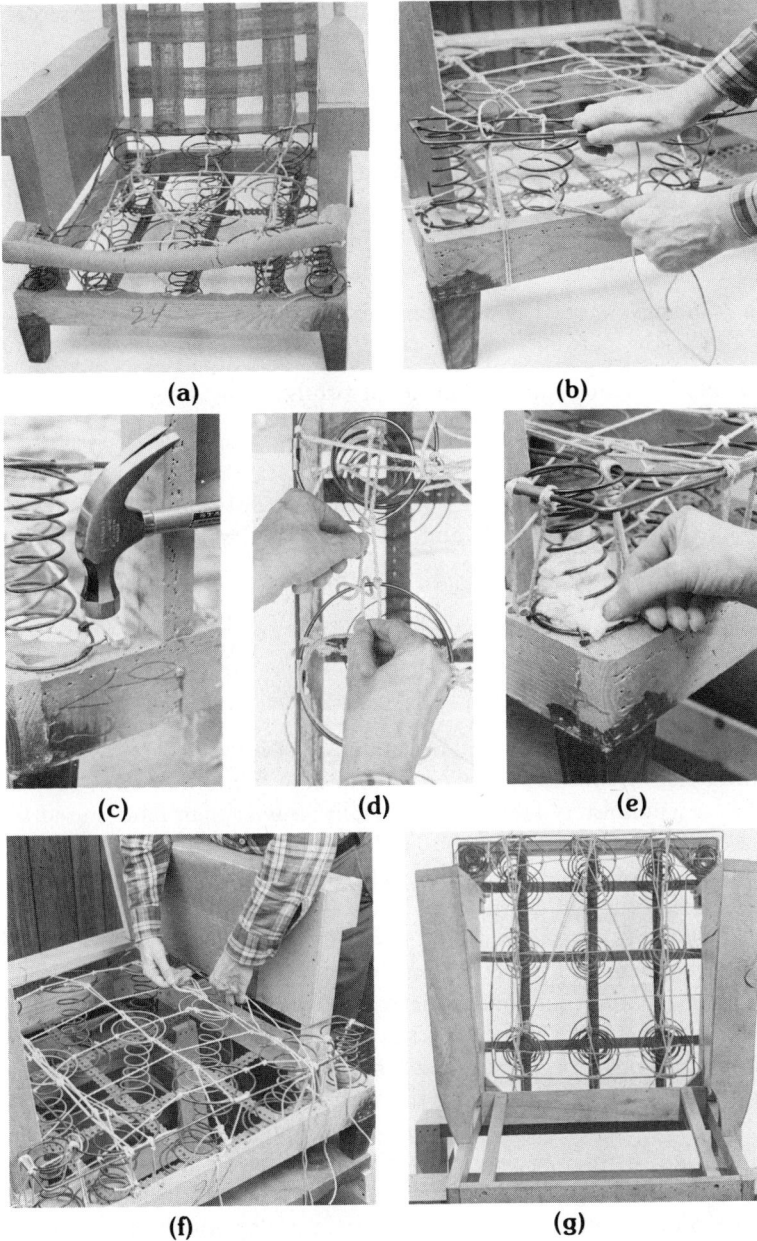

Spring tying details: (a) Before retying (spring assembly sagged forward with all ties to frame broken). (b) Temporary lashing pulls springs down to correct height so that tying can be done more accurately. (c) Secure spring to frame with bent rosined box nail. (d) Clove hitch is used for all spring tying. (e) Cotton batting is stuffed into spring to keep it quiet. (f) Double front-to-back ties. (g) Finished seat springs are neatly tied and back in position.

you want it, retie the springs using clove hitches and a second piece of spring twine.

- Springs are attached to webbing by sewing them down four places per spring with stitching twine.

- Attach springs to wood framing with staples—the kind used for fencing, not the kind in staple guns. Or use rosined box nails hammered partway in and bent over the spring wire. The staples do the job better.

- Springs fastened to wood tend to be noisy. Put a ball of cotton inside the bottom coil. It's called an insulator, or silencer.

- Spring twine must be anchored firmly to the wood frame.

- Springs are tied with either a two-way or four-way tie system. A two-way tie produces a more resilient seat, a four-way tie makes for a stronger seat because the load is distributed more evenly over all the springs, and springs have less freedom to move sideways.

Final Covers

What is and what isn't suitable material for a final cover? While the difference between drapery and upholstery fabric may exist only in the use, upholstery fabrics are generally heavier than fabrics used for other purposes because of the harder wear they will be subjected to. Don't try to save money by using a lightweight material for upholstering because it won't last.

Also, heavier materials are easier to install. They will withstand your rough handling better, and their nubby surfaces will hide all manner of minor installation defects. However, corner pleats have to be neatly made to avoid unnecessary bulkiness, and you might as well assume from the beginning that some sewing machine needles are going to be broken when trying to stitch several thicknesses.

Don't use velvet for your first try at upholstering. Every mistake you make, no matter how small, will show. If you are going to reupholster in either a solid color, stripe, or small pattern the surest way to determine how much material you need is to lay out all the old pieces on the floor between 54″ lines (that's how wide upholstery fabric generally is) and simply measure the resultant yardage. Be sure all pieces run the right direction. Don't forget welting. However, if your new cover will have a large vertically and horizontally repeating pattern, you must allow for being able to center the pattern on chair backs and seats. Fabric shops have charts indicating yardage for different pieces of furniture, and these should be used for large patterned cover material.

Recovering a Removable Pad Seat

Loose pad seats are typical of many side and dining room chairs. The procedure for recovering a removable pad seat is shown in Figure 6–11. This is a very simple upholstery job.

**FIGURE
6-11**

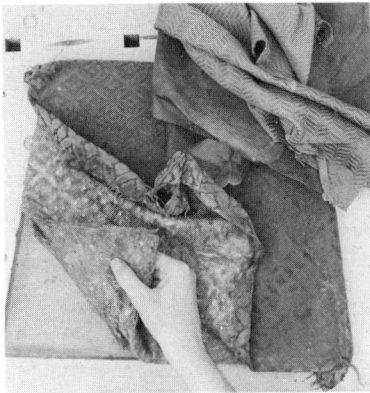
(a)

(b)

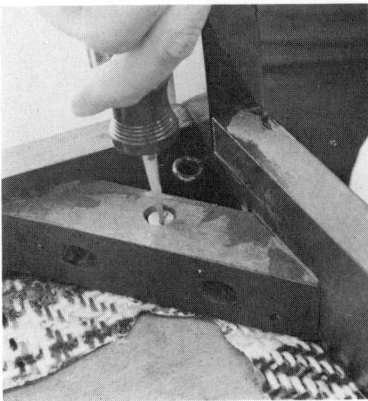
(c)

(d)

Recovering a removable seat: (a) Chair had been covered three times over many years—with each cover over the last. (b) After removing old covers, new cover is stapled to seat. (c) Pad set seat is attached to chair gluing blocks with wood screws. (d) Completed seat.

FIGURE
6-12

(a)

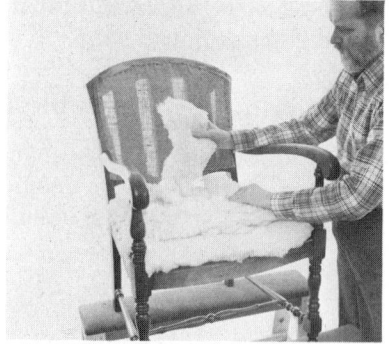

(b)

(c)

(d)

(e)

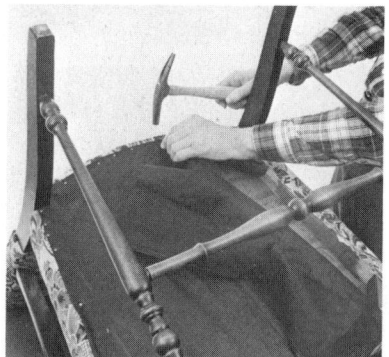

(f)

Recovering a chair with a pad seat and back: (a) Large patterns in the fabric requires careful layout so that the pattern can be centered on the seat and the front and rear of the back. (b) New cotton padding is put in place before adding muslin undercover. (c) Webbing pliers are used to grip the narrow edge of the fabric for tacking. (d) Tack the cover to arm (the best way to determine how the pieces go is to save all scraps from the old cover). (e) The hollow of the back behind the webbing is filled with foam slab to maintain shape of the chair back. (f) Finally tack on the black cambric.

Replacing a Pad Seat and Back

The chair in Figure 6–12 was bought at a garage sale. The chair was stripped, and, as the webbing was sagging and torn and we knew not where the chair had been, everything was replaced. The frame was disassembled and reglued, the finish was stripped, and the show wood restained and given two coats of satin polyurethane varnish.

New webbing was tacked down in the same location as the old using No. 12 (11/16″) tacks. Burlap was then tacked over the webbing with No. 3 (3/8″) tacks. The chair did not have role edge installed; as the loose fiber stuffing was going to be replaced with a formed slab of rubbarized hair, none was needed.

The rubberized hair slab was cut 1/2″ undersize as measured from the outside of the wood frame, and the edge was beveled with shears. The horsehair was stitched in place, which was probably unnecessary as the rubber coating on the hair reduces any tendency to move.

A layer of cotton was put on next with the edges brought over the hair stuffing edge and formed with extra cotton to produce a smooth rounded surface at the edges of the chair seat.

Loose cotton padding was mounded in the center of the seat, with all lumpiness eliminated. Over this was placed a top padding of a second cotton pad, this one with the edges extending over the sides of the wood frame and taper-torn evenly on the sides of the framing.

Using the old cover as a pattern, a muslin undercover was cut out, leaving extra material on all sides. This was tacked over the top padding, pulling the padding and stuffing down to the desired contour.

The pad back was made in a similar manner. In the case of the back, the rubberized hair slab stuffing was securely stitched to the burlap and webbing to prevent sagging downward. The burlap was drawn tight and tacked to the top and bottom frame, then to the side frames, but not drawn so tightly as to not be able to be pressed against the webbing with light pressure.

The back was completed in the same way as the seat except that no loose cotton padding was mounded between the two layers. To prevent a hollow appearance to the back of the back, one-inch foam was placed inside the frame.

Reupholstering an Overstuffed Chair

Reupholstering the overstuffed chair shown in Figure 6–13 was no more difficult than the previous example. Springs had to be tied and back webbing replaced. As the chair came from my own house, the original arm stuffing and the back padded spring unit were retained; the 1/2″ foam padding had to be replaced. Spring retying is shown in Figures 6–9 and 6–10.

FIGURE
6-13

(a)

(b)

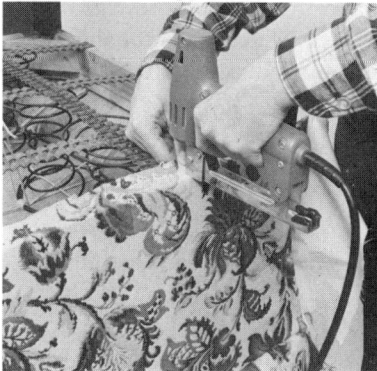

(c)

(d)

(e)

(f)

Recovering an overstuffed chair: (a) Fabric with small patterns allows flexibility in layout, produces less waste than large pattern. (b) Old stuffing and padding go back over arms (stuffing is foam). (c) Staple cover to bottom of chair frames. (d) Tack arm cover to underside of arm using cardboard tacking strip. Great care is required to get strip down straight; after checking, tacks are added, one inch apart. (e) Cushion is installed in chair as a unit. (f) Finish off with cambric. (Notice skirt installation.)

Other
Repairs

7

Many of the chair frame repair techniques described in Chapter 5 are applicable to other furniture too—disassembly, cleanup and regluing, repairing and replacing broken spindles and stretchers, and so forth.

Additional repairs are discussed in this chapter along with two techniques important in furniture repair and restoration—how to design and make dowel joints, and veneering.

7-1 REPAIRS

Splits

Table tops, leaves, chest tops, and other flat-board furniture parts frequently split and warp. Often both at the same time. (If so, take care of the split first.)

Short splits in the ends are caused by the wood drying out and shrinking. There is no point in trying to close the split and glue it back together. You would just be putting the split-producing stress back into the wood. Fill the split with patching compound, then treat it as a deep surface scratch.

Longer splits (half the board length, for example) and completely separated pieces are worth trying to glue together if the break is fresh and the sides of the split are still clean. It is a major clamping job usually requiring pipe or bar clamps. How many clamps? Assuming the split is located at the middle of the board, you should have one

FIGURE
7-1

Chest (left) was restyled from 1930's style (right). Sides were shimmed and veneered; new drawer fronts and top were added; the box was removed; the legs were cut; and a new base and false panel added at the bottom.

FIGURE
7-2

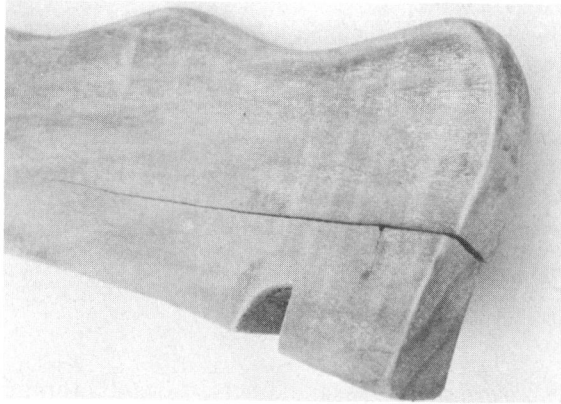

Warped and split chair crest rail: In this case, nothing would be accomplished by completing the break before regluing, because it is possible to dowel the joint from the bottom edge and end of the rail.

clamp for every board width the split is long. If the split is near one edge use a piece of wood as backup. You will also need C-clamps or equivalent to hold the board flat on your bench while in clamp. This is most important. The best glue to use is epoxy cement. It is the strongest and will give you adequate time to get the adhesive worked into the split and the clamps in place. If the force needed to close the split seems not excessive, then use white glue.

134

If the long split is old and dirty, you will not be able to reglue using those surfaces. Break or saw the board into two pieces, dress the edges, and reglue. Are dowels needed? If the board isn't warped, dowels will be useful only to aid clamping alignment, which you can also accomplish with blocking and clamps.

If the two separated pieces are warped and they probably will be, clamping pressure is required to bring them into alignment, then dowels should be used. Alignment is more important than dowel size. (See Figs. 7–2, 7–3, 7–4, and 7–5.)

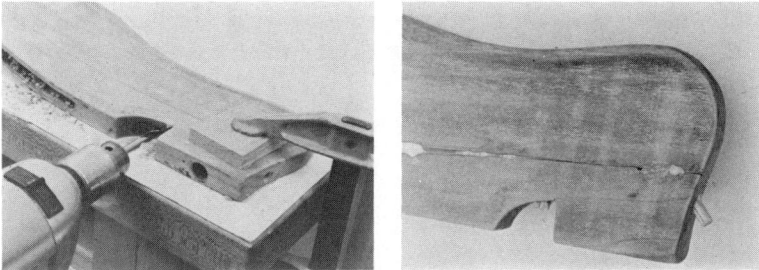

FIGURE
7-3

Split chair rail repair: (a) Drill for dowels. (Extending the backpost dowel is not possible because the end of the hole already broke through the surface.) (b) Repair is made. The dowels do the holding; the glue in dirty break serves mainly as a crack filler.

FIGURE
7-4

Split table top: Four boards of table top were edge-glued and originally fastened to the apron with screws up through the side aprons into the outer boards. At a later date additional screws were used through the ends of each board into the end aprons. Both attachments made no allowance for top expansion across the grain and resulted in wide paint-filled cracks between the boards.

FIGURE
7-5

Table top repair: The edges of the slightly warped boards were planed true and the boards were drilled for dowels. Dowels were necessary because of the warp. The table top was then glued up and sanded flat.

Warp

The best kiln-dried lumber will warp if its moisture content changes; and that in a nut shell is what causes warp. In old furniture, the tendency to warp is aggravated by more moisture getting into one side than the other, or moisture drying out of one side of the board more than the other. Warp is less likely in boards finished equally on both sides, with a finish impervious to moisture, and least a problem in boards securely fastened down, such as a table top screwed to an apron frame.

You get warp out of a board by applying moisture to the concave side, and clamping pressure to straighten it out. It is not an overnight operation. It can take days, weeks, sometimes months, depending on the wood and the degree of warp. All warped wood should be clamped cautiously. Apply only a little straightening distortion at a time and increase the pressure only when the wood is actually yielding to the clamping—or you will have a split board on your hands.

You must keep the wood moist and in clamp for a long time. This can involve setting up a special clamping frame just for the board, using 2 x 4's, and locating it somewhere besides on top of your bench so you can get other work done meanwhile. Excelsior packing is usually advised for keeping the board moist, but excelsior is not that common anymore. Pads of upholstery foam, moistened periodically and held against the wood will also work well, perhaps even better.

A simple one-plane warp like cupping or bowing (one or the other) can be taken out completely. Combinations of warp and uneven warping usually result in a board straighter, but still warped, because, you are actually, by clamping, replacing one set of warps with another, lesser set. The board, in other words, doesn't know it's supposed to go straight, but only reacts to the clamping forces.

After the board has straightened out, remove the moisture pads and leave the board in the clamps until it is thoroughly dry. It should then be finished on both sides, even if it is a table top, and the finish should be applied equally.

Warped Veneered Wood.   First, you cannot apply moisture to the veneered side. It will not help or it will ruin the veneer. Clamp without moisture, or clamp with the other side moistened. (See Fig. 7–6.)

**FIGURE
7-6**

Clamping a warped desk lid. (The lid was re-veneered before clamping.)

FIGURE
7-7

Table leg attachment.

Table Frames

Loose and wobbly table frames should be treated as loose chair frames—take them apart completely and reglue, unless the problem is merely loose legs. The legs of many tables particularly large tables, are held to the apron frame by one screw each. The screw is usually a hanger bolt (see Fig. 7-7), and tightening the nut is often all that is required if the apron framing is sound. If you do take the table apart for frame regluing, after applying glue, loosely screw the frame to the top to hold it in alignment—but only if the top itself is not warped.

Tops should not be glued to table frames. If they are not allowed to expand and contract with changes in the weather, they crack and split. Figure 7-9 shows several ways tops can be attached without this happening.

Chest and Cabinet Carcasses

Loose joints mean disassembly and regluing. Often, the whole carcass does not have to be taken apart. Great care must be exercised when reassembling a carcass to ensure that it is glued and clamped square.

Drawers

Drawers can give you trouble several ways. They can stick or go into the carcass too far, or go in crooked. They can fall apart, which should

FIGURE
7-8

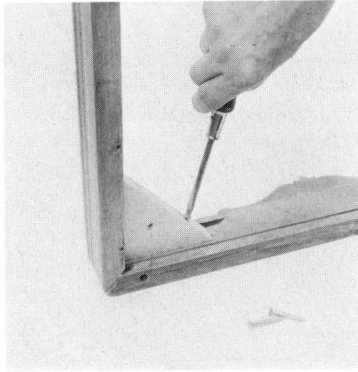

(a)   (b)

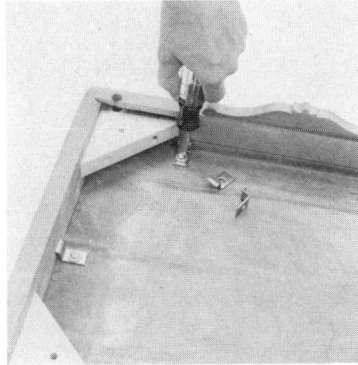

(c)   (d)

Table repair: Legs were attached to table apron by cross members (set in slots at each end), which may not have been original. (a) Legs are attached to the new corner blocks. (b) Attach corner blocks with glue and screws. (c) Mounting studs are pieces of threaded rod epoxied into threaded holes in the crossed legs. (d) The table top is secured to the apron with special clips made for the purpose.

not be too surprising as every time you open a drawer you are in effect trying to pull the front off. They can also be missing.

Sticking Drawers. Before doing anything, find out where precisely the drawer is sticking and why. If both sides are rubbing top and bottom against the guides, the wood of the drawer sides is probably swollen due to absorbed moisture, but the drawer could be in the wrong opening. Before sanding or planing, try rubbing a wax candle on the rubbed parts. All that may be needed is a little lubrication. A tight drawer in summer will usually be a loose drawer in winter. Sanding from the bottom of the drawer sides is preferred because you won't have to refinish the surfaces, but sand from the sides evenly or the drawer can tip backward when it is closed.

139

FIGURE
7-9

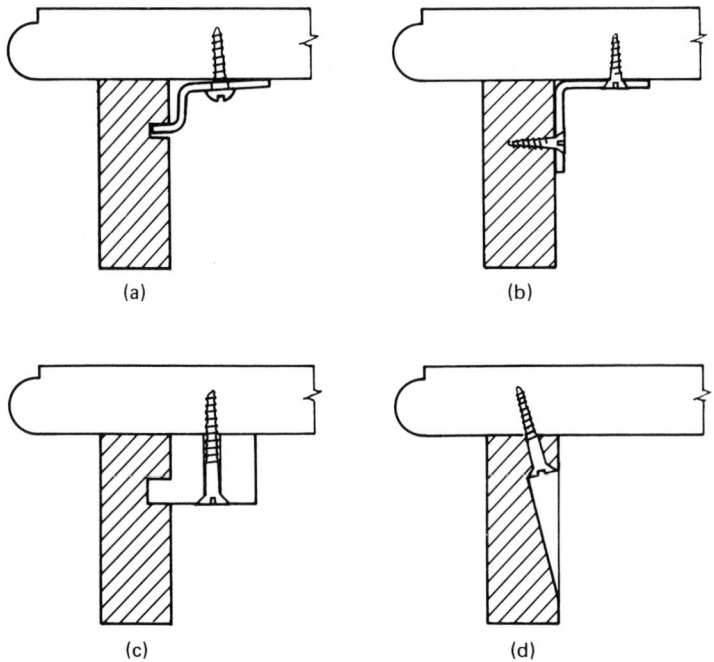

Methods of attaching table and cabinet tops that allow expansion and contraction without cracking: (a) Metal table-top fastener, (b) steel mending angle, (c) rabbeted wood block, and (d) woodscrew in pocket in rail.

If the drawer sticks only on one side, swelling wood could still be the problem, but it might also be that a guide is out of position. Check before sanding. If the drawer sticks on the top of one side and the bottom of the other, it usually means that the carcass is racked—leaning sideways at an angle. The cure for this usually means disassembly and regluing the carcass.

Loose Drawers. Drawers that go in too far are caused by missing drawer stops; usually they have broken off. Drawer stops are blocks of wood that limit how far in a drawer can go. They can be located in the back of the opening and come against the back of the drawer, or they can be on the front rail under the drawer and come against the back of the drawer front. Their location depends normally on the design of the drawer. Replacement blocks should be glued and screwed in place.

Broken Drawers. Most better-quality drawers are assembled with dovetail joints, which are the strongest construction possible (see Fig. 7-10). With age and constant stress, the joints fail—or to be more accurate, the glue fails, and the joints work apart. If this has

FIGURE
7-10

Drawer construction and joints: (a) Side-guided drawer, (b) center-guided drawer, (c) handmade dovetails, and (d) modern machine-made dovetails.

happened awhile back, the drawer bottom falls out and is often lost. A replacement drawer bottom should not be glued in the slots. If the bottom is located under the drawer back rather than slotted into it, the bottom should be nailed to the back. Reassembling most drawers usually involves nothing more than gluing up the dovetail joints. Be very careful that the joints are fully closed and that the drawer is clamped square while the glue dries.

Hinges

Broken hinges must of course be replaced. This should be no problem unless the hinges are decorative. Screws loose in the holes should not be replaced by bigger or longer screws. The holes in the wood should be reamed to clean wood and packed tightly with wood putty. When dry, drill pilot holes and insert screws. Using wood pegs in the holes or toothpicks is not too good an idea for remounting any hinge subject to high stress, such as a desk lid hinge, because the screws will not hold well in the end-grain wood.

Mouldings and Turnings

Replacing missing parts if not too extensive, can be done with hand tools only. Wood is the easiest repair material to work with. (See Fig. 7–11.)

The break surface must be clean and smooth. Cut and fit an oversize piece of wood for the repairing. If the glue line is in one plane only, drill holes for reinforcing dowels. These simple butt joints are

FIGURE
7-11

(a)

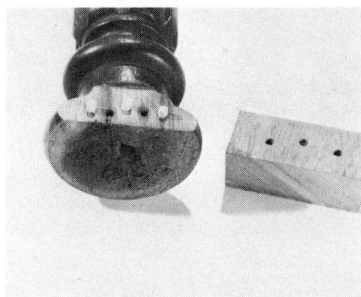

(b)

(c)

(d)

Replacing a missing part of a turning (technique can also be applied to mouldings): (a) Before (the folly of depending on nails to hold anything is shown by the old repair). (b) The face of the break is dressed smooth and the oversize block is glued and doweled (the dowels are 1/8" in diameter and about 3/8" long). (c) Remove wood cautiously to avoid trouble carving the repair. (d) Sand to final dimension.

too weak without dowels. The grain of the repair piece should run in the same direction as the repaired wood. After the part is glued in, start carving. The procedure is simple. Remove wood that doesn't look like it will be part of the finished repair. Go slowly, starting with the obvious waste wood. As you progress, your carving perception will improve. Shave the wood off, don't take it out in big chunks. When the repair looks about finished, sand.

Moulding and turning repairs can also be done with patching materials such as Duratite Wood Putty and Miracle Wood, or an acrylic polymer modeling paste containing pulverized marble. You might want to use these materials on repairs requiring detailed modeling, but for most wood repairs, wood is faster and easier, and it is wood repairing wood.

Missing Turnings. If you have a wood lathe you don't need suggestions on how to make replacements for missing turnings. If you don't, the question becomes one of where to get them made. The first choice, obviously, is a friend with a lathe. Or you could sign up for an adult-education woodworking course so you can use a school lathe. A better way, after making an accurate and neat drawing of the part you need, is to contact a shop teacher to see if he can have a student make the part. You would have to provide the material. The teacher is usually happy with the idea because it gives a student a chance to make something that is not a regular assignment. As a last resort, take your drawing, or the piece you want a duplicate of, to a cabinetmaking shop (look in the Yellow Pages). It will cost but not as much as buying your own lathe.

Marble Tops

Missing marble tops can be replaced either with natural marble or a product made by Du Pont called Corian® . You will have a greater range of colors using natural marble, but you will have to purchase the top finished because marble working requires specialized tools not often found even in a well-equipped home shop.

Corian looks, feels, and is heavy like natural marble. The coloration is moulded right through. Colors available are white, beige, and olive. Thicknesses made are 1/4″, 1/2″, and 3/4″,. The material is a filled methyl methacrylate.

You can saw, rout, drill, and sand Corian (see Fig. 7–12). The material is very hard. For all sawing, protect the surface with tape.

Saber Saw. Use 12 to 14 tpi metal-cutting blade.

Circular Saw (any). Use a carbide blade, the more teeth, the better. The blade should project 1/4″ through the Corian to ensure for smoothest cut.

FIGURE
7-12

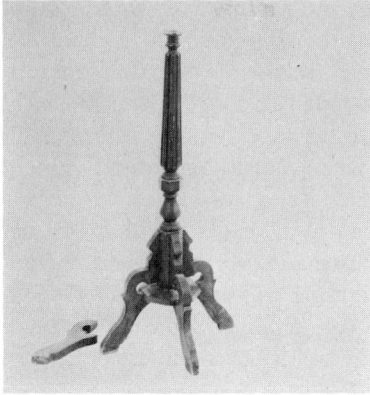 

before   after

(a)   (b)

 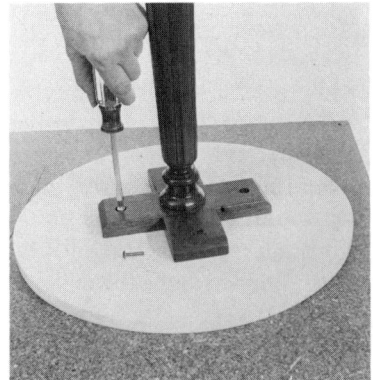

(c)   (d)

Replacing a marble table top with du Pont's "Corian": (a) When sawing, use metal-cutting blade and protect Corian surface from scratching. (b) Sand the Corian with silicon-carbide paper (nothing else is hard enough). (c) After sanding, buff with Scotchbrite pad under sander. (d) Crossed supports are fastened to post with lag bolt. Holes in Corian are tapped for machine screws.

Router. Use carbide blades only, and light cuts. Guide the router with a fence or ball-bearing pilot, never a plain pilot. To make a cutout, use a templet and a router instead of sawing. Relieve all sharp edges.

Drilling. Use ordinary twist drills.

Tapping. Same as for cast iron, but use water as the lubricant. Careful chip cleanout required.

Sanding. Use silicon carbide paper only. Start with 50 grit on belt sander, finish with 180 and 220 grit on pad sander.

Buffing. Use a Scotchbrite pad under the pad sander. High gloss polishing is not recommended because all minor scratches and other surface imperfections will show.

Scratches and cigarette burns can be removed, depending on depth, with abrasive cleanser or 400-grit silicon carbide paper, then buffed.

Plastic Laminates

Plastic laminates go under several trade names—Formica, Micarta, Textolite, and so forth. The thin, hard and brittle material comes in a wide variety of patterns including solid colors, woodgrain and mineral patterns. Their most usual use is in the repair of table and chest tops; a sheet of the material can quickly refinish an impossibly ugly or damaged top.

The material is not difficult to work with if you will keep in mind its brittleness. It can be sawn without objectionable chipping with a saber saw and a Sears No. 28761 superfine finishing blade. Support the laminate carefully when you cut it.

After cutting, glue laminate to your core with contact cement. Edges can be filed and sanded, but the best way to trim edges is with a carbide router bit made for the purpose. Such bits used with a router attachment and router can, by adjustment, trim square or bevel.

7-2 DOWEL JOINTS

Doweled joints are widely used in furniture. The joints have high strength, are easy and economical to make in new work, and not too difficult to repair in old furniture (see Fig. 7–13).

A dowel is a pin or peg of wood that fits in mating holes in two joined wood pieces. A dowel joint always consists of two or more dowels, necessary to prevent the joined parts from twisting. A rung into a chair leg, for example, is not a dowel joint.

145

**FIGURE
7-13**

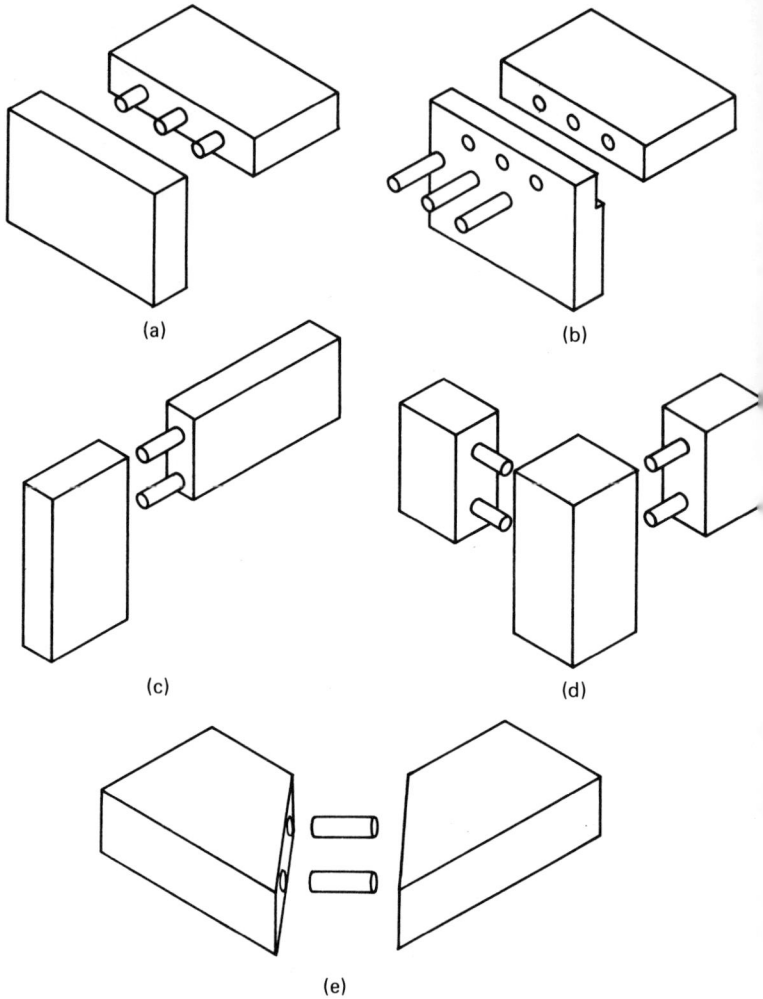

Doweled joints: (a) Doweled butt joint, (b) doweled rabbeted joint, (c) doweled frame joint, (d) doweled rails into a corner post, and (e) Doweled miter joint.

**TABLE
7-1**

Recommended Dowel Diameters

Wood Thickness	Dowel Size
1/2"	1/4"
5/8"	1/4" or 5/16"
3/4" or 13/16"	3/8"
1" or 1 1/8"	3/8" or 1/2"
1 1/2"	3/4"

A doweled joint is held together by the strength of the glue line between the sides of the dowels and the wood they are fitted into. The dowel joint, whether new or repaired, must be tight fitting for good strength; woodworking glues must be used. A poorly fitting doweled joint will also be strong if glued with a gap-filling adhesive, such as epoxy cement.

New Work

The dowel diameter should be 1/3 to 1/2 the thickness of the wood—the common 3/8" dowels are the right size for 3/4" to 1" wood. (See Table 7–1.) If one piece of wood is thicker than the other, go by the thinner piece. Locate the dowels on the centerline of the wood if possible, for the strongest joint. Keep dowels their own diameter away from the edges of boards when you are putting the dowel into the end, and two diameters away from the ends when putting the dowels into side grain. This will reduce the possibility of splitting the wood. The dowels should go two to three times their diameter into each piece of wood, further in softwood for maximum joint strength.

Making Dowels

You can buy dowels or make them. Purchased dowels are inexpensive, but they are usually available only in 3/8" diameter. You will have to make your own for other sizes. Start with a birch dowel stick from a hardware store or lumberyard. Cut dowels to length. Chamfer the ends for easier joint assembly and saw a groove lengthwise to let air and glue out of the joint.

Dowel Holes

The best drill bit for making dowel holes is a spur wood bit (see Fig. 7–14). These can be purchased individually or in sets. These drill bits are used in an electric drill or drill press and work best at high speeds.

FIGURE
7-14

Drills: (From left) auger bit used in a brace, (b) spur wood bit, (c) twist drill, and (d) spur wood bit made from a twist drill.

147

Twist drills should be used only when you suspect you might run into hidden nails or screws. Twist drills are for metal, they are difficult to control in wood and often leave a messy hole. If you have a grinder, you can easily make spur wood bits from twist drills. If you have the skill to keep the holes straight, drill them with a brace and auger bit.

Dowel holes should mate, which is sometimes easier said than done. The best way to make up the holes in new work is with dowel centers, but in repairs, particularly when you have a splintered surface, you will need a doweling jig.

Metal dowel centers transfer dowel hole locations from one mating piece to the other. To use these lay out the dowel hole locations on one piece, then drill dowel holes. Insert the dowel centers in the holes, line up the two mating pieces of wood and press together. Points on the dowel centers will mark the second piece of wood (see Fig. 7-15).

A doweling jig will hold your bit perpendicular to the mating surface while you drill the hole. It will also help you locate holes. (See Fig. 7-16.) A doweling jig is indispensable when redrilling to replace a broken-off dowel.

Dowels should fit in the mating holes fingertight when dry. In furniture repairs this is not always possible. Sometimes holes have to be deliberately oversize to compensate for misalignment, either in hole angle or location. Loose fitting dowels whether new or old can be corrected several ways.

The best way is to use a filled epoxy cement, such as Sears No. 80606 in place of white glue or aliphatic resin glue. This adhesive comes in two tubes from which equal amounts are mixed. This epoxy will solidly fill the gap between the dowel and the hole. Wrapping

FIGURE
7-16

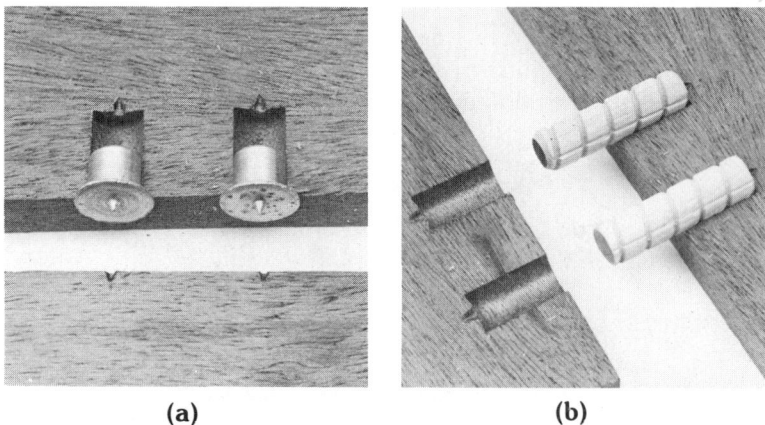

(a)   (b)

Dowel centers (sets contain two of each size—1/4", 5/16", 3/8", 7/16" and 1/2"): (a) Centers aligning with holes in second piece, shown in cutaway. (b) Aligned dowels.

string around the dowel is another solution, but it is not as good; neither is lining the hole with a thickness of veneer or toothpicks.

(*Note:* Cleaning up old joints, removing dowels, and so forth is discussed in detail in Chapter 5.)

7-3 VENEERING

Many times in furniture repair and restoration you will have to use veneer to match a repair to the rest of the piece. Veneering is not complicated or difficult, but careful workmanship is required to avoid making a mess of the effort. Except for sanding, veneering is a hand-tool operation.

Tools

The tools required for veneering are shown in Figure 7-17.

Veneer Saw. Veneer saws come in several forms. The teeth are not set, instead they form a knife edge. A veneer saw must be used with a straightedge.

Utility Knife. When an accurate cut is not essential (which is most of the time), you can also cut veneer with a utility knife. Scribe the veneer, then break.

Straightedge. This tool is used to guide the veneer saw for accurate cutting.

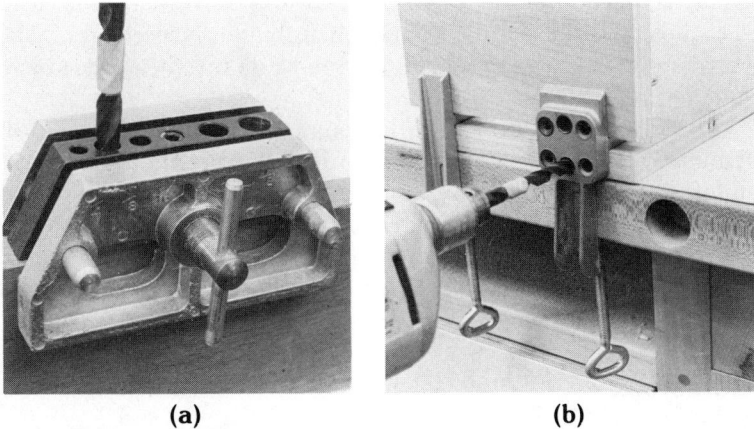

FIGURE
7-15

(a) (b)

Doweling jigs: (a) Dowl-it® jig locates holes on centerline; it is used for doweling edge-to-edge joints. (b) Coastal jig is used for making corner joints.

**FIGURE
7-17**

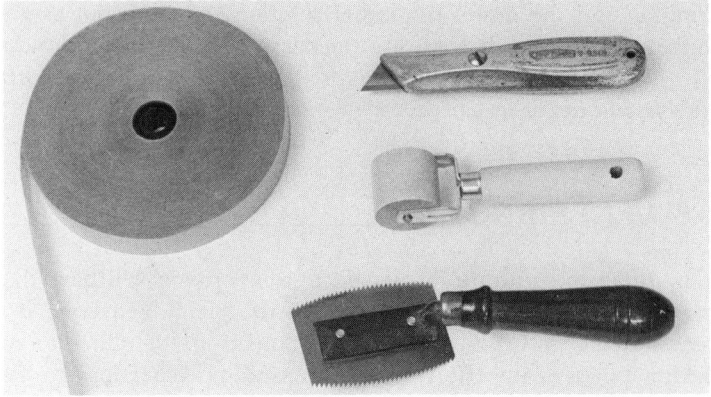

Veneering tools: Gummed tape, utility knife, roller, and saw.

Veneer Pins. These are used to temporarily tack veneer in place while you start getting it clamped. Buy expensive ones that are glorified thumb tacks, or use any 18-ga. nails.

Veneer Tape. Tape is used to join pieces of veneer accurately for one-shot gluing. Veneer tape is actually thin kraft tape. You can also use masking tape provided you remove it quickly. Even then, it can be difficult to get off the veneer. Kraft paper veneer tape can be sanded off.

Veneer Roller. This tool is used to press down veneer for good contact when using contact cement, or to squeeze out excess glue when using conventional glues.

Veneer Press. Veneers must be glued under clamping pressure evenly applied over large surfaces. This is difficult to do with C-clamps, and the normal solution is to build a veneer press. The press can be a bench-top model that can be set up when needed and stored at other times.

Both veneer presses shown in Figure 7–18 consist of a series of frames. The width of the opening in the frame determines the maximum width work you can clamp, the length of the work is determined by the number of frames you build.

For good clamping, the machinist's jacks or press screws should be placed not more than 9″ apart in both directions. The vertical opening of both presses can be adjusted for clamping convenience.

Corestock

Three materials are used as corestock under veneer—lumber, plywood, and particleboard, both chipboard and flakeboard. All have advantages and disadvantages.

FIGURE
7-18

(a)

(b)

Veneer presses: (a) Machinist's jacks are used in this press in place of
more expensive press screws. (b) Press with press screws.

Lumber core. If the edge of the panel is going to show, a lumber core is best as the wood can be finished to a close match with the face of the panel. A lumber core also provides the best holding power for screws (hinge screws, for example) that must be driven into the panel edge. There is usually more work involved in veneering on a lumber core, however. The wood must be smoothed, and the panel may have to be made of edge-glued strips. Also, crossbanding is required. Lumber cores should be used only for curved panels where you can't use plywood.

Plywood. Plywood is the best all-around core material for veneering.

Veneer plywood—plywood with face plies of white pine, birch, other hardwoods, and mahogany instead of fir—should be used. Face plies are smooth and core is relatively solid. This plywood can be obtained in 4 x 8 panels from lumberyards, and as leftover part panels from cabinet and millwork shops. Check the Yellow Pages and look around.

Fir plywood in A-C Exterior and A-D Interior grades should not be used for corestock. The back veneers in both grades are allowed too many defects such as knots, knotholes, and splits. Also the surfaces are not smooth. In addition, the low-grade internal cores have the same knotholes and splits as back plies. This results in a plywood whose structural integrity cannot be trusted. Delamination is another problem.

The only construction plywood that can be used for veneering corestock is *underlayment* grade, and the best, and most available plywood of this grade is imported Lauan. The plywood is sold in a nominal 1/4″ thickness. Plies of this plywood can be glued up for thicker cores.

Particleboard Cores. Two types of particleboard are used for veneer cores—chipboard and flakeboard. Both are heavy materials and are best worked with carbide tools. Neither has much screw-holding ability, particularly in edges. Flakeboard edges can be smoothly moulded with a router and can be given an opaque finish to match the color of the face veneer; chipboard edges are worse looking than plywood when not covered.

Crossbanding

Crossbanding is the layer of veneer directly under the face veneer and back veneer. The grain of crossbanding is always at an angle to the grain of the solid-wood corestock, preferably at a right angle. If your corestock is plywood or particleboard you do not need crossbanding. When using veneer plies to build up core thickness under the face and back veneer, you must also maintain symmetry by using the same number of plies on each side of the corestock.

While any veneer that glues well can be used for crossbanding, poplar is generally used because it is cheap and comes in wide pieces.

Joints in crossbanding must be tight and neatly made. There should be no holes in the crossbanding. It is better not to use the part of the veneer containing the hole than to fill the hole with compound because you will have to sand the repair smooth.

Gluing Veneer

White glue, yellow glue, and urea resin glues are the best choices for gluing veneer. Which of the three glues you use depends on the size of the glue job and how long it will take you to get the glue spread, the pieces aligned, and the press closed. The whole problem really comes down to how fast you can spread the glue. Spreading glue with your finger may be fine for gluing joints, but a notched spreader is a lot more efficient for large surfaces. Make one from a paint scraper. It spreads the glue quickly and evenly.

Yellow glue is the best choice for gluing veneer panels if you can get the work clamped fast enough; otherwise, use white glue or urea resin glue. Do not be generous with the glue, which need only go on one surface, usually the core, but be very thorough in getting even and complete coverage.

When you clamp, excess glue will come right through the pores of most veneers and spread on the good surface. Remove excess glue first with a hand scraper, then sand.

Brittle and Rippled Veneer

Most veneers can be glued down without any ceremony other than applying the glue. Crotch and burl veneers and many highly figured veneers are brittle and ripply, and, therefore, difficult to glue down without their splitting and breaking.

Wetting the veneer, and drying it in a press usually doesn't do much good. Sizing the veneer is a better solution. The following size contains a glue to give the veneer strength and glycerine to provide flexibility. Measurements are by volume. The alcohol simply speeds drying.

- 3 parts urea glue resin (powder)
- 4 parts cold water
- 2 parts glycerine
- 1 part denatured alcohol

Mix powder and water, then add glycerine and alcohol. Soak the veneer in this solution for one to two minutes and drain dry. Then place veneer between sheets of aluminum foil backed by pads of newspaper, and press on a flat surface under a board weighted to slowly flatten the veneer as it dries. Several days drying will be required.

Flat Panel Veneering

To apply veneer to a panel, start with oversize veneer, and also an oversize panel in new work, if possible. Crossbanding is not necessary with plywood or particleboard—only with solid wood. Crossbanding is also not necessary on board edges or other small pieces, whether you are veneering with or across the grain.

FIGURE
7-19

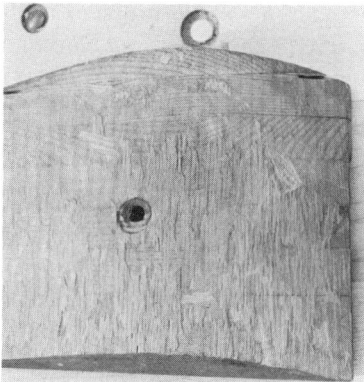

(a)

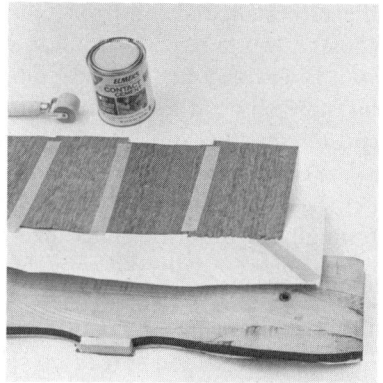

(b)

(c)

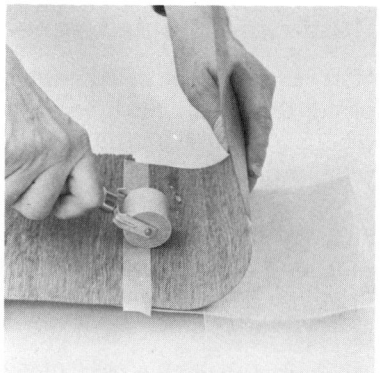

(d)

Re-veneering a curved drawer front for a Victorian Queen Anne Desk: (a) Veneer was completely missing from drawer front when acquired; surface of glue residue indicates that crossbanding was not used originally. (b) To run veneer grain vertically, crossbanding has to be installed diagonally. (c) Contact cement is applied. (d) Roll veneer for good contact and adhesion.

Spread glue evenly and thinly, then clamp core, crossbanding, and veneer in one operation. When the glue is dry, trim.

If you are veneering the edges as well as the face, do the edges first. Allow 1/8'' waste on each side. and at the end of the edge. After the glue is dry trim the ends first. A coping saw tears the scrap veneer less than a veneer saw. Next clamp the panel and slice the scrap from the side, down to 1/32'' or 1/16'' depending on how adventurous you are. The final bit of veneer scrap should be filed off using a flat second-cut file with double-cut teeth. Wrap the end of the file with masking tape to protect the panel surface.

Veneering Curved Surfaces

The easy way out is to use contact cement. (See Fig. 7–19.) With contact cement you can veneer many materials besides wood, including metal. However, contact cement leaves a very visible glue line. (The better way to glue veneer to curved surfaces is to use conventional glues and forms called *cauls,* which are shaped to support the corestock and ensure that clamping pressure is applied evenly over the whole work surface.)

Marquetry

Marquetry is the assembling of pieces of different kinds of veneer to form a pattern or design (see Fig. 7–20). Many designs can be purchased ready-made, and can be used as is, or can be taken apart and used as material for a design of your own. The carefully fitted parts are pasted good side down to a sheet of kraft paper. When the whole design is assembled it can then be glued to the corestock, with the kraft paper out. When dry the kraft is peeled and sanded off. The sheet of kraft paper can be most easily made up in parallel strips of 3'' packing tape.

Inlay

Letting decorative strips, pieces of veneer, or other materials such as metal, ivory, tortoise shell, mother-of-pearl into the surface of solid wood is called inlaying. The hard part is routing the surface to take the inlays. It is usually done with an electric router and elaborate jigging, but it can also be done with a hand router plane.

FIGURE
7-20

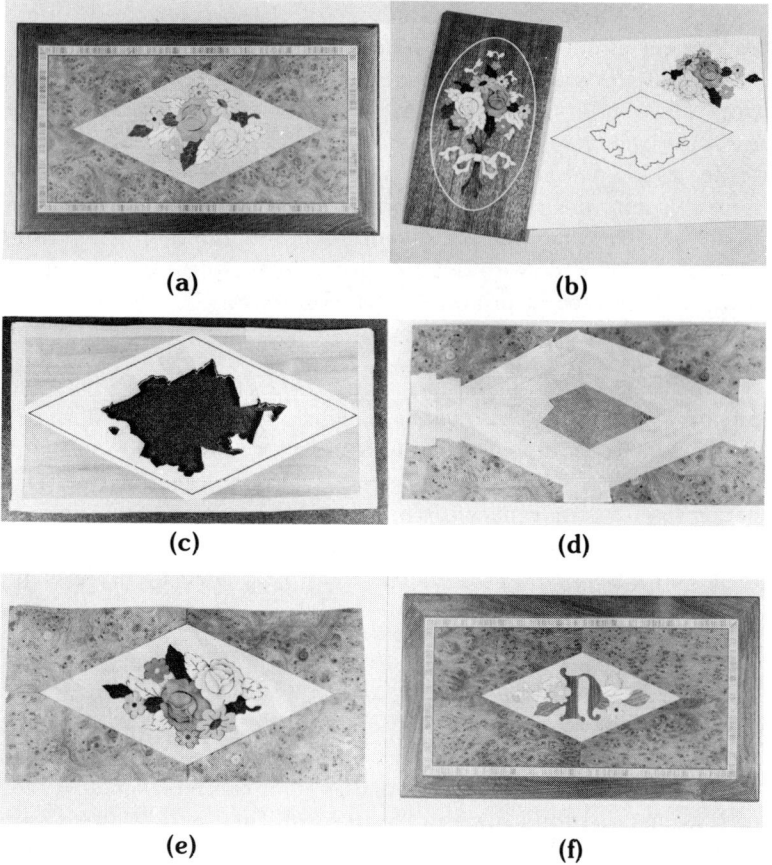

(a)   (b)

(c)   (d)

(e)   (f)

Marquetry (making the top of the jewelry box, which is pictured in Fig. 4-14): (a) The finished top (the outside frame is solid rosewood). (b) The floral inlay was purchased, cut from its mahogany background, partially disassembled, and some parts were rearranged to fit diamond avoidire inset. (c) For cutting out on scroll saw, avoidire is sandwiched between scrap veneer. (d) Veneer is assembled for gluing to core stock (shown from "good" side). Floral inlay is covered with and held together with kraft paper, which will be sanded off. (e) Assembled veneer (shown from side that will be coated with glue). (f) Another jewelry box lid with rosewood initial worked into floral design.

The Original Finish – Rejuvenate or Remove?

8

Decisions, decisions. What should you do? There are many options.

An old finish can (1) be admired for its age, (2) cleaned up and then admired for its age and beauty, (3) cleaned up, repaired, and then admired for its age, beauty, and good condition, (4) removed and replaced with a modern finish with similar characteristics and admired for the way in which the finish brings out the figure in the wood, or (5) removed and replaced with a completely different finish. (See Fig. 8–1.)

If you are restoring a piece of furniture, you should first consider cleaning or reviving. Don't go overboard. Old furniture should look old—but not disreputable, dirty, dingy, and disfigured. If 100 years old, the piece is most handsome and valuable if it looks its age. The fancy word for this attractive old glow is *patina* which no one seems able to define, or even agree on how to pronounce. An antique has it when it looks good, but a new piece of furniture doesn't have it no matter how good it looks. There is another reason for cleaning or reviving a finish—both are a lot less work than stripping and refinishing.

8-1 CLEANING AND REVIVING FINISHES

Some old furniture finishes are just plain dirty. Scratches, white and dark marks, dirt, and grime can be easily taken care of. However, if

**FIGURE
8-1**

**Revive this finish? Except for a few chips, veneer appeared sound,
rosewood seemed to be lurking under the very dirty finish. However,
when careful cleaning got underway, "rosewood" turned out to be a
painted finish, much of which was no longer on the wood. The clock
case was stripped and repaired (Chapter 7), and a new "Rosewood"
finish was painted on (Chapter 11).**

the finish is chipping and not smooth you will probably have to
remove it. Try cleaning first.

The first step is to get the wax (if any) off. Rub down the surface
with a cloth wet with paint thinner, or a product made for the purpose with somewhat stronger solvents, such as Mohawk's Silicone
Wash. Burlap is better than a soft cloth because it won't clog up as
fast. If the surface is veneered, stick with the soft cloth and be careful
not to pick up loose veneer. Many times just removing the layer of
wax built up over years and decades is all that is needed.

Next, identify the finish. Begin by testing for shellac. (See Fig.
8-2.) Moisten a wad of cotton with denatured alcohol and rub the
finish in an inconspicuous spot. If the finish comes off, it is shellac. If
none of the finish comes off, moisten cotton with lacquer solvent and
rub. If the finish softens or comes off—probably not as readily as
shellac rubbed with alcohol—the finish is lacquer. If the finish
doesn't come off with either alcohol or lacquer solvent, it is varnish.
(Don't spend all day at this test, lacquer solvent will eventually cut
varnish too. Give it about 10 seconds.)

If the finish is lacquer, varnish, or paint, you can wash the piece
with mild soap or liquid dishwashing detergent and water. (A shellac
finish washed with water will turn white.)

Never slop water on the surface. Use a damp cloth with the soap,
then wipe with another damp cloth to remove the soap film, then
wipe dry and polish with a third cloth. Regardless of the finish be very
careful about getting water into the glue under veneer.

**FIGURE
8-2**

**Test for a shellac finish: If the finish comes off quickly when rubbed with
alcohol on a cotton swab, it is shellac.**

Washing removes surface dirt, but doesn't get at the dirt imbedded in the finish itself. For that, you need a cleaner that will get the
dirt out of the finish, but you must realize that any cleaner that will
do that will also remove some of the top coat of the finish, whether
the top coat is shellac, lacquer, or varnish. You need a slow-acting
cleaner that you can control. Control includes being able to stop the
cleaning action instantly when you have decided that it has gone far
enough. This cleaner below meets all of these requirements.

Furniture Finish Cleaner

Mix together by volume:

- 3 parts—steam-distilled turpentine (not paint thinner or
  mineral spirits).

- 5 parts—anhydrous alcohol. That means alcohol without any
  water in it. Ordinary denatured alcohol will do if it has not been
  standing around open for a long period of time (alcohol absorbs
  water from the atmosphere).

- 1 part—ethyl acetate.

  Put up in several small sealed bottles.

  To use, set out two containers, one with some of the cleaner, the
other with turpentine. You will need wads of absorbent cotton. Be
sure you have good ventilation. Work small areas of the finish at a
time. Moisten a wad in the cleaner, rub the area you are cleaning with
a circular motion. Rub, don't scrub. Let the cleaner do the work. The
surface being cleaned should be horizontal. Watch the wad. What
you are doing is dissolving the finish by extremely thin layers and
picking up the dissolved finish with the wad. As one side gets dirty,
turn it over. As soon as the wood no longer looks dirty, or when it has
a slight yellow color or paint color (if you are cleaning a painted sur-

face), stop wiping. Take a clean wad dipped in straight turpentine and flood the surface you are working. This will stop the dissolving action of the cleaner almost instantly, leaving the rest of the the finish intact.

Cleaning a finish with this procedure will not be fast. This cleaner is primarily used for cleaning varnish from oil paintings, which should give you an idea of the slowness of the action—and the preciseness with which it can be stopped short.

Refinishers

These products claim to quickly restore the natural beauty of old wood furniture shellac, lacquer, and varnish finishes without stripping. The cautions and ingredient lists on the back of the can—*Danger, Poison, Extremely Flammable, Contains Methylene Chloride, Methyl (wood) Alcohol, Toluene*, etc.—make these refinishers close cousins chemically to paint and varnish removers. The main differences appear to be that they are liquids and slower acting.

Refinishers are applied with steel wool; you rub, then rinse with fresh refinisher until the top coat is liquified and removed. The one observable difference between refinishers and removers is that you can stop the action before the stain and the filler (if filler was used) are removed. Whether this activity should be classed as restoring the finish or almost removing the finish is a good question. The fact that the next step after "refinishing" is hand-rubbing a tung-oil varnish *into* the wood might give you a clue.

Reviving the Finish

Before you go any further, stop and reconsider whether you want to, or really have to remove the finish. Crazing, fine cracks, alligatoring, and white spots in clear finishes can all be repaired by a process called *amalgamating* (see Chapter 9).

Old paint finishes, especially those many-layered encrusted, cracking, and chipping jobs, leave little choice—they must come off. Minor or localized chipping in an otherwise sound paint finish that is going to be repainted can be repaired by patching the surface (see Chapter 9).

8-2 REMOVING FINISHES

There are many other ways you can get paint or other finishes from a wood surface—blowtorch, scraper, belt or disc sander—but dissolving the finish chemically is the only procedure to use on furniture. Chemical removers are the only way you can go about it without removing some of the wood with the finish. You simply can't sand, scrape, and scorch that carefully.

Packaged paint and varnish removers—the better ones anyway—will remove just about any finish. (See Fig. 8-3.) Actually, they don't remove anything—they soften the finish, and you do the removing. There are many formulations for paint and varnish removers on the market. The best kind are the semipaste varieties with methylene chloride as the principle working ingredient accompanied by various combinations of methanol (wood alcohol) and petroleum distillates. While nonflammable, the fumes are toxic, and the removers should be used with good ventilation. There is something else to consider: unlike fumes from lacquer, alcohol, and paint thinners that tend to rise into the air, methylene chloride fumes are heavier than air and can accumulate near the floor, particularly in basements, as do the fumes from carbon tetrachloride.

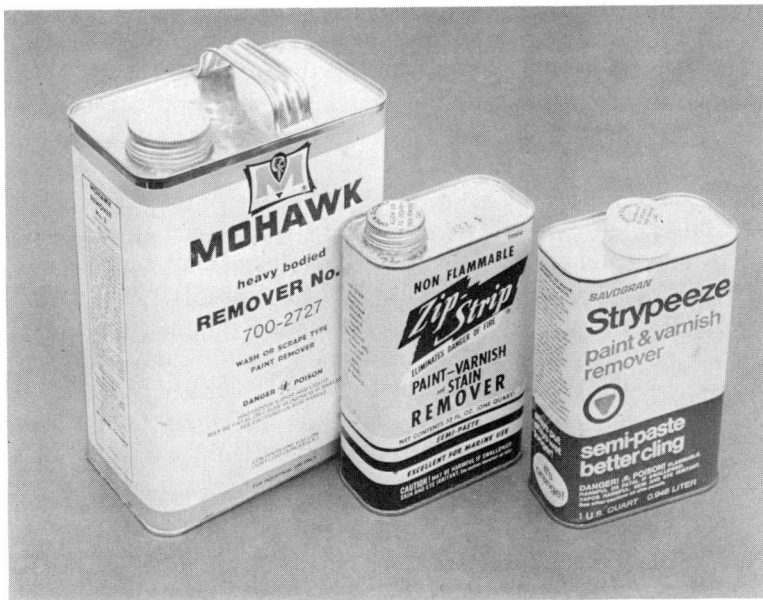

**FIGURE
8-3**

Paint and varnish removers: Methylene-chloride based industrial and consumer paste-type paint and varnish removers (all are about equal in effectiveness).

Lower priced removers are usually not only flammable, but contain wax (it won't be listed on the can) as a thickening agent instead of methyl cellulose. This wax leaves a residue on the surface which has to be cleaned off before you can start any refinishing. And the wax sometimes doesn't come off easily.

The purpose of the semipaste consistency is to help the remover lay on the work in a thick coat whether the surface is horizontal or vertical. It also slows down the evaporation of the solvents allowing them more time to get at the finish.

Polychrome Finishes

Many pieces of furniture were originally finished with decorative painting. This included Colonial and anything else earlier than Chippendale (his Chinese was in effect painted too), Adam, Hepplewhite, Sheraton, late American Federal, plus a lot of stencil work in all periods. Often this decoration was later painted over and painted again and again.

If you attack a paint finish with paint and varnish remover, you will go right through the first decorated finish often never knowing it was there. This is not to say you will do it with one application of the remover, but you will have no control and no way of stopping the action if you do by chance discover something interesting under all those coats of paint. The same goes for refinishers. You have little control with them either.

What to do? You can forget the above and remove the finish to bare wood anyway, because removing the top layers to expose the original finish is going to be tedious if you do it yourself, and prohibitively expensive to have it done professionally, if you can even find someone to do it. Unless the piece is very valuable, or you are a fanatic about those things, it might not be worth the effort.

But, before stripping anything, it is always a good idea to pick an obscure spot and sand a small area down to bare wood so that you can identify the layers of finish applied over the years. The black table in Figure 8–4 was painted many times. Working from last to first coat, black, dark green, applegreen, cream, and white paint was discovered. The crude bailing wire repair was made early on, way back when the white coat was applied. However, there was no hint of any polychrome decoration. (After stripping, evidence was found of an original cherry-colored transparent finish.) But you never know.

Procedure. If there is only one coat over the polychromed coat, use the furniture-finish cleaner, doing a small area at a time. It will be impossible to clear away the top coat without also removing some surface from the polychrome coat, but if you are careful you can keep it to an acceptable minimum.

For a heavy buildup of paint, carefully try lacquer thinner, acetone, or one of the prepared refinishers to get down into the last coat *over* the original coat. Then switch to the cleaner.

Stripping Procedure

Shake the semi-paste paint and varnish remover and pour some into an open container. Load your brush, and flow on a thick, uniform coat. Brush in one direction only. Do not brush out as you would paint. Let the remover work until a test scraping shows the old finish is ready for removal. Do not rush the job—let the remover do the work. Remove old finish with a paint scraper followed by 1 or 0 steel wool or heavy burlap. If there are several layers of old paint, you will probably have to repeat the process several times. Wear gloves. (See Fig. 8–4.) Scrape carefully, with the grain.

After all of the finish is removed, go over the entire surface with grade 00 steel wool and fresh remover. Allow the surface to dry thoroughly before applying a new finish. Some finishes can be removed with less effort. If by testing, you have found that the piece has a shellac finish, you can remove it with nothing more than a can of denatured alcohol and cloth, burlap, Scotchbrite pad, or steel wool. Do the work outdoors because you need a lot of ventilation.

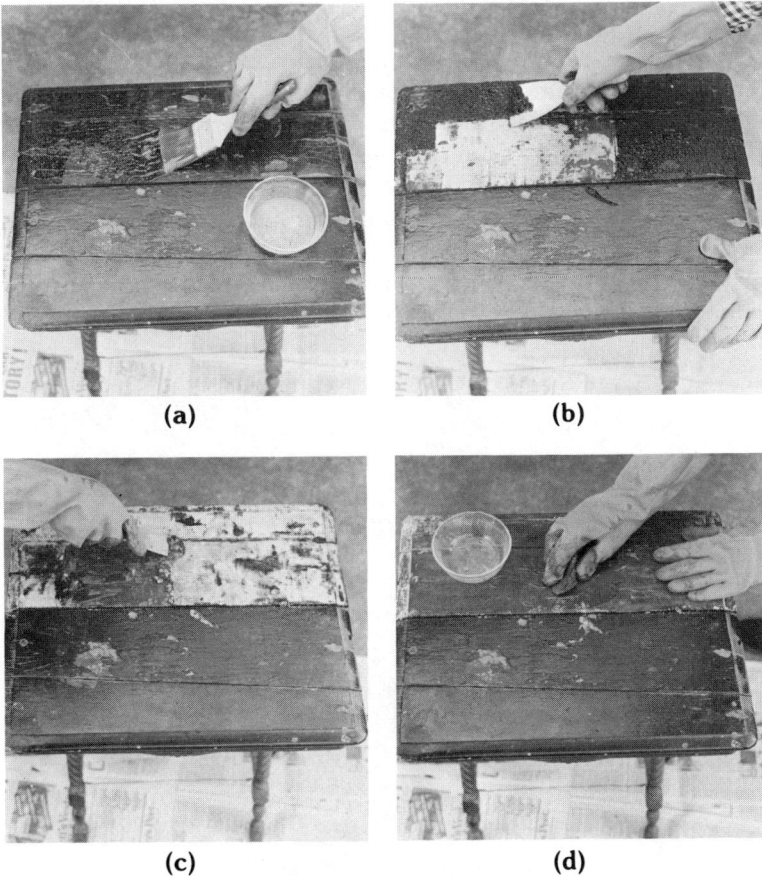

**FIGURE
8-4**

(a)

(b)

(c)

(d)

Using a paste-type paint and varnish remover: (a) Slop on a thick coat without a lot of brushing out. (b) Wait until remover has softened finish and then scrape it off. (c) The many coats of paint on this table required several applications. Black and green paint coats revealed cream and white coats. (d) Finally, clean up with remover and steel wool.

Scrub first with alcohol and steel wool or Scotchbrite to get most of the shellac off, then switch to burlap and soft cloth to finish up. (See Fig. 8-5.)

Lacquer thinner will soften lacquer so you can remove it, but the action is not as fast as alcohol on shellac. Used carefully, however, lacquer thinner can be used to clean up a lacquered finish. Small pieces are practical to strip with lacquer thinner; for large pieces use regular paint and varnish remover. Again, have adequate ventilation.

Strip Joints

Stripping furniture is a messy, time-consuming pastime that fortunately can be avoided. You can let someone else do it by taking the furniture to a professional stripping shop. Many methods are used commercially—all chemical—but most use the dip and strip method. Your piece of furniture is submerged in a vat of liquid remover, usually a mix containing methylene chloride. After soaking a few minutes, the piece is moved to an open-front area and whatever finish hasn't already fallen off is brushed and hosed off with more remover. The piece is then water rinsed and dried. Typical costs for chairs is $8, small tables $10.

Now, what should you worry about when taking a piece to a strip joint, and what should you expect? First, make all glue-joint repairs,

FIGURE 8-5

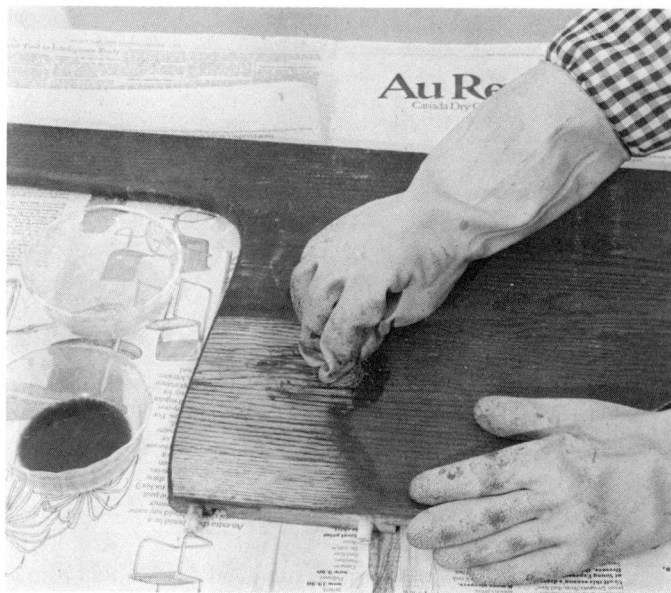

Stripping a shellac finish: The finish on 19th century furniture is shellac in many cases; it can be stripped easily with alcohol and grade #0 or #1 steel wool, followed by a cloth-and-alcohol cleanup.

and particularly veneer repairs beforehand. Also, remove all hardware. The furniture is in and out of the vat normally before any of the liquids have a chance to get at the glue, but if the liquids get under loose veneer or into a loose joint they aren't going to come pouring out that fast.

When you get the piece home you will still have some crevice and corner cleaning to do. This is where you use toothpicks, knife blades, sandpaper, and anything that will get at the paint, plus a little remover, to finish the job. This additional work is usually run into only with paint finishes; shellac, lacquer, and varnish finishes come off fast and clean in the vat. Usually you can wait while they do it.

Lye

No furniture refinishing book is complete without mentioning *lye*. Lye is a dangerous caustic alkali which will powder refractory (stubborn) paints that resist lesser paint and varnish removers. Fortunately, you will not encounter such paints very often, if ever.

You have to use lye with proper precautions. A prepared solution will burn holes in your cloth—and in you. Wear old clothes, apron, heavy rubber gloves and a full face shield. Work on a concrete floor. Lye is applied to the furniture surface with a cotton mop, and hosed off with lots of water after it eats through the finish. All this water is not exactly good for your furniture, especially anything veneered. You have to get *all* the lye off too. It burns most wood black, so you have to get it out of all crevices, cracks, and loose joints. Wherever the runoff lye and water mix goes, nothing grows. So don't work on your lawn.

If you find you have a finish you can't remove with a semipaste methylene chloride remover, don't go to all this hazardous trouble. Take the piece to a professional stripper and let him worry about it. The price is right.

Lye is not recommended as a paint and varnish remover for the home shop. I won't even tell you how to mix it.

8-3 SANDING

Furniture wood surfaces, whether stripped old wood or newly repaired wood, have to be smooth before you apply any new finish. (Sanding with abrasive paper is the usual, but not the only method of smoothing the wood. Steel wool and hand scrapers can also be used to advantage.)

In new wood, tool marks, cross-grain sanding scratches, surface glue deposits, and standing wood fibers must all be sanded out so as not to be a cause of uneven staining or a muddy appearance in a finish that is supposed to be transparent. Good sanding takes time. If it is not done right, you can waste long hours staining, filling, hand rubbing and top coating. When you look at the finished result, you may decide that you have to clean it all off and start over with sanding again.

Successful furniture sanding comes down to using the correct abrasive for each sanding step and using power and hand sanders to get the finish you want with the least expenditure of effort and time.

Coated abrasives (sandpaper) are made up in sheets, belts, discs, and sleeves. All have a working surface made up of sharp cutting particles bonded to a backing of paper or cloth. These particles are graded by size (grit number). The higher the number, the finer the abrasive, and the smoother the surface that they can produce. Several abrasives are available for woodworking.

Flint, which is natural white quartz, is the least durable. It is not intended for machine sanding and is never used wet. Flint is cheap and sold in most hardware stores. It is grayish white in color. Don't buy it. It wears out too fast to be useful except possibly when sanding off paint by hand, where it would clog faster than wear.

Garnet is next up on the hardness scale. It is a natural reddish brown–colored mineral that makes a good abrasive for hand and machine wood sanding. Garnet cabinet paper has a heavy paper backing, garnet finishing paper, a light paper backing which will not crack when folded. Both are used with pad sanders and for hand sanding. Use dry only.

Aluminum oxide is harder than garnet. This artificially produced abrasive is the best all-around choice for furniture work. It can be used on softwood and hardwood, particleboard, and hardboard, plastics (except fiberglass-reinforced), and most metals. Aluminum oxide paper is made closed-coat and open-coat. In closed-coat paper, the abrasive grains completely cover the surface. In open-coat, they cover only 50 to 70 percent of the surface. Open-coat papers clog less than closed-coat and are especially useful when sanding softwoods. Use dry only.

Silicon carbide is a very hard artificial abrasive, grayish black in color. Finer grades of this paper are used in furniture work primarily for sanding between coats and rubbing down the final top coat. The paper backing is waterproof, and the abrasive is normally used wet with either water or oil. It is also used for sanding hard materials.

Sanding, as mentioned, involves several steps, each requiring the correct grade of abrasive paper, sanding tool, and technique.

Rough sanding is aggressive stock removal without concern for the smoothness of the surface left. Primary concern is for fast cutting.

Semifinish sanding is the operation in which all tool marks from previous operations are removed, bringing the stock to dimension, or as close to dimension as you dare. It usually takes several steps with progressively finer abrasive paper. Depending on the tools used, semifinish sanding may or may not leave tool marks of its own.

Finish sanding removes all of the scratches left from the final semifinish sanding step, and smooths the surface for applying the finish.

Rubdown sanding is done between coats of the finishing schedule to smooth the coating, remove dust particles, or if required, to roughen the coating slightly to provide a tooth for the next coat.

Sanding is not recommended as a general method of removing finish from furniture, except for getting it out of crevices, for example. Table 8–1 lists the type of abrasive paper, grit, and power sanding tool that should be used for each of the sanding steps.

Sanding Techniques

● Always begin sanding with the finest grit you think practical. You want a balance between fast cutting and smallest residual scratches left to be removed by the next sanding step.

● Don't try to make it from rough sanding to finish sanding in one big step. You will spend too much time and sandpaper getting out the scratches left by the coarse sanding. Or, you will sand "thoroughly" thinking you have removed the scratches and discover they are still there after you have the stain on. Go from 60 to 80 to 120 to 180, etc.; not directly from 60 to 180.

● If you are going to apply stain, sand all surfaces of a piece equally so all parts will take the stain evenly.

● Use a five-power magnifying glass and an oblique light from a bare bulb to inspect for scratches before staining. It is the only way you will find them.

Steel Wool

Steel wool is shaved steel, matted and rolled up in pads. The shreds have a rectangular cross section rather than circular, like wire. This gives them four cutting edges per strand. Steel wool is sold in sleeves of 16 pads of one grade, and in assortments. Don't waste money buying assortments. Steel wool is made in seven grades—3, 2, 1, 0, 00, 000, and 0000. Steel wool can be used wet or dry.

Use grades 1 and 0 for stripping with paint and varnish remover, alcohol, or lacquer thinner. Use grade 00 for final cleanup with fresh remover. Use grades 000 and 0000 for rubbing down between finish coats and before waxing.

On the American market, there is no *good* quality grade of steel wool. Steel wool is steel wool. There are minor differences in the exact thickness of wire in grade 0000 between manufacturers, but the difference is academic. All grade 0000 wire is finer than human hair anyway. The rest of the grades are essentially identical.

Using steel wool in finishing wood furniture has problems. The

TABLE 8-1

Abrasive Applications

	Hand Sanding	Pad Sander	Portable Belt Sander	Stationary Belt and Disc Sander
Rough sanding				
Softwood	Use Stanley Surforms, or rasp	NR	50–80	60–80
Hardwood		NR	36–60	60–80
Semifinish sanding				
Softwood	Use Diston Abrader or file	50–100	100–120	100–120
Hardwood		50–80	80–120	100–220
Finish sanding				
Softwood	120–220	120–180	NR	180 +
Hardwood	120–220	100–220	NR	150–220
Between coat sanding				
All finishes	220	220	NR	NR

NR: Not recommended.

finer grades of steel wool disintegrate into minute particles which not only get into the air (don't work with fine steel wool outdoors in the wind), but also get into the pores of wood and can be difficult to get out. If not cleaned out completely they can oxidize and cause black spots in the wood. Being sure you have left no residue of steel wool particles on the wood surface is a particular problem when using a refinisher, as the original finish is not completely stripped.

Hand Scrapers

Hand Scrapers are very useful in furniture repair and finishing (see Fig. 8-6). Once you get the hang of how to sharpen them and use them, you will wonder how you ever got along without one.

A single scraper can be used for both rough and finish work. It can scrape surface glue, rub down flat surfaces between coats without leaving metal particles imbedded in the finish, and does an excellent job shaving off varnish and lacquer sags.

After you have semifinish sanded an edge true, use a scraper instead of a pad sander to remove sanding marks. Do all but the last bit of smoothing. Unlike a pad sander, a scraper will not round over a square edge. Used after semifinish sanding, a hand scraper can cut surface preparation time in half.

The working edge of a hand scraper is a burr as shown in Figure 8-7, running the length of each working edge. A scraper as you buy it

FIGURE
8-6

In many furniture finishing operations scraping produces better results than sanding. Shown are three scrapers and a burnisher used to form the scraper working edge.

FIGURE
8-7

(a)   (b)

(c)   (d)

Sharpening a hand scraper: (a) File the edge flat and square. (b) Stone the edge to remove all file marks. (c) Burr the edge with a burnishing tool. (d) This is the appearance of the working edge.

will not be ready to use. To sharpen a scraper you first file the edge square, then stone and hone it smooth. The next step is to put the burr on the edge. This is done with a burnisher, or any smooth piece of steel harder than the scraper itself, such as a flat chisel blade. Lay the scraper on the bench with the edge to be burred over the edge. Hold the burnisher at an 85° angle with the edge and stroke it. Not too much—you don't want a big burr. If you can feel it with your finger, it is enough.

A scraper is held at an angle of 70° to the wood. Bow it slightly and either pull it towards you or push it away, whichever you prefer. The scraper, of course, is tilted in the direction of travel. A sharp scraper will produce tiny shavings. A dull one, sawdust. Dull or sharp, a hand scraper will smooth wood. (See Fig. 8-8.)

**FIGURE
8-8**

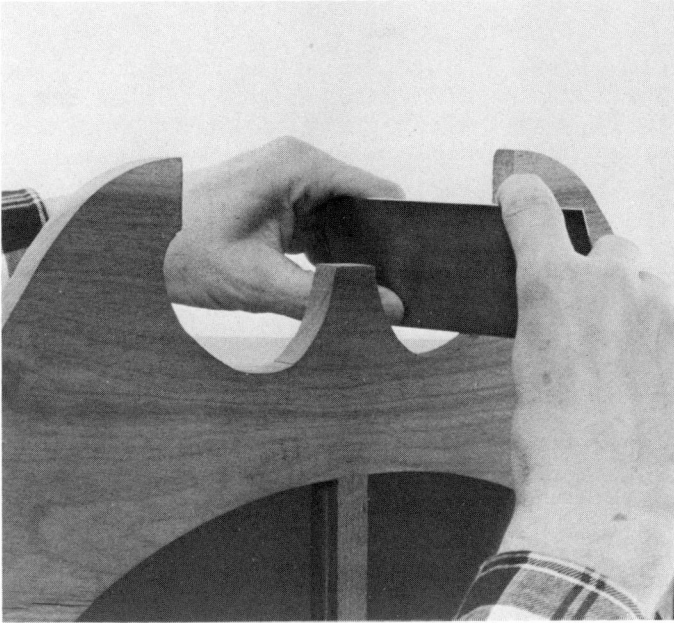

Using a hand scraper.

When a scraper becomes dull, you can burnish off the burr and reburr several times before you have to rework the blade by filing, stoning, and honing again.

8-4 BLEACHING

Staining adds color to wood. Bleaching lightens wood by removing color. It does not change the color of the wood.

Why bleach? If you want to finish wood a color lighter or different from the natural color of the wood, you must first tone down or remove the natural color. The wood may contain off-color areas or mineral streaks; these can be lightened by locally applied bleach. When woods of more than one species are used in a piece of furniture, the darker ones can be bleached to match the rest. Bleaching can also be used to take any remaining stain color from stripped pieces. Before bleaching, it is important to first remove all stripper residues, particularly wax. Use silicone wash or lacquer solvent.

Three bleaches have been commonly used on wood: household bleach (Clorox, for example) which is an approximately 5 percent solution of sodium hypochlorite, oxalic acid, and prepared two-solution bleaches. Household bleaches do the least bleaching, the prepared bleaches the most. Regardless of the bleach you select to use, test it first on a part of the furniture that won't show. It is not enough to test it on a scrap of wood of the same species from your stock.

171

FIGURE
8-9

Bleaches. Results can vary from wood to wood. All bleaches do not work alike.

Results obtained in bleaching wood can be unpredictable. (See Fig. 8–10.)

● *Household Bleach.* These bleaches are best for spot removing. Use the others for large areas. Apply the bleach full strength to the wood. If doing spot work, use an eyedropper. After 15 minutes, wash the area with water. After the area has dried, inspect. If the wood is still too dark, repeat. When you get the right color, wash the whole surface and let it dry.

● *Oxalic Acid.* Oxalic acid is intermediate in bleaching power, used to be cheap, and has the additional advantage of not smelling like a household bleach. It is also becoming hard to find in paint and hardware stores. One company that formerly packaged oxalic acid for retail sale now has a product they call "Substitute for Pure Oxalic Acid," which they decline to identify. Oxalic acid is packaged in one-pound boxes of powdery crystals. You can sometimes buy it in drugstores in the same form.

To use oxalic acid, prepare a saturated solution in a glass container. Fill the container with boiling water, then add oxalic acid crystals at the rate of four ounces to the quart. When dissolved it is ready to use. Excess crystals will come out of solution as the water cools.

Use oxalic acid bleach hot. Apply it to the wood surface with a brush or to a spot with an eyedropper. Spot work is chancy, but try. If you fail you can always do the whole surface. After 10 minutes, wipe the surface with a damp cloth. Repeat if bleaching is insufficient. When you get the bleaching you want, wash off the surface with a mixture of one part household ammonia and ten parts water to stop further action and neutralize the bleach. Then wash with water and

	No Stain	Alcohol Stain	Oil Pigment Stain
No Bleach			
Clorox Bleach			
Oxalic Acid (Substitute) Bleach			
Industrial Two-solution Bleach			

FIGURE
8-10

Results of a bleach test.

let dry. Some prefer to neutralize with full strength white vinegar instead of the ammonia-water mix.

You can store made-up oxalic acid bleach in a glass jar. Replace evaporated water with hot water when the bleach is needed again.

Prepared Two-Solution. There are several two-solution bleaches on the market. All have two things in common: They are powerful bleaches and they are dangerous to use and handle. Wear heavy rubber gloves, protective clothing and a full face shield when using. The exact procedures for using the bleaches differ somewhat. The following steps for using one product are typical.

Set up three wide-mouth glass containers for working quantities of solutions A and B and the neutralizer. Mark the jars.

Surfaces to be bleached must be absolutely dry, free from dirt, and free of all glue deposits. Apply all solutions in the direction of the grain to prevent spotty bleaching. Apply the solutions evenly; do not saturate or flood the surface.

173

Apply solution A to the wood with a brush or rag. The brush should have tampico or synthetic bristles or be expendable. Wait five minutes, then apply solution B. If you use the same brush for both bleaches rinse it thoroughly between bleaches. This is not stuff to be played with carelessly. Let the work stand four hours or overnight, then wash off with neutralizer. Bleaching will be speeded by exposing the wood to sunlight, but forced drying reduces bleaching action. Repeat the procedure for lighter bleaching if required. Apply neutralizer if you get either bleach on your skin, then flush thoroughly with running water.

Unused materials must not be returned to their original containers. Don't mix the solutions together. The solutions must not come in contact with metal of any kind. Discard wiping pads and newspapers, etc., when finished.

8-5 DISTRESSING

Distressing is a finishing technique used to make a piece of new furniture look used, or to put it more truthfully, to make something new look very old. The operation is a major step in the production of fake antiques and a normal step in the manufacture of new French and Italian Provincial furniture. Some of the tools used in distressing are shown in Figure 8–11.

Minor Distressing

Small, randomly scattered scratches, nicks, gouges and dents applied to the surface with chains, hammer, screwdriver, stones, or an awl and

FIGURE 8-11

Distressing tools.

174

treated with paint speckling make the surface and finish look used. Nothing is done that could come under the heading of fakery. This distressing is done after staining and sealing, and before filling. If the wood is not to be filled, then it should be glazed after distressing (there's no sense doing all that work and then not being able to see the depredations). (See also the discussion of glazing in Chapter 10.)

Major Distressing or Out-and-Out Fakery

How to make instant antiques. Essentially, you beat the piece up, then restore it to whatever extent required. Round off edges, tops of rungs, bottoms of legs, and so forth. But think before you file—Could wear ever occur there? Rumble edges with a tire chain, preferably rusty. Bash the piece with a clump of grass with moist dirt attached. Stand back and throw one rock at the piece. Repair the break in a primitive way.

Make worm holes. They gather in groups. Worm holes go in 1/8" or less, turn parallel to surface. Use 1/16" or 3/32" round bur in a hand grinder.

9 Spot Surface Repairs and Spot Refinishing

Holes, chips, gouges, scratches, cracks, loose veneer, discoloration, marks, stains, and finish deterioration can be repaired in a variety of ways. The value of the furniture is most often the determining factor in the choice of repair method. Another factor is the availability of the tools and materials needed for the repair procedure.

Even with identical defects, repairs are made differently in unfinished, partially finished, and completely finished surfaces, and repairs can also be different for different top coats. Some of the repair techniques used on wood can also be used on laminated plastic table and counter tops and on moulded polyurethane carving, trim, and doorfronts.

Most of these repair methods require some skill to do well. This skill can best be obtained from practice on scrap before you attempt a real repair.

Table 9–1 provides a quick cross-reference of surface defects and recommended repair methods.

9-1 BURNING-IN

Indentations, chips, and holes in transparent-finished furniture surfaces can be repaired several ways. The most satisfactory and professional way to do it is by the burn-in method. In this procedure, the defect is filled with material melted from the end of a burn-in stick

TABLE 9-1

Spot Repair and Refinishing

Defect	Clear Film Top Coat	Penetrating Top Coat	Opaque Top Coat	Unfinished Wood
Surface scratch	Fill with liquid scratch filler, putty stick, or wax stick	Steel wool area, refinish with penetrating finish	Touch up with acrylic paint	Sand out
Deep scratch	Stain bare wood, fill with liquid filler, pad if required	Stain bare wood, fill with liquid filler, spot refinish	Fill with composition wood filler, sand, paint	Fill if to have opaque finish, sand out for clear finish
Dent	Burn-in	Burn-in	Fill with composition wood filler, paint	Steam or hot water to raise wood, or fill
Gouge, chip, or hole in solid wood	1. Burn-in 2. If deep, fill or plug to below surface, then burn-in	1. Burn-in 2. If deep, fill or plug to below surface, then burn-in	Fill with composition wood filler, paint	Plug with wood, or burn-in if to have clear finish, fill with composition wood filler if to have opaque finish
Chipped or missing veneer	1. Patch 2. Burn-in	1. Patch 2. Burn-in	Not applicable	Patch
Loose veneer	Reglue	Reglue	Not applicable	Reglue
Blistered veneer	Slit, reglue	Slit, reglue	Not applicable	Slit, reglue
Worn off finish; edges, etc.	Pad on blending stain, apply padding lacquer	Pad on blending stain, spot finish with penetrating finish	Touch up paint	Not applicable
White rings, cracks, and alligatoring	Amalgamator, padding lacquer	Steel wool, spot refinish	Not applicable	Not applicable
Discolored finish	Pad on blending stain, apply padding lacquer	Pad on blending stain, refinish	Clean	Not applicable

composed of shellac, resin, and lead-free pigment. The technique is very much like applying melted sealing wax.

The sticks are made in many colors—one manufacturer carries 143 shades—and you can get the exact shade needed for a repair. Sticks are made in opaque and translucent colors. Opaque sticks are used to refill defects where the finish is removed exposing bare wood. Translucent sticks are used for shallow repairs where only the top coat is damaged and the color of the finish does not have to be restored.

It is not necessary to stock all shades that are made. Colors can be matched by buildup of several layers of different opaque and translucent colors. A defect extending down to bare wood can also be stained before you start filling the cavity.

Basic Burning-In

Tools and materials required are shown in Figure 9–1.

- *Burn-In Knife.* The best knife is a flexible steel spatula.

- *Alcohol Lamp.* The lamp is used to heat the spatula. You cannot use a candle or kerosene lamp because both smoke and the soot will discolor the filling material.

- *Burn-in Sticks.* Set of 12 sticks.

- *Abrasive Paper.* 280-grit garnet paper and 400A wet or dry paper.

- *Rubbing Block.* For flat surface work, a block of wood with rounded edges and a flat face, surfaced with felt is required. This is used with the abrasive paper. The block should be no bigger than 2″ by 4″, smaller for small defects.

Procedure. Clean foreign matter from the defect. If the defect goes to bare wood, apply a stain with a small brush or Q-tip. (See Fig. 9–2.) The color should be close to the finish color. You can also color exposed unstained wood with an opaque stick.

Select a translucent stick that matches the finish color. If none of your sticks exactly match the color, pick a somewhat lighter colored stick. You can always darken the repair slightly with blending stain.

Heat the spatula in the flame; then out of the flame, melt a little of the stick with the tip of the blade. Pass the blade through the flame again, then pack the material into the defect. Be careful not to get the material so hot that it bubbles and runs. It should be just tacky for filling the hole. Reheat the blade and work the filler in the hole to make good contact with the wood surface for complete filling and good adhesion. Add material until the hole is slightly overfilled. Use the hot blade to feather the edge and be sure there are no bubbles. Be careful that the blade is not too hot during this step as you can damage the surrounding finish.

FIGURE
9-1

Tools and materials for burning-in (basic kit).

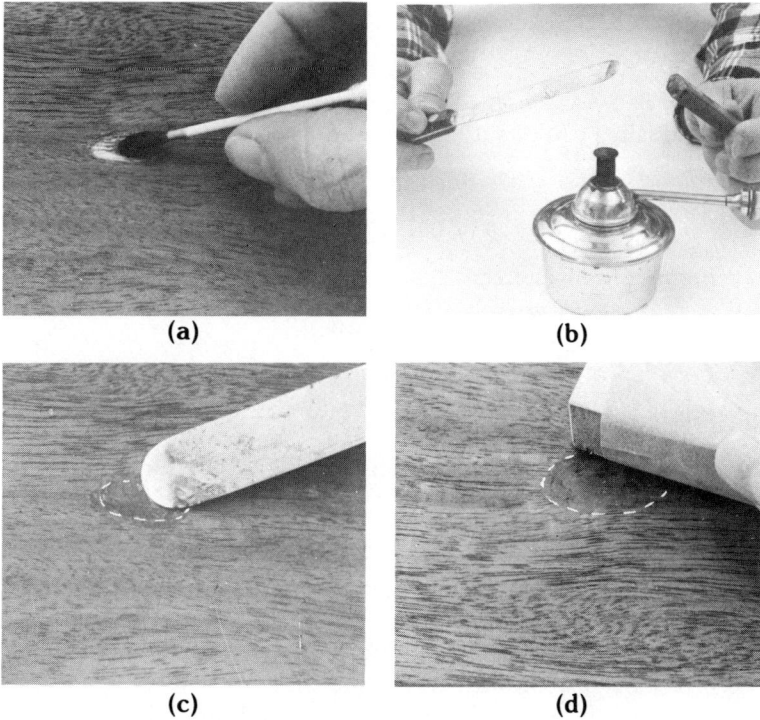

FIGURE
9-2

(a)   (b)

(c)   (d)

Burn-in procedure: (a) Stain the exposed wood approximately the same finish color. (b) Select matching or slightly lighter burn-in stick. Melt a little of the stick with the tip of the blade. (c) Pack the material into the defect. (d) Sand the repair (first with 280 grit garnet paper, then 400A wet or dry paper) wet. When sanded smooth, pad a finish over the repair.

The material in the hole will be very brittle. Any attempts to save smoothing time by scraping with a chisel or knife blade will produce more chipping than progress. Some initial scraping can be done successfully with a curved hand scraper and very light passes, however.

Next, sand the repair smooth and flush with the surrounding surface. Fingertip sanding is difficult because it is hard to prevent waves. Use the block, first with dry 280-grit garnet paper, then finish with the 400A paper wet. Use water only if you know the finish is varnish or lacquer. Use oil if the finish is shellac, or if you don't know what the finish is.

The final step is to pad a finish over the repair. (See "Padding Lacquer" on the following page.)

Professional Burning-In

Tools and materials required are shown in Figure 9–3.

- *Electric Burn-In Knife.* An electric knife permits more accurate temperature control. When repairing plastic furniture, the heat level must be reduced. Use any solid-state voltage control having characteristics similar to the Dremel model 219.

- *Burn-In Sticks.* No-lift Sticks (made by Mohawk) are available individually or in sets of 12, 44, and 88.

- *Abrasive Paper.* 280-grit garnet paper and 400A wet or dry paper.

- *Steel Wool.* Grade 0 or 00.

- *Brasiv.* Dissolves excess filler.

- *Felt Block.* Use for applying Brasiv.

- *Cork Block.* Use for sanding repair.

- *Rubbing Oil.* Use for sanding repair.

- *Burn-In Balm.* Protects the finish on the surface surrounding the repair.

Procedure. Clean foreign matter from the defect. If the defect goes to bare wood, apply a stain with a small brush or Q-tip. The color should be close to the finish color. You can also cover the exposed unstained wood with an opaque stick.

Select a translucent stick that matches the finish color. If none of your sticks exactly match the color, pick a stick slightly lighter. You can always make the repair a little darker with blending stain. If there is prominent grain marking, match the background color.

Melt a little of the stick with the leading edge of the knife blade. (See Fig. 9–4.) Place the tip in the defect and allow the filling material to flow from the blade into the hole. Repeat these steps until the hole is slightly overfilled. Wipe the blade clean with steel wool or a cloth. Always keep the blade clean.

Now, with your finger, apply Burn-in Balm to the wood surface around the area of the repair. The balm will protect the furniture surface from the knife in the next steps.

Hold the knife in one hand and a clean wiping cloth in the other. Apply the blade to the repair with a circular motion until the patching material softens. Be careful not to let the blade touch the surrounding surface. Without waiting, pull the blade across the burn-in repair scraping off excess material. After each stroke, quickly wipe the knife clean, and repeat careful scraping until the repair is almost flush with the surface. Never let the blade stop on the surface or you will damage it and have additional repair work on your hands. Keep it moving.

Now apply Brasiv to the felt pad and remove most of the remaining burn-in material by rubbing. Then wet sand using the cork block, 400A wet or dry paper and Brasiv as a lubricant.

If an exact color match has not been obtained, the next step is to apply blending stain to the patch (see later discussion of spot coloring).

9-2 PADDING LACQUER

Padding lacquer is the modern-day French polish. The finish is applied by padding—rubbing—and must not be confused with wipe-on finishes. While a wipe-on finish is laid on with a wet cloth and then

FIGURE
9-3

Professional burn-in tools and materials.

181

wiped to remove the excess, a padded finish is applied a very little at a time with a lot of padding required to apply what is really a very thin film to the surface.

FIGURE
9-4

(a)

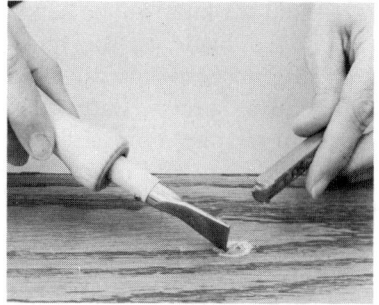

(b)

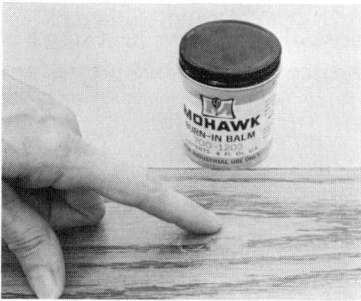

(c)

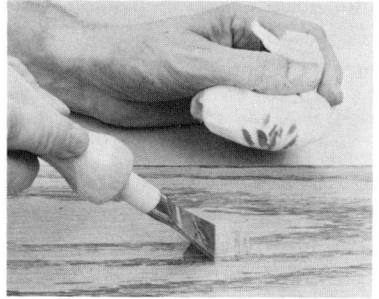

(d)

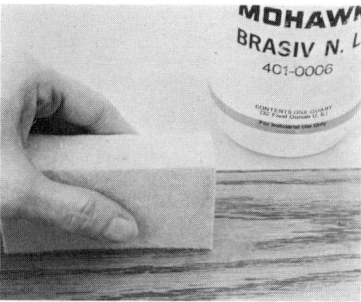

(e)

(f)

Professional burn-in procedure: Clean and repair, stain exposed wood. (a) Select a matching or slightly lighter stick. Melt a little of the stick with the knife blade. (b) Place the tip of the blade in the defect and allow the material to flow into the hole. (c) Apply burn-in balm around the repair. (d) Scrape the repair with a blade to remove most of excess material. (e) Apply Brasiv to felt pad and remove almost all of the remaining material. (f) Wet sand with 400A paper and a cork block.

The finish can be used several ways:

- As complete one-step procedure on bare wood finish—a favorite finish on turnings.

- As film top coat over stain, filler, glaze, and so forth.

- As refinishing film over a varnish, lacquer, or shellac top coat.

- As spot or area touch-up finish.

- As overall, area, or spot color changing finish when used with blending stains.

To make a padding pad, you will need a 12″ square of lint-free cloth (do not use cheesecloth), white absorbent cotton (the first-aid kind, not the upholstery stuffing variety), and a piece of string. (See Fig. 9-5.) Fold the cloth to a 6″ square and place a ball of cotton on the center. Bring the edges of the cloth over the cotton to form a ball and tie tightly with the string.

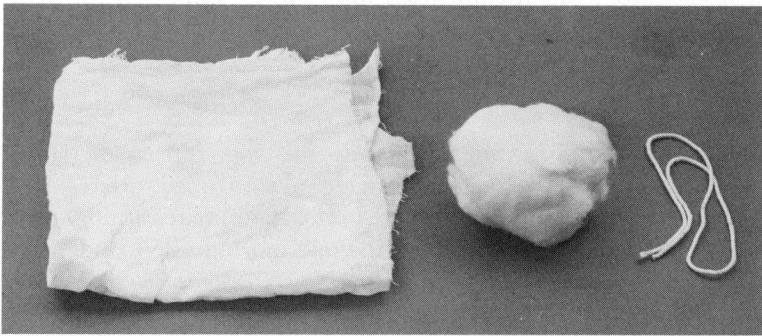

FIGURE 9-5

(a)

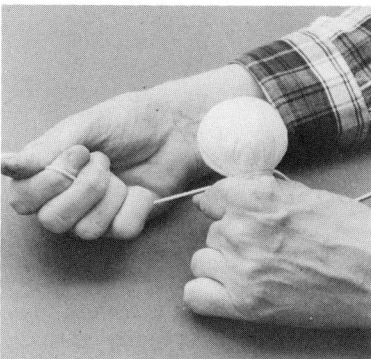

(b)

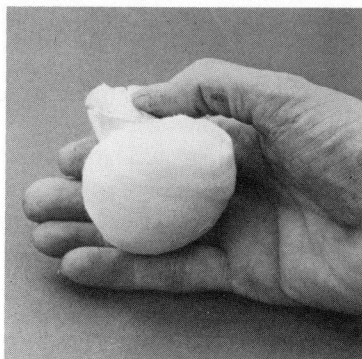

(c)

Making a padding pad: (a) Materials include lint-free cloth, surgical cotton, and string. (b) Make a ball of cotton, pack it inside cloth, tie tightly with string. (c) pad is ready for use

Padding a Top Coat: A Complete One-Step Finish

The surface to be finished must be smooth and clean. All repairs must be made beforehand. Padding lacquer used by itself has zero ability to hide defects. If the old finish is varnish or lacquer, wipe with a cloth damp with alcohol.

Load about 1/4 oz. of padding lacquer into the pad. (See Fig. 9–6.) Disperse the padding lacquer through the pad by tapping the pad on a clean sheet of white paper. This will prevent a wet spot. You want the pad just damp, never wet.

Now apply the finish with a quick circular motion. Never, repeat, never, start the pad on the surface or lift it off the surface. Always slide onto the surface from beyond an edge and finish by sliding off the edge. Otherwise your pad will leave a sitzmark. Continue until you have a thin coat on the entire surface. After 24 hours repeat, until you have about 4 coats on. Now switch to applying the finish with the grain to eliminate swirl marks, but be careful to slide on and off edges. Continue the process. The actual number of coats will depend on the condition of the surface or finish you are restoring. Waxing is optional.

Padding Turnings

To French polish a turning, do it with the work still on the lathe. Make up a pad of a size that can get at all of the turned surfaces. Run the lathe at a speed slightly slower than the appropriate turning speed and apply padding lacquer. Keep the pad moving side to side. The polish will go on fast and you will have to recharge the pad often. A fair amount of pad pressure can be applied. Finally, buff with a clean soft cloth.

Refinishing with Padding Lacquer

This is done with straight-line padding only. The job can usually be completed in one session.

Note: Repairs to Danish oil and other penetrating finishes should not be made with padding lacquer. Rub the area with grade 000 steel wool and apply oil finish following the directions on the can.

Spot Coloring

Patched and burn-in repaired defects, and other discolored surfaces can be matched to the surrounding wood with a combination of blending stain and padding lacquer, without harming the surrounding finish.

First select the blending stain that matches your finish. If none of your stains provide an exact match, select the two or three colors that

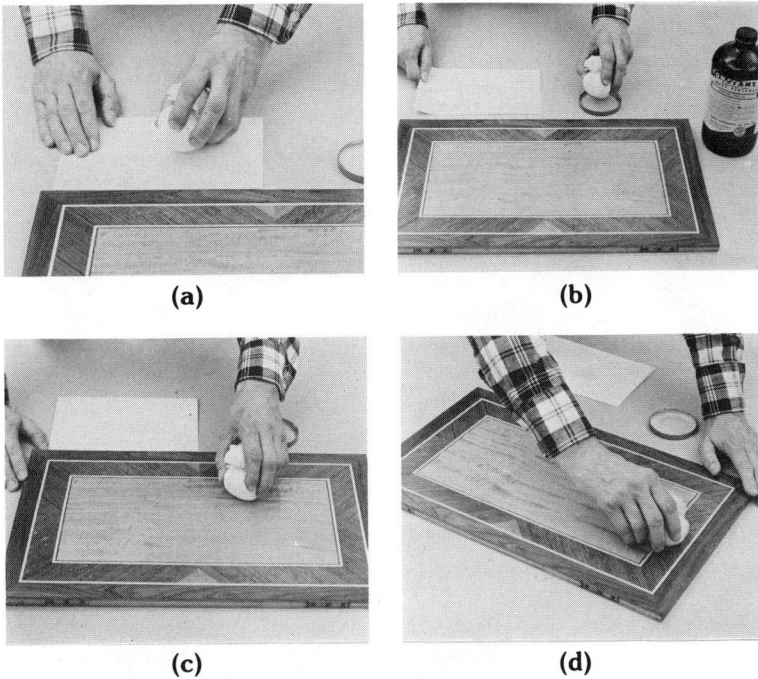

FIGURE 9-6

Padding a finish: (a) Load pad. (b) Disperse the padding lacquer in pad by tapping on clean white paper. (c) Apply padding lacquer with circular motion until a thin coat is built up. Repeat four times, allowing each coat to dry for 24 hours. (d) Now apply the finish with the grain, using long sweeping strokes to eliminate swirl marks.

come closest. Shake a small quantity of each onto a piece of white paper.

Clean the surface and apply padding lacquer to a padding pad, then pick up a bit of blending stain on your index fingertip. Pad the repaired spot lightly several times, then immediately apply stain by rubbing lightly with the grain. Then continue padding the area. If more color is needed, repeat the procedure. If the color is not right repeat with a color selected to bring the color closer when applied over the first color. You should be able to get an exact match by careful blending. If you miss the color completely, clean off the area with padding lacquer solvent and start over.

Edges

Touching up the edges of tables and parts of chairs where the finish has worn off exposing bare wood is more involved. The procedure is shown in Figure 9–7.

185

FIGURE
9-7

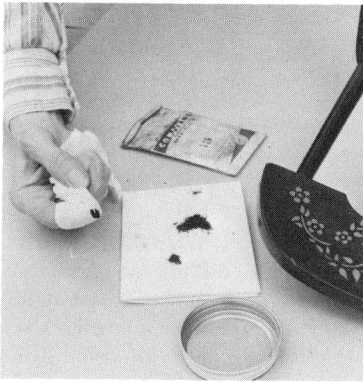 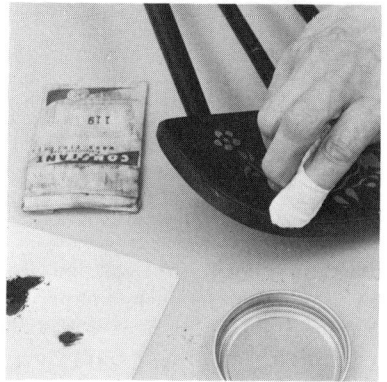

(c)   (d)

Spot coloring an edge: (a) Edge is shown with worn finish. (b) Clean
edge with padding lacquer solvent, then steel wool to provide a tooth for
the finish. (c) Take up some blending stain, dip in padding lacquer in lid,
and tap off excess. (d) Apply to edge. Repeat until a solid color is built
up.

Procedure. Clean area to be refinished with the solvent to
remove dirt, wax, and any traces of silicone polish. Lightly rub the unfinished area with the steel wool to put a tooth on the surface. Put a
few drops of padding liquid on a jar lid and, beside the drops, a bit of
blending stain.

To color an edge, fold the cloth twice. Hold it tight over a finger,
then dip lightly in padding liquid and work the cloth a bit to
distribute the liquid evenly. The cloth should be only damp, not wet.
Now rub a bit of blending stain on the cloth and apply to the edge
with light strokes back and forth until the color is built up. This
method also works well on carvings.

Graining

A neat repair burned-in the furniture surface of exactly the right color still can stand out because the repair has no grain. The same is true for compound-filled patches. You can apply grain by brush or pencil.

Brush Method.

- *Blending Stains.* Select a color to match the wood grain lines.

- *Graining Liquid.* This is similar to padding liquid, except that it is formulated to dry slower, leaving you some time to load your brush and apply it.

- *Artist Brushes.* Use pointed, No. 1, No. 0, or smaller.

- *Steel Wool.* Use grade 0000.

Put a few drops of the graining liquid (or padding liquid) on a jar lid or some other nonporous surface. Mix in some blending stain of the grain color, then with the brush, draw in the grain, connecting the lines on either side of the repair. Keep the strokes light and the lines indistinct, copying the wood grain as best you can.

When dry, buff lightly with the steel wool. This is to avoid a high spot. Apply a padding finish to the repair area.

Pencil Method.
The procedure is shown in Figure 9–8. Graining pencils are sold individually, or in sets of 12 assorted colors. The range of assorted colors is black, brown, dark fruitwood, maple, burnt umber, raw umber, and walnut. There is some duplication in the standard set.

Sharpen the right colored pencil and draw the grain on the surface. Afterwards, apply padding finish.

Brush and pencil graining of course can be combined in a repair to get the right grain reconstruction. Brush first, then buff before using the pencil.

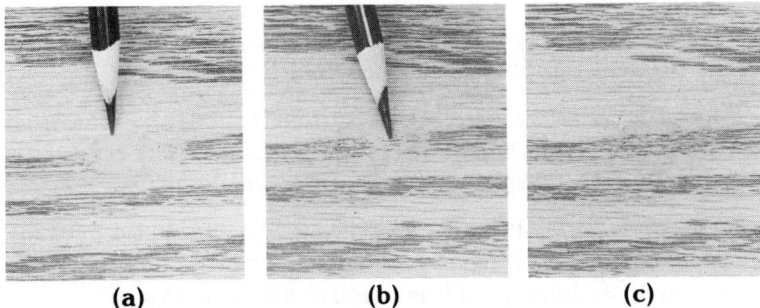

FIGURE 9-8

(a)　　　(b)　　　(c)

Pencil graining: Adding grain to the burn-in repair shown in Fig. 9-4.

Patching

Holes, chips, gouges, dents, and cracks both large and small in unfinished wood are repaired by patching. Some of the many available patching materials are shown in Figure 9–9. For most repairs, puttylike materials are used, even when the wood is to be stained and given a clear finish. The exceptions would be repairs in conspicuously grained veneer or large repairs that can be more easily handled with a wood plug. These patching materials should not be used to repair finished surfaces (except painted) because of the damage that can be caused to the surrounding finish by the solvents.

Do not expect any of these materials to take stain the same as the surrounding wood except by oddest chance. They don't, and it is a waste of time trying to find a patching material that will. Coloring the repair to match the wood later in the finish cycle is no problem. Some patching compounds are put up in colors; but even these require matching with blending stain.

The following patching materials work well:

1. *Elmer's® Professional Carpenter's Wood Filler.* This patching material is nonflammable, latex-based, odorless, and water-resistant. It can be nailed, screwed, or drilled. It can be painted, shellacked, varnished, and French polished, but not lacquered. The material dries very fast and very hard; small repairs can be sanded in 15 minutes. Scrape or shave off as much excess as possible before you sand. Sand intermittently with a machine sander to avoid heating and softening. When hand sanding use a sanding block, otherwise surrounding softer wood will be sanded away faster than the harder patch.

2. *Duratite® Wood Dough, Miracle Wood®* . Both are similar. Both have a slightly granular texture. Use for large repairs (over 1/8″ wide or deep). They are extremely flammable. They can be purchased in natural (light tan) and wood colors, but don't expect exact matches. Fill deep holes in thin layers. Wait until layer is dry before packing in next layer. Dries medium hard. Scrape or shave excess before sanding. Can be nailed, screwed, drilled. Can be painted, varnished, shellacked, and lacquered.

3. *Duratite Surfacing Putty.* This patching material has properties similar to Wood Dough, except that it has a buttery consistency and is used for cracks and other defects smaller than 1/8″.

4. *Spackling Paste.* Prepared spackling paste is a useful patching material for preparing pine or other softwoods that are to be painted. Its principal advantages are low cost, easy application and rapid sanding.

**FIGURE
9-9**

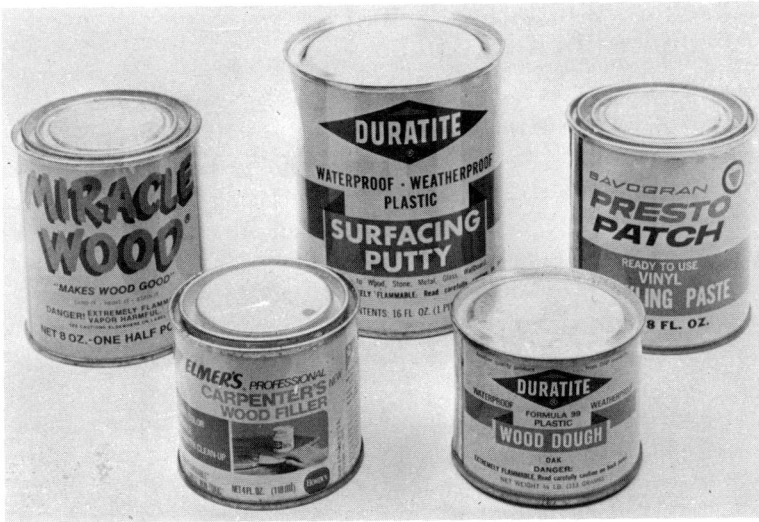

Patching materials.

Scratches

Scratches are physically caused surface defects. The method of repair depends on (1) whether the scratch goes through the finish into the wood, and (2) the kind of finish on the wood.

Shallow Scratches in Film Finishes. If the stain is not damaged, repair consists of filling the scratch level with the surface. The alternative, abrading the surface down to the level of the bottom of the scratch, is not recommended except for very shallow scratches where you know you have a film of adequate thickness.

Scratches can be filled with prepared paste scratch fillers, which are similar to wood putties but are smoother in texture. They come in many colors. The paste filler is applied with a putty knife or spatula, sanded when dry, and then padded over with padding lacquer. Some color-matching may be required when using a blending stain.

Scratches can also be filled with clear liquid scratch fillers, applied with a small brush or spatula, and sanded when dry.

Deep Scratches. These are defects that cut through the finish and expose the bare wood. They should first be stained. Use any water or oil stain on hand that matches; or use blending stain mixed in padding lacquer. After staining, remove any excess stain from the surface with the appropriate solvent and proceed as for a shallow scratch.

Scratches can also be filled by using stick putty. As these products are formulated to be used on prefinished paneling you may not be able to successfully apply any finish over the repair.

189

Checked, White-ringed, and Alligatored Finish Repairs

The defects all have one thing in common—the defect is in the finish not on it (see Fig. 9–10). Checking and alligatoring are caused by age. White stains are caused by water or alcohol getting into the finish. Often these defects—all of them—can be cured by a moist application of padding lacquer diluted one-to-one with padding lacquer solvent, but a more permanent and satisfactory repair can be made with a *penetrating* padding lacquer called an *amalgamator*. The amalgamator is better absorbed by the finish, where it draws together and solidifies the macro- or micro-granulations of the finish.

Procedure. Load amalgamator into a padding pad and disperse by tapping on clean white paper. The pad should not be saturated, but it should be more moist than when applying padding lacquer.

Apply amalgamator to the surface by padding with a circular motion. Do a small area at a time about the size of a saucer. As soon as the area is repaired (you will see it easily) move on to another area until the whole surface is padded. Allow amalgamator to dry 15 minutes, then pad with padding lacquer as previously described.

Blistered Veneer

Blisters on veneered surfaces are usually caused by excess moisture from the air or a spill getting through the veneer, softening the glue and swelling the veneer. The moisture also might be causing the wood to swell in a spot where there was insufficient glue, or no glue.

Unless you happen to know that waterproof glue was used under the veneer, the first method of repair to try is to apply heat to the

**FIGURE
9-10**

(a)   (b)

Repairing defects in the finish with amalgamator: (a) White spot on wood edge frame of card table. (b) Repair with amalgamator.

blister. Use a warm (not hot) flatiron on the blister to heat the glue for a few minutes, then clamp the blister.

If that doesn't work the next procedure is to get some glue under the blister. There are two ways to do it: (1) drill a hole and inject a very small amount of white glue; or (2) slit the blister with the grain, place glue under one side only, clamp it, and when dry repeat for the second side. The second procedure is better than the first because you can use epoxy cement, and you may get the veneer to lay down better. The halves may overlap; in this case, trim the second side edge to lie flush.

Loose Veneer

Loose veneer on old furniture is repaired by gluing it down again, whether it is in the middle of a panel or conveniently at an edge. (See Fig. 9–11.) The most important thing to watch out for is getting all loose dirt out from under and getting enough old glue off the veneer and off the core surface to allow new glue to hold the veneer down.

Applying heat to the veneer or heat to the veneer and moisture under the veneer in the hope that the animal glue originally used will reconstitute itself and hold the veneer down is most of the time a waste of time and effort. First, if the veneer has been loose for long, there is so much dirt under it that the glue couldn't stick if it wanted to. Second, there might not even be any animal glue under the veneer.

After the veneer and core surfaces have been cleaned and dusted, inspect with a good light and magnifying glass. Does the core surface look clean? If it does, glue the veneer down with white glue or epoxy. Press the veneer down and wipe away excess adhesive. Then lay on wax paper and clamp under a block of wood. If the veneer is completely loose, tape it in place with masking tape. Be sure to remove the masking tape as soon as it is possible to unclamp, otherwise it can become difficult to peel off. Clean off excess glue.

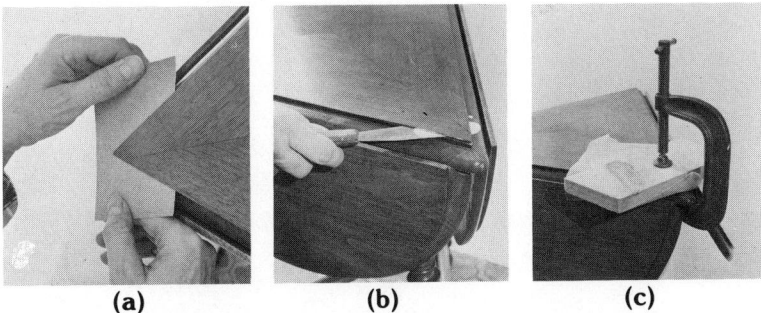

FIGURE 9-11

(a)   (b)   (c)

Loose veneer repair: (a) Clean surfaces with abrasive paper. (b) Apply white glue with blade. (c) Clamp until dry, then clean up.

Missing Veneer

Missing veneer can be repaired several ways. A chip of veneer or inlay in a finished piece of furniture is best repaired by burning-in. In unfinished or stripped wood, the repair is best made by fitting in a replacement piece of matching veneer. The repair can also be made by patching with a crack or patching compound and correcting the color mismatch with blending stain after the piece has been restained.

Fitting in a replacement piece of veneer—called *keystoning*—is tedious but not difficult. With a sharp chisel, cut out a rectangle around the defect. Select a piece of veneer of the same species that closely matches the grain of the veneer surrounding the defect and trim it to fit. This is the tedious part. The better the fit, the less visible will be the repair. Glue and clamp the patch. If this repair is made in finished work, finish off the patch with blending stain and padding lacquer.

Clear
Finishes

10

All furniture finishes can be neatly divided into two groups—transparent, or clear, finishes that display the grain and figure of the wood, and opaque finishes that hide the surface of the wood. Opaque finishes are discussed in the next chapter.

Transparent finishes must be thought of as finish systems, in which the several components of the system accomplish different purposes. The following are the components of a transparent finish:

- Stain—to color the wood.

- Filler—to fill the pores in the wood surface in order to obtain a smooth surface for the top coat.

- Sealer—to isolate one component of the finish from another or to prepare the wood for staining.

- Glaze—to vary the color over the surface of the wood or to match color over the surface.

- Top coat—to impart a hard, attractive protective surface to the wood.

- Wax—to protect the top coat.

In many instances, one finishing material may perform two or more of the component functions, and not all components are necessary in all finishes on all woods.

FIGURE
10-1

This desk has been given a stain, filler, and varnish finish, and has been rubbed to a satin finish and waxed.

FIGURE
10-2

(a)   (b)

How stain enhances the figure and grain of wood (samples are birch): (a) No stain and (b) oil pigment stain.

10-1 STAINS

Each natural wood has characteristic figure pattern, grain, and color (or colors). A stain is a transparent (more or less) liquid that is used to modify the color of a wood without obscuring the grain and figure.

Staining can also accentuate the contrast between the grain color and the background color (see Fig. 10–2). A wood can be stained a color lighter than its natural color only if the wood is first bleached. A filler can be used to enhance the contrast between grain and background, but the primary purpose of any filler is to fill the pores of the wood (see Fig. 10–3).

Staining is not hard work, but you can get into trouble fast. If you are not careful your efforts can end in disaster and there is no remedy short of stripping the piece and starting over again.

Color charts—particularly four-color printed charts—are not reliable guides to the real color of the stain nor to how the stain will look on your wood. Colors can even look different from one batch of color charts to the next—same brand, same product.

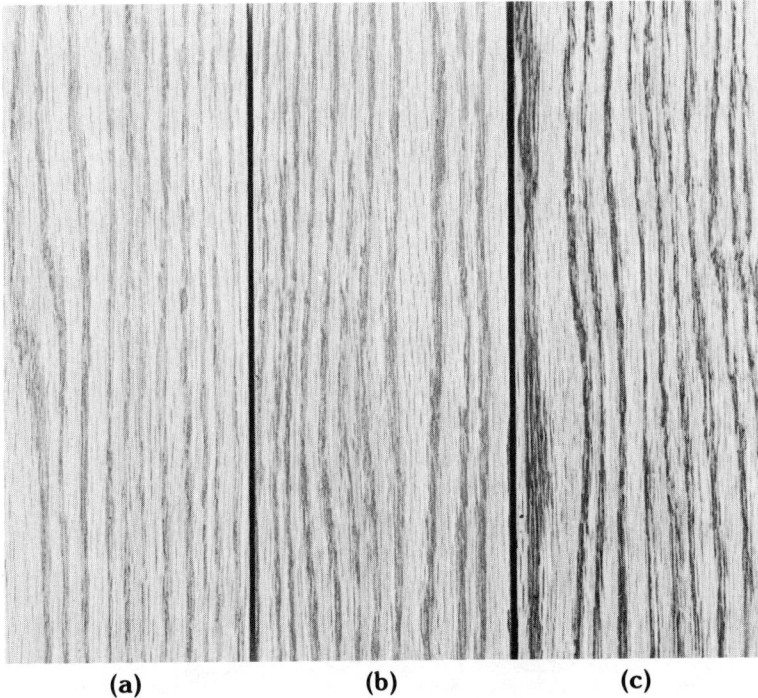

FIGURE
10-3

(a)   **(b)**   **(c)**

How filler changes the appearance of wood (samples are oak, stained with Colonial Maple NGR stain): (a) No filler, (b) filler of the same color as the stain, and (c) black filler.

The coloring material in a stain is either a finely ground pigment—a fine powder—or a dye, usually aniline. The coloring material is suspended or dissolved in a liquid vehicle. The liquid can be alcohol, water, lacquer solvent, or oil (petroleum distillates). The purpose of the liquid is to enable you to spread the colorant thinly and evenly on the surface of the wood. Pigmented and dye stains produce different results. And the results will not be the same using different vehicles, different kinds of woods, or even different brands of the same type of stain (see Figs. 10–4 and 10–5).

Stain from one can will color different pieces of wood differently. The color you get will depend on the kind of wood, whether it is new raw wood or old stripped wood being refinished, and the amount of stain you apply.

Oil Stains

Oil stains are the most widely used stains outside of furniture factories because they are conveniently packaged and easy to apply by brushing, wiping, dipping, and spraying. As they dry slowly, they can be brushed and rebrushed to eliminate lap marks. Excess stain can be wiped off—thus they are often called *wiping stains*. Oil stains do not penetrate the wood surface as deeply as do water and alcohol stains.

There are two kinds of oil stains—stains colored by oil-soluble aniline dyes and stains colored by finely ground pigments. The difference is important.

Oil aniline stains are called *penetrating stains*. The colors in these stains penetrate into the wood surface. They are transparent and reasonably clear. The stains are not as permanent as water stains, and because of this, are used only in medium and dark colors.

These stains must be used with caution on softwoods such as pine as they can leave porous places almost black. Surface pretreatment

FIGURE 10-4

Oil stains are the easiest to use, but results and color will vary widely among brands. All stains shown are sold as "Fruitwood".

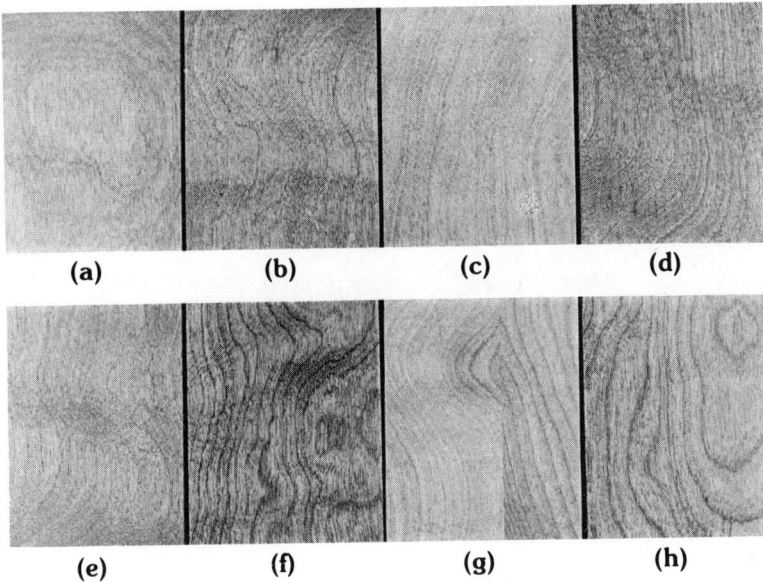

FIGURE
10-5

Results of staining birch samples with eight of the stains shown in Fig. 10-4. Not apparent in black and white illustration is the significant variation in what the stain manufacturers think "Fruitwood" should be. The manufacturers are (a) Sears, (b) Formby, (c) Sherwin-Williams, (d) Zar, (e) Tungseal, (f) Deft, (g) Woodkote, and (h) Minwax.

with oil or dilute shellac is customary. Use a mixture of one part boiled linseed oil and four parts mineral spirits, or one part four-pound shellac and four parts of alcohol (see Fig. 10–6). Sand lightly afterwards if you use shellac.

Most stains sold in paint, hardware, and department stores are pigmented stains. Even if not so stated and even if the ingredients are not listed, the sure identification is the direction on the can to stir well before and during use.

Oil pigment stains are made by dispersing finely ground tinting colors ground in oil into a vehicle consisting of linseed oil, mineral spirits, and other petroleum distillates. The important distinction is that the powdered pigments are not dissolved in the vehicle as are dye pigments. The powdered pigment remains a powder—even when you brush it on the wood.

Pigment stains do not color the wood as do dye and chemical stains, but leave a thin coating of microscopic pigment particles on the surface and in open pores.

This coating action does not produce a clear, transparent finish, and there is some hiding of the grain.

Oil pigment stains do have advantages. The colors are permanent, and a repair piece stained with a pigment oil stain will look a lot less new than it would with any penetrating stain.

197

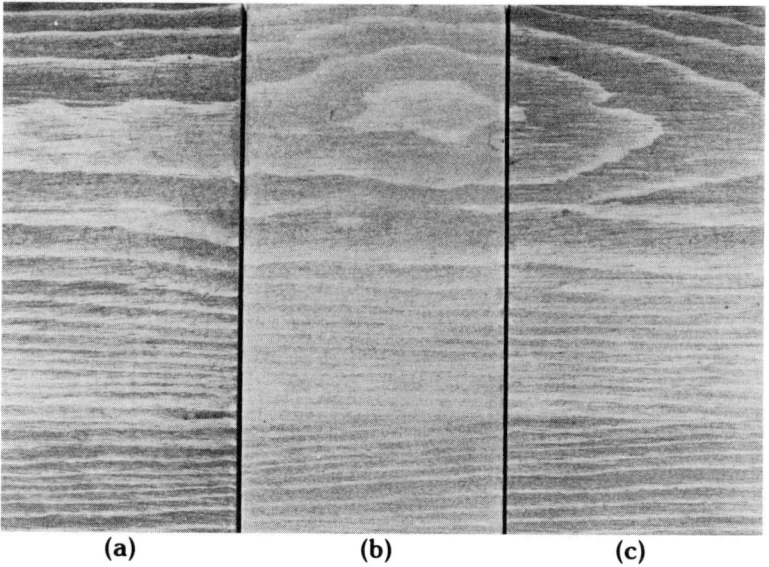

FIGURE 10-6

(a)   (b)   (c)

Staining pine (some pretreatment of pine is usually desirable to tone down the contrast): (a) No pre-treatment. (b) Wash coat of shellac (diluted 1-to-4) applied in a thin coat and sanded lightly when dry. (c) Coat of boiled linseed oil (diluted 1-to-1 with paint thinner); excess is wiped off immediately.

Lacquer Stains

Lacquer stains are colorfast nonfading stains recommended for use under lacquer. They can be applied by dipping, brushing, padding, or spraying. Spraying is the preferred method as it produces the best results. Grain raising is slight, requiring little sanding. These stains can be mixed with lacquer and sealer to produce a shading stain. The solvent for these stains is lacquer thinner. Lacquer stains are not widely available.

Water Stains

Water stains consist of a water-soluble colorant, and water as the principal constituent of the vehicle.

The ability of a water stain to penetrate the wood—rather than lay as a coating on the surface—is superior to all other stains. The wood cells in their natural state are filled with water. When lumber is kiln dried, the water is replaced by air. Dry wood absorbs water more readily than it absorbs oil or alcohols. Also, the water evaporates more slowly than alcohols, making it easier to get an even distribution of the stain.

Water stains containing aniline dyes are the best stains that can be used in furniture finishing. They are available either in powders that you mix with water to make a concentrated stain, or as a liquid concentrated stain. (Aniline and coal-tar stains are not exactly the same thing, but the differences are academic as far as wood staining is concerned. Both are classes of dyes.)

In the long run water stains are the cheapest. An ounce of powdered stain—enough to make a quart of stain concentrate—only costs around $1.10.

Water stains containing these colorants are clearer (more transparent), more brilliant in color, and enhance the natural shadings and grain figure of beautiful wood to greater advantage than other stains.

The permanency of water aniline and chemical stains is far greater than alcohol anilines and oil anilines. This permanence includes light colors as well as dark colors.

Now for the bad news. Water stains are more work to put on properly. The water stain raises the grain in the wood, requiring additional sanding to cut off the raised fibers to regain a smooth surface. For this reason, particularly on pine, poplar, gum, and fir, it is customary to wet the wood with water after completion of the sanding in order to raise the grain. The raised grain is then sanded after the wood dries, and the steps repeated, until the grain is no longer raised. The wood is then ready for staining with water stain. At least by then, the grain will not raise as much as it would have initially. If the wetting and grain-raising steps are not done before staining, so much sanding may be necessary after staining that the stained finish is destroyed.

The best way to control the application of water stains is with a spray gun. You can also brush or sponge it on.

Do not apply water stains to thin veneer, or for that matter on any thin or delicate wood. The water swells the wood and raises the grain too much, and will weaken the glue (unless a waterproof glue has been used).

Dyewood water stains—the traditional stains—are obsolete. These stains were made by cooking and messing around with various combinations of dyewoods, bark, nuts, berries, leaves, and minerals. The biggest problem, aside from the amount of time required to make up the concoctions, is that results vary from batch to batch; that is, the formulas require constant doctoring, and matching new and old work is practically impossible.

Chemical Stains

While dyes color wood by simply penetrating into the surface and producing a color that is dependent on the color of the stain and the color of the wood, chemical stains color the wood by chemically reacting with substances in the wood. Chemical stains are not commonly used today, as there are dye stains available to match just about any of the colors traditionally obtained with chemical stains. Besides, mixing and using some of these chemical stains is downright dangerous.

Staining with chemical stains is not the instant operation of dye or pigment stains. The chemical reaction between the stain and the wood takes place slowly, more slowly with some woods than others, and the color obtained can be quite different with different woods.

The number of colors obtainable with chemical stains is limited, but the color is superior to anilines and coal-tar stains in both transparency and permanence. Some of the stains are acid, some alkali, some both in successive coats.

Tannic acid produces browns; dilute nitric acid turns wood yellow, or in less-dilute solutions brownish or reddish yellow, depending on the wood. When diluted, sulfuric acid turns wood yellow; when used full strength it turns oak brown and pine green or gray.

Hydrochloric acid produces blacks, browns, and grays, depending on the strength and the wood. The violet crystals of permanganate of potash when dissolved in water produce an attractive brown on hardwoods. When first applied the wood turns violet, then brown as the stain dries. The deep red once so popular on mahogany is produced by a solution of potassium dichromate, in raw form a yellow crystal.

Alcohol Stains

Alcohol, or spirit stains, overcome the principal disadvantage of water stains. They do not raise the grain most of the time, and what grain they do raise is nowhere the problem that it is with water stains. Alcohol stains are also sold as NGR—nongrain-raising—stains.

The fact they dry so much more quickly than water stains means that they penetrate less into the wood, but at the same time, wood stained with an alcohol or NGR stain can be stained, sealed, filled, and varnished (one coat) in one working day. This makes them very useful in furniture repair work.

The colors of alcohol stains are transparent, brilliant, and enhance the natural coloring and grain of wood—but not quite as beautifully as do water stains. The colorants used in alcohol stains are aniline dyes that are soluble in ethyl or methyl alcohol.

It is sometimes claimed that alcohol-type stains will penetrate through old varnish enabling you to change the color of a finish without stripping off the old finish. Don't believe it.

Naturally, there's bad news here too. As a class, alcohol stains fade badly in sunlight or strong artificial light. Some colors are better than other colors, but the container won't tell you. All last better if coated immediately on drying with shellac or varnish to exclude air and light. (This is not necessarily a recommended finish system sequence, just a note.) Trying to get a light color with an alcohol stain is a waste of time. They are good, however, for medium and dark browns, and nigrosine SSB will produce a permanent black. Nigrosine is actually an extremely dark blue.

When you seal an alcohol stain with dilute shellac, it is important to do as little brushing as possible because the alcohol in the shellac dissolves and raises the stain letting it bleed into the shellac.

Alcohol stains are packaged as concentrated liquids or powders which you will have to dissolve in alcohol. The prepared liquids are recommended over the powders for convenience.

Varnish Stains

Varnish stains are simply varnish to which enough colorant has been added to produce a definite color. A lot of it is sold, most going onto floors or on low-priced "mahogany" or "walnut" furniture that is finished to look like a wood that it isn't, and for fast and furious home furniture refinishing.

These varnish stains do have their good points. Varnish stains dry quickly, four hours to overnight. They can cover up a lot of mismatching in wood. The colors of those containing pigments are permanent; those made with aniline dyes may or may not fade, depending on the dye used, which is difficult to determine until long after the finish is applied.

Paint as Stain

Any oil-based interior flat wall paint can be used as a stain on open-grained wood (such as oak) to finish the wood any color of the rainbow. Thin the paint to a watery consistency with mineral spirits, brush out thoroughly, then wipe off excess with clean cloths before the paint can dry. (*Note:* Oil paint–based finishes are taken up in more detail in Chapter 11.)

Stain properties are summarized in Table 10–1.

Preparation for Staining

Wood to be stained must be clean, dry, and smooth. All repairs should be made before staining. If the wood has been sanded, it should be brushed or vacuumed and wiped with a tack rag. Stripped wood must be free of any remains of old finish, paint, varnish remover, and wax. Wipe stripped wood with silicone wash, or lacquer solvent.

Sealing Before Staining

Softwoods (notably pine) sop up stains in sometimes strange ways and produce results usually far from what you desired unless first sealed to limit and control the penetration of the stain. It does not matter what kind of stain you use.

Stain Summary

TABLE
10-1

Stain Vehicle	Colorant	Transparency, Brilliance	Color Permanence	Raises Grain	Penetration	Bleed	Application Brush	Application Wipe	Spray
Water	Aniline dye	Excellent	Excellent	Yes	High	No	X		X
	Chemical	Excellent	Excellent	Yes	High	No	X		
Alcohol NGR	Aniline dye	Good	Poor	Slight	Moderate	Yes	X		X
Oil	Aniline dye	Good	Poor	No	Slight	No	X	X	
	Pigment	Fair	Excellent	No	Slight	No	X	X	
Varnish	Pigment	Fair	Varies	No	None	No	X		X

Pitch streaks should be scrubbed with paint thinner to remove as much pitch as possible. It may take more than one try. When the surface is dry, seal with shellac cut one to four with alcohol. The shellac will seal in the rest of the pitch. Seal knots with two applications of one to four shellac sealer. Apply the shellac carefully to the knot only with a small artist's brush.

Applying Water Stains

Water stains are bought as powders which you mix in hot water to make a concentrated stock stain. They should be stored in closed glass bottles. Dilute the stock stain for working stain. Colors can be inter-mixed for intermediate shades. Wood to be colored with a water stain requires special sanding, as mentioned earlier.

Staining will be more uniform on most woods if the wood is dampened with a moist cloth immediately before staining. Oily woods such as rosewood and teak should be wiped with lacquer thin-ner instead. Stain strength should be such that a wet coat will give the color desired. If you are inexperienced with water stain, dilute the stain further than you think necessary and plan to apply two coats. Wait until the first coat is dry before putting on the second coat.

Brush on the stain with a wide brush or use a sponge. Wipe im-mediately. If it looks too dark wipe the surface with clear water.

You can also apply water stain with an airbrush or spray gun. This is the most trouble-free and neat way to do it.

After the water stain has dried, you will note most likely that there has been some raising of the grain no matter how carefully you sanded beforehand. Before you do any sanding, apply a seal coat of diluted shellac or prepared sanding sealer.

Applying Alcohol (NGR) Stains

Alcohol stains purchased as liquid NGR stains are far too concentrated to use straight out of the bottle. With these stains it is important that you dilute them (with the appropriate reducer as recommended by the seller) to produce the shade you want on the wood with one coat. (See Fig. 10–7.)

To get an even finish, you should slop on a wet coat and wipe im-mediately. More problems befall users of NGR stains through trying to brush on or wipe on a dry coat than from any other cause. Darken-ing with a second coat does not work as well with alcohol stains as it does with water stains.

Applying Oil Stains

First time out, follow the directions on the container. Get an idea of how that particular brand of stain handles. Different brands of the same kind of stain can vary greatly in the way they color wood. Experi-ment.

203

FIGURE
10-7

Applying alcohol stain (NGR stain): Dilute stain to get the color you want with a wet coat. Quickly brush on a wet coat, wiping excess as you go, then wiping entire surface. A second coat can be applied immediately, but the degree of additional color darkening will be slight.

End-Grain Staining

End grains of wood and plywood edges take stains differently than do side grain. Stain is absorbed more readily into the end grain, which always leaves this wood darker than the rest. There are several ways you can handle this end-grain problem besides ignoring it. For boards, the best solution is to seal the end grain with dilute shellac, then sand the end, and stain the whole piece. Be careful not to get any of the shellac on the side or long edge of the board. You don't want those surfaces sealed in spots. It is a good idea to do some precautionary sanding after sealing the ends.

If the stained end is too light, sand lightly and restain. Repeat sanding and staining until you get a match.

For plywood edges, the best solution is to veneer the edge. Otherwise, paint the edge with japan color to match the rest of the wood. (See Fig. 10–8.) Board ends can also be colored with japan color.

10-2 SHELLAC

Shellac is an easy finish to apply. In the past it was used extensively as a top coat. Now it is used principally as a sealer. Moisture will turn a bare shellac finish white. It does not produce a tough furniture surface, but shellac can be protected to some extent by wax.

**FIGURE
10-8**

Staining end grain: For some woods, such as mahogany, no special procedures are required. Softer woods, such as those used in veneer plywood core veneers shown, require special treatment. The top piece is stained the same as the other surfaces; the bottom piece is stained with matching japan color on the side. Some unevenness in the coverage enhances its appearance as wood.

Shellac begins as a resinous deposit left by tiny insects, call lac bugs, on twigs of certain trees in India and other Eastern countries. The twigs are harvested twice a year and ground up, sifted, soaked, melted, and broken into flakes forming dry shellac.

Shellac in its natural state is bright orange. White shellac is orange shellac that has been chemically bleached white. The difference between best-grade shellac and lower grades is freedom from impurities.

Dry shellac is soluble in alcohol. It is not soluble in water, turpentine, oil, mineral spirits, or lacquer thinner. Grain (ethyl) alcohol is best for cutting gum shellac, but for practical and economic reasons, denatured alcohol is used. Denatured alcohol is grain alcohol mixed with something to keep you from drinking it. A variety of substances can be used to make denatured alcohol; the best combination for shellac cutting is grain alcohol denatured by 5 percent methanol. Methanol is wood alcohol which is poisonous, fumes included. Shellac cut in methanol is difficult to brush because it sets quickly—and then is slow to dry hard.

Liquid shellac is normally sold as *four-pound cut,* but many stores are now carrying *three-pound cut.* This means that four pounds (or three pounds) of dry shellac gum flakes have been dissolved in each gallon of alcohol. This is too heavy for brushing and must be diluted—with more alcohol—for use. Pure shellac gum is expensive, so, naturally, ways have been found to extend the shellac by adding in cheaper gums. This reduces not only the price, but also the quality, resulting in products unfit for furniture work. Pure shellac can be sanded 30 minutes after brushing on without gumming your paper; extended shellacs can't be. If it isn't marked *pure* shellac, orange or white, don't buy it.

Shellac deteriorates in the container; this is the reason containers are dated. Don't try to save money by buying in quantity. Buy what you think you will use in two or three months, and throw anything a year old away. Orange shellac usually keeps better than white shellac because of the difficulty of removing all of the bleach. Anytime you discover undissolved pieces of gum shellac in white shellac, don't waste time trying to strain it for use, dump it.

Shellac is an excellent filler for all but the coarsest of open-grain woods when put on in thin coats and sanded after each coat so only the shellac in the pores remains. It is also a good seal coat for stains, fillers, glazes, and it is useful as a raw-wood sealer on pine under both paint finishes and transparent finishes. With shellac as a sealer, you can varnish the same day.

Orange shellac dries translucent, white shellac dries transparent. Use orange shellac as a sealer with dark finishes, white shellac with light finishes, or use white shellac for all.

Shellac shouldn't be applied over any stain the same day, nor should more than two coats of shellac be applied in one day no matter how dry it seems. Rub down shellac with 220-grit or finer paper, or pumice in oil—never pumice and water which will cloud the whole surface.

No finishing should be done when the humidity is high, least of all shellacking. And, there is no way you can protect shellac enough with varnish for it to be used for anything that will go outdoors.

For brushing shellac, use the largest brush practical to keep the number of strokes to a minimum. Brush shellac on rapidly without cross brushing and rebrushing because it drys fast.

10-3 FILLERS

The surface of woods such as oak, ash, mahogany, and walnut are covered with large, visible pores. No amount of sanding will eliminate these characteristic surface depressions, and it would take too many coats of well-sanded varnish or shellac to smooth them over to be practical.

Fillers can be applied to raw wood, over a shellac sealer or over stain. The results obtained will be quite different in appearance. Paste filler put on raw wood will stain the wood the same color as the filler, but the color won't be very concentrated.

Filler applied over a shellac sealer can be removed from the surface and left only in the pores where it belongs by sanding. The sealer keeps the filler from penetrating and staining the surface, but you will not then be able to get much penetrating with any staining after the filling, but this again may be what you want. The usual furniture finishing schedule is stain—sealer—filler—sealer or stain—filler—sealer.

Wood fillers are used to fill these pores in order to obtain a smooth finish on the wood, whether it is to be a clear finish or an opaque finish. It should be noted that it is not always desirable to obtain a totally smooth finish. With some finishes such as fumed oak, antique oak, and Jacobean, the wood would not be filled. (See Table 10–2.) The tools and materials used in wood filling are shown in Figure 10–9.

There are two kinds of fillers—paste and liquid. Paste wood filler can be used on all open-grained wood. The liquid kind is only practical used on open-grained wood with small pores, such as walnut, teak, and rosewood.

Paste Wood Fillers

These wood fillers are packaged as concentrated pastes that must be reduced for use. These pastes are essentially silica, or silex (the materials that do the filling), boiled linseed oil, turpentine or mineral spirits, and japan drier. Silica is finely ground (140-mesh) sand; silex is very finely ground (240-mesh) sand. It is claimed that silex produces a transparent filler, while plain silica makes for an opaque filler. As pigment-colored filler goes into pores with measurable depth, this is straining credibility a bit. The filler concentrate may be a natural gray color or may contain a pigment to match the color of common wood finishes.

Paste filler should be reduced to the consistency of varnish for use on oak, ash, and chestnut, and a little thinner for mahogany and walnut. The preferred reducing medium is mineral spirits. Wood distilled turpentine should be avoided because it produces a filler that doesn't dry well, and improper drying is an inherent filler problem.

In clear finish schedules, the filler is normally applied after the stain and sealer coats. The filler is usually colored the same as the

TABLE 10-2	**To Fill or Not to Fill, Filler Color, and Tinting**	

Wood and Finish	Fill	Filler (Natural Paste Filler)
Brown mahogany	Yes	Very dark filler. Tint with Van Dyke brown and small amount of rose pink.
Light brown mahogany	Yes	Match stain with Van Dyke brown as tint.
Red mahogany	Yes	Dark filler. Use mixture of Van Dyke brown, drop black, small amount of rose pink to tint.
Walnut	Yes	On unstained walnut, use natural (clear) liquid filler.
Antique walnut	Yes	Light gray filler, tint with zinc white and enough drop black added to produce gray.
Golden oak	Yes	Natural paste or tint with Van Dyke brown.
Weathered oak	No	—
English oak	Yes	Very dark filler, tint with Van Dyke brown and drop black.
Mission oak	No	—
Jacobean oak	No	—
Bog oak	Yes	Black filler. Tint with drop black.
Olive oak (wood stained green)	Yes	Black filler. Tint with drop black.
Rosewood	Yes	Seal first with two coats shellac or lacquer sealer. Dark filler. Use Van Dyke brown and rose pink 3:1 to tint.
Van Dyke brown	No	(This finish is used on close-grain wood to give the appearance of walnut.)
Driftwood	Yes	White filler. Do not completely fill pores.

stain, but interesting effects can be obtained with both darker and lighter fillers.

If the piece to be filled has had a sealer coat, sand and dust before filling. Coat the surface with the filler, using a stiff-bristled brush (see Fig. 10-10). Brush the filler on with the grain, then finish brushing across the grain. The pores of the wood before filling are filled with air. The filler is not going to get into the pores unless vigorously brushed in. You won't hurt anything by brushing too much. Be sure to stir the filler often as the silica settles rapidly.

When the surface dries to a dead flat appearance (five to ten minutes), rub the surface with a burlap pad, across the grain as much as possible, but at least with a circular motion. Avoid rubbing with the grain because the burlap will lift the filler out of the pores. The object of this wiping is to remove all of the filler that is not in the pores. Any filler remaining on the surface will cloud the finish. If you don't have burlap, use a piece of terry cloth.

After getting most of the filler from the surface with burlap, finish with a soft cloth, first across the grain, then with the grain, lightly, to remove the final traces of filler and all fingerprints.

To apply filler to carvings and moldings, use a toothbrush to scrub it in. When the filler has dried dead flat, use terry cloth to remove excess filler. You may have to use it over the rounded end of a dowel stick to get it into carvings. Q-tips are also handy for this. Finish with a soft cloth.

Was the filling operation successful? If the filler was reduced and mixed correctly, it rolled up and crumbled off the wood when you rubbed with burlap. If it was tough going and hard to remove, you waited too long before wiping. If this is the case, some of the filler is still likely to be on the surface leaving it with a muddy appearance.

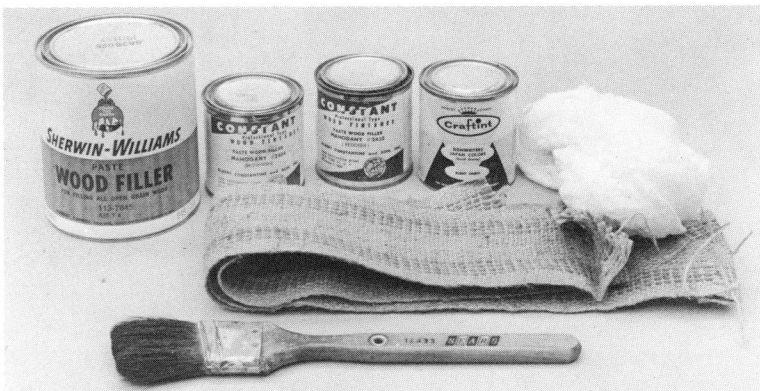

**FIGURE
10-9**

Wood filling tools and materials: (From top left) natural color paste wood filler of the kind most readily available, colored paste wood filler, japan color for coloring paste wood filler, stiff brush for application, burlap for scrubbing filler into pores, and clean cloth.

FIGURE 10-10

(a)

(b)

(c)

Steps in filling: (a) Brush on an even coat of filler, brushing it across the grain to get the material into the wood pores. (b) After the filler has partially dried (goes dull), scrub the surface across the grain with burlap to pack filler into the pores and remove most of excess filler. (c) With soft cloth, rub surface across the grain; finish by rubbing with the grain.

You may have to wipe the surface quickly with a cloth dampened with mineral spirits, and then fill the surface a second time because the wipe down will probably lift some of the filler from the pores.

If the filler lifts out of the pores when you wipe after the surface has dried flat, it means there is too little japan drier in the filler. Add japan drier, at the rate of one ounce per pint. If the filler dries too rapidly for you to wipe the whole area clean, you are trying to do too large an area at one time. Get help wiping or do smaller areas.

Are the pores filled and the surface flat? Look at the pores with your magnifying glass to see if they were filled completely. Don't be surprised if the piece requires a second filling, particularly if you are working on oak or one of the other really open-grained woods.

The next step in filling is very important. Let the filler dry before you do any subsequent sealing, glazing, or top coating. Oil-based fillers should dry 24 hours. You have not applied an even thin coat in filling—the filler is all clustered in the pores. If not properly dried, the solvents in the filler can bleed through succeeding coats and can prevent or delay drying.

There are on the market products that are combination stains and fillers. They do not contain enough silica to do an adequate filling job—at least not on oak and similar open-pored wood. In use, these products are brushed on, brushed into the pores, then wiped off.

Liquid fillers function more as sealers than as fillers. Their ability to fill open-pored wood is questionable. Some cannot be used under lacquer. Shellac and lacquer-type sanding sealer are to be preferred.

Shellac

Shellac works well for filling woods classed as open grained but do not have the large wide-open pores that oak does. Shellac can be used as a filler on these woods, particularly if they are not stained. Use white shellac for light woods, orange shellac for dark woods. Use at least two coats of shellac cut one to one with alcohol, and sand afterwards. The purpose of sanding is to leave shellac in the pores but remove most from the surface.

10-4 GLAZING

Glazing, in furniture finishing, is either a second stain or paint applied over the stain or enamel coat to give richness and color depth to the final finish. With transparent finishes, glazing is also used to match up different colored woods in which case it is called *shading*. Glaze is applied with cloth, brush or spray gun, then wiped to obtain the desired effect. When applied over stain, the change of color in heavily wiped areas is subtle. (When applied over enamel, the change in base-coat color can be drastic.)

Glaze is widely used in the art of antique imitation as, if applied with not too heavy a hand, it produces an instant appearance of age. One problem with glazing over enamel is that the glaze will accentuate all brush marks and other surface defects in the enamel coat unless they have been completely sanded out.

Glazing over Stain.   Glazes used for this purpose are heavy bodied pigmented stains. It is important that the stained surface be sealed and the sealer sanded before glazing to prevent the glaze from being in effect another stain which could change the color of the piece overall rather than permit selective color changing by wiping.

How you put the glaze on is not critical. Rag, brush, spray, and sponge all work. Apply a wet coat. If the object of glazing is a uniform color change, wipe the surface uniformly with clean cloths.

Shading.   This is a form of glazing over stain in which edges and corners of panels and the indented parts of carvings and mouldings are colored a darker color than the rest of the piece. The purpose is to add some interest to large plain areas and to accentuate the carved and moulded detail. After wiping, and when the glaze is dry, prominent areas of carvings and edges can be highlighted by removing a little of the glaze, usually with steel wool.

Spattering.   This is adding specs to the surface by flipping glaze droplets off the ends of a stiff bristled brush. To be effective, spattering should not be overdone.

FIGURE
10-11

Topcoat materials (there is no one best furniture topcoat).

Hours of careful work—stripping, sanding, repairing, staining, filling, sealing, and glazing—can come to nothing if the wrong top coat is applied. The choice of clear top coat materials is wide—varnish, lacquer, shellac, oil, oil-resin—and there is no one best universal finish for all furniture. (See Fig. 10–11.)

Clear top coats, also called *natural finishes,* can be classified in two groups—surface finishes and penetrating finishes. The surface finishes are applied in multiple coats and are built up on the surface of the wood in films of measurable thickness. These finishes include varnish, lacquer, and shellac. Penetrating finishes soak into the wood where they solidify and leave a minimum film on the wood surface, even when several coats are applied.

Choice of top coat material depends on many factors. These include the desired appearance, the wood or woods used, durability, and ease of application. Table 10–3 summarizes these factors.

Varnish

Varnish is a very loose term. Defined broadly, varnish means any liquid containing no pigment which is used for the protection and decoration of wood surfaces when spread on the surface in a thin homgeneous film, and which will dry to a hard essentially transparent coating. (According to this definition, lacquer and shellac would be varnishes.) In our discussion varnish means *polyurethane* varnish.

Varnish is the best all-around top coat that you can put on a piece of furniture. Today's polyurethane varnishes are still slower drying than shellac or lacquer, but the drying is a lot faster than it used to be for varnish, and the problem of dust settling on the wet surface is not the disaster of years ago. Polyurethane varnish is easier to apply by brush than lacquer, and there is less hazard to your safety and health. In resistance to spills and wear, varnish and lacquer are essentially equal. Furniture varnishes tend to be brittle and do not withstand impact and scratching as well as lacquer, however. Both top coat materials are available in a wide range of formulations.

Varnishing Tools

The usual first recommendation is to use a good varnish brush, which is not a bad idea. A good varnish brush will be made with pure black Chinese hog bristles formed to a chisel edge and vulcanized in hard rubber. (The very best varnish brushes have all white Chinese hog bristles.) Keeping the brush good is another problem. It requires careful cleaning and storage, usually under lock and key in the typical household. These brushes are not cheap either. Use lacquer thinner instead of mineral spirits for really thorough cleaning.

Clear Top Coat Comparison

TABLE 10-3

	Polyurethane Varnish	Brushed Lacquer	Shellac	Linseed Oil	Oil-Resin	French Polish (Padding Lacquer)
Type of finish	Film	Film	Film	Penetrating	Penetrating	Film
Appearance: overall ability to enhance wood grain and figure	Good	Good	Good	Poor	Good	Excellent
Durability: ability to withstand physical abuse; e.g., surface scratching	Good	Excellent	Good	Good	Excellent	Good
Repairability: surface scratch	Fair	Fair	Good	Fair	Good	Good
Moisture resistance: alcohol and water	Good	Good	Poor	Fair	Good	Poor
Application: how best described	Fairly easy	Difficult	Fairly easy	Tedious	Easy	Hard work
Goofs: ease of correcting application errors	(Easy) Sand and recoat	(Difficult) Recoat, possibly remove and start over	(Easy) Remove and recoat	(Easy) Clean and recoat	(Easy) Rub and recoat	(Easy) Remove and recoat
Sheen	Satin, gloss, mirror	Satin, gloss, mirror	Satin and gloss	Dull	Satin	Satin and gloss

A better and inexpensive alternative for applying varnish is to use a foam polybrush as described in Chapter 1. With a foam brush, you will have no trouble getting on a thin coat.

The room where you varnish should be at least 70° F, dust free, and ventilated (for your protection) without being drafty. How dust free? Brush and vacuum the piece you are going to varnish, preferably in another room. Otherwise, wait until the dust settles. Wipe down your bench with mineral spirits, then put the work on the bench and wipe it thoroughly with a tack rag. Be careful to get into all the corners. Work alone in the shop. When the varnishing is finished, get out of the shop until it is dry. This procedure also applies for lacquering and shellacking.

Varnishing Procedure

There is no one proper way to apply varnish. Any method you use to get the varnish on the wood in a smooth thin coat without bubbles, and without holidays, brush marks, and sags is a proper way to do it. Whether you brush crosswise first and finish with the grain, or lay on the varnish with the grain, brush crosswise, then brush with the grain, or any other procedure, is unimportant so long as it works for you.

Pouring varnish from the can to another container for use is a waste of varnish, time, and containers and should be done only when your brush is too big to get into the can.

Never shake varnish to mix it. That only makes bubbles. All satin varnishes must be thoroughly stirred before use, and stirred during use. Stir with a smooth stick so you can use it to strike excess varnish from your foam polybrush rather than use the side of the can lip which only makes more bubbles.

While varnishing, keep a folded face tissue handy to run under edges to get up excess varnish.

Varnish, after drying, should be sanded between coats. Use *used* 220-grit paper. Sanding is always needed to remove dust specs. (There will always be a few.) Sanding is sometimes also needed to provide a tooth for the next coat, but this depends on the varnish used and the time elapsed between coats. Read label directions. Sags will not be dry in a few hours but they can be shaved flush with a sharp chisel or hand scraper without waiting.

Lacquer

Lacquer has meant different things in the past than it does now. The word is derived from *lac*, the gum resin produced by lac insects. The finish material made from this resin is now called *shellac*. Chinese and Japanese lacquers were not and are not made from this lac resin, nor are they in any way related to modern lacquer. They are varnishes made from resins and oils available in those countries.

215

As we know them today, lacquers are composed of nitrocellulose or acrylic bases, resins, plasticizers, and solvents.

Lacquer is inexpensive, fast drying, and produces a durable top coat that is less prone to chipping than most varnishes. Almost all wood furniture manufactured today has a sprayed-on lacquer finish.

Lacquers are formulated for either brushing or spraying. The difference is that a spraying lacquer dries faster than a brushing lacquer. You can slow down the drying time of a spraying lacquer by thinning it with a retarder rather than regular lacquer thinner so it can be brushed. Both types of lacquer must be thinned for use. If you are going to apply lacquer by brush, you are better off buying a brushing lacquer to begin with.

Solvents differ slightly between lacquer brands. Some manufacturers insist you use their own solvent exclusively, which may or may not be necessary. These special solvents cost more than good old plain lacquer thinner (solvent) which you buy in any paint or hardware store, even in stores that don't carry cans of lacquer anymore. I have experienced no problems with plain lacquer thinner.

With lacquer, you can produce any finish from high gloss to dull satin right out of the can by buying the right lacquer. You can also rub a gloss lacquer dull, or rub and polish a dull lacquer to a glossy sheen. The colors of lacquers range from a very pale yellow (called "water-white") to amber. Lacquer darkens the color of finished wood less than any other top coat, but over long long periods of time and with exposure to sunlight, most lacquers will yellow.

The difficulty encountered in brushing lacquer and the high cost of lacquer spraying equipment—professional spray gun and compressor, spray booth, and forced-air ventilation—to say nothing of the health and safety hazards of lacquering, have made varnish a very attractive alternative for refinishing furniture.

Lacquering Procedure

Brush lacquering should be confined to small articles (e.g., chairs and pedestal tables) and not used for large pieces like dining tables and dressers. The best choice of brush for small article and touch-up work is a very soft, really good-quality sable or squirrel hair (camel hair) brush. A one-inch brush is about the minimum useful size for flat surface work. Depending on where you buy it, it may be called a lettering, lacquering, or lacquer touch-up brush. Don't use the brush for anything else and keep it locked up. You can also use foam polybrushes, discarding them as soon as the side seam starts coming unglued.

Applying lacquer is completely different from laying on paint or varnish. You cannot lay on lacquer crosswise and then smooth it by brushing out. You must lay it on smooth right out of the brush. Flow on a wet coat with long sure strokes and avoid rebrushing. Clean up

216

sags at the ends of your strokes immediately. Keep a wet edge. The time the edge of your lacquer will stay wet is measured in seconds rather than minutes as for varnish. Keep moving and work fast. If you discover a holiday, leave it. Just hope you remember to catch it on the next coat.

Varnish usually can be used right out of the can or thinned only slightly. Lacquer must be thinned until it is quite watery in order for it to lay on with one stroke.

Spray-can lacquers are often used for finishing small repair areas. There are difficulties that must be overcome to do it successfully. Nozzles are chronically unreliable, can pressure is marginal, and fast skin drying tempts one to apply coats too close together.

Lacquer skins over before it dries. The surface is dry, but there are still solvents below the surface that must evaporate before you apply the next coat. Four hours between coats at temperatures above 70° F is usually adequate; allow more time if you are brushing on heavy coats, which you shouldn't be doing.

You don't have to sand lacquer between coats to provide tooth for the next coat, as you have to do with varnish. Sanding is necessary only to remove high spots and dust particles. Use 220-grit finishing paper. To remove sags, use a hand scraper. The solvent in the coat being applied will dissolve the previous coat sufficiently for a good bond. If you don't work fast when recoating and avoid brushing over at all costs, the old coat will be so softened that it will lift off.

Lacquering, more than the application of any other finish, requires good ventilation. It is also essential that you work well away from any open flames, cigarettes, or sparks. The solvents in lacquer are very rough on the mucous lining of your nose and throat, and a face mask won't do much to help. You may discover that you cannot tolerate lacquer solvents at all. Keeping sour balls or hard candy in your mouth while lacquering will help.

The solvents in lacquer are potent paint and varnish softeners. Putting a lacquer top coat over an old finish can often end in disaster. Varnish is a better choice of top coat over any old finish. In new work, pigmented wiping oil stains and paste fillers have a bad tendency to bleed into a lacquer coat. Use water, alcohol, or NGR stains intead of an oil stain. Let paste wood fillers dry 48 hours, then seal with a wash coat of shellac. If you use an oil stain, seal it with shellac.

Linseed Oil Finish

Linseed oil by itself is a poor finish and has nothing to recommend it, except perhaps historical accuracy on some antique furniture. If anybody wants a finish procedure that is all work and no results, this is it.

The material is boiled (polymerized) linseed oil cut two parts to one with turpentine. Raw linseed oil will never dry. Boiled linseed oil contains drying agents. You brush on the oil, allow it to penetrate, then wipe off the excess. You do this once a day for a week, once a week for a month, once a month for a year, then once a year for the rest of your life. For all this work you get a finish that gives wood a murky natural look, spots with water and alcohol, gets tacky in warm humid weather, and almost never looks clean.

If you do apply a linseed oil finish, wash out the rags afterward because otherwise they can ignite spontaneously.

Oil-Resin Finish

If you combine boiled linseed oil, a natural resin, and turpentine you have a crude oil-resin wiping finish that was used in the old days on fine furniture in what was called a *hand-rubbed* finish. You can make your own. Start with two parts alkyd interior gloss varnish, add one part boiled linseed oil and three parts mineral spirits. Mix it, seal it and let it stand a day before using. This finish can go on over raw wood, stained wood, or be used as a top coat over stained and filled wood.

You can apply it to the wood with a brush, rag, or your bare hands. Let it soak in. Apply more to areas that go dry. When the wood will absorb no more (after about an hour), wipe off the excess with cloths. Be sure you get all the loose finish off the surface. If the surface is tacky (indicating that the finish has started drying on the surface) wet the wiping cloth with mineral spirits.

Wait a day, then apply a second coat. Two coats will probably be enough to saturate the wood. Now you can do the final dressing. Using the same mix, apply a small amount with a cloth pad as you would apply paste wax. With a clean soft cloth burnish the finish into the surface. If the rubbing isn't going smoothly, mix a lubricant consisting of equal parts of boiled linseed oil and mineral spirits. Very slightly dampen the burnishing pad with the lubricant—use as little as possible for best results. You can also use your bare hand for the polishing—nothing works better—or wear a leather glove dampened with the lubricant. If this sounds like a penetrating oil finish or a wipe-on oil finish, you are right.

Penetrating Oil Finishes

Penetrating finishes are especially attractive on modern styled furniture, or any furniture made of walnut, rosewood, teak, and many other exotic woods.

These top coats are easier to apply than varnish, shellac, and lacquer, with no need to worry about brush marks, shedding brushes, dust, or sags. Techniques vary with the different products, but basically you brush or wipe them on, wait, then wipe off to remove the excess.

The main difference between varnishes and penetrating oil finishes is that the latter contains more solvents in relation to resins and oils making them thinner—more watery—and thus more penetrating.

Tung oil is a popular finishing product today. But all penetrating finishes do not contain or need tung oil. Alkyd and other synthetic resins are also effective pore fillers. (Watco's Danish Oil Finish, for example, does not contain tung oil.) Most of these products contain a mixture of resins and oils, both natural and synthetic.

There is nothing magically new about tung oil. Tung oil, also known as China wood oil, is a natural aromatic oil extracted from the nuts of the tung tree. Originating in China, tung oil has been used for centuries as a wood sealant and preservative. It has been used in American paint and varnish manufacture for decades, and most of the tung oil used today comes from trees growing in our own southern states.

Application procedures vary among products. The first time you use one, follow the can directions. Then you might want to experiment. Basically, the procedure is as described earlier in our discussion of oil resin finishes.

French Polish

This is the most attractive clear finish you can put on a priceless antique, marquetry, or a turning of any kind (except food vessels). The finish in several versions is close to 300 years old. It involves a lot of work and considerable skill to do right, except for applying it to turnings, which is a snap. But on the right kind of furniture, the results can be well worth the effort.

French polish is a rubbed-on shellac top coat. In application, the shellac is mixed with linseed oil. As it is shellac, you should not expect it to be as durable as a varnish or lacquer finish. It should not be applied to surfaces exposed to water or other spills. French polish can be applied to raw wood, over water stains, and over oil and alcohol stains if first sealed with a wash coat of shellac.

There are procedures that use French polish with pumice to serve as a filler. It is more practical to use brushed and sanded coats of shellac or a liquid filler instead, sanding between applications. French polish finish should not be attempted on open-grained wood.

One of the big advantages of a French polish finish is the ease with which it can be repaired. It is also an excellent procedure for repairing other clear finishes. With appropriate powdered stains, you can change the color of a finish (within reason), match color in repair work, and touch up edges that have worn through the stain.

It is not necessary to buy the ingredients and mix your own French polish. It can be purchased ready-mixed as *padding lacquer* in several formulas under the names Pad-Lac, Qualasole, or Lacover.

How to apply a French polish finish using padding lacquer is covered in Chapter 9.

Polishing

Varnish and lacquer can be purchased gloss or satin, which eliminates the necessity of rubbing for a satin finish. If you have applied gloss varnish or lacquer, however, you can rub them for either a satin or mirror finishing.

Rubbing for a Satin Finish. The first step is to wait until the finish is thoroughly dry—a week is a good minimum drying time for either varnish or lacquer. Rub varnish with 320A wet or dry paper and water. Fold the paper over a felt-faced pad and rub lightly with the grain. Be careful not to rub so much that you cut through the finish. Be particularly careful on edges. Wipe the surface clean and check often. When the surface is smooth, stop rubbing and clean off. Now rub with dry grade 0000 steel wool. Buff with lint-free cloth and wax.

For lacquer, use oil with the 320A paper instead of water, then steel wool with oil. Clean off with mineral spirits, buff, then wax.

Mirror Finish. A mirror finish—also called a piano finish—is the ultimate high-gloss finish. It can be obtained with both varnish and lacquer but it is easier with varnish because you will need more coats to begin with and it is difficult to get on more than two lacquer coats by brush.

The mirror finish starts with wood surface preparation. The wood must be as smooth and flat as you can get it. The tiniest depression, crack, or ripple will show in the finish.

Put on two coats of gloss varnish, sanding as required between coats. Now, using a sanding block, rub the entire surface with 320A paper until the gloss is removed. Slight depressions in the surface will still be glossy. Rub them with grade 0000 steel wool to remove gloss. Now clean the surface, and put on another coat. When dry, sand again.

Then varnish again. Keep sanding and varnishing until the glossy spots all disappear when you rub with 320A paper.

When you have achieved that condition, rub the surface with pumice and oil, using a felt pad. Wet the surface with rubbing oil, then sprinkle it with pumice. Now with the felt pad and light pressure, rub with the grain, going over the whole surface evenly. To check your progress you have to clean a spot or surface. You are finished with the pumice when the surface is satin smooth. Now clean thoroughly with mineral spirits. Be sure to remove every trace of pumice.

The next step is rubbing with rottenstone. Rottenstone is finer than pumice. Rub with oil in the same manner as with pumice, but use a different pad, reserved for rottenstone only. The surface should be just about glossy.

Compounding is next. Compound comes as a paste or as a liquid. Make a cheesecloth pad. Dampen the cheesecloth with water. Pick up some compound on the cheesecloth and rub the surface evenly with the grain until you get a mirror finish. Buff the surface to clean.

Waxing

The final step in any finish sequence (except a linseed oil finish) is to apply a thin coating of paste wax, then buff it until it shines. Wax only twice a year. When the wax builds up too much, remove with mineral spirits, then rewax.

11 Opaque Finishes

For the last 300 years, paint has been a normal finish on furniture of many periods and styles. Colonial American furniture was painted, if finished at all; Louis XV and XVI furniture was painted, as was Chinese Chippendale, and Sheraton, Windsor, and Hitchcock chairs. Contemporary furniture is painted.

Such furniture, if restored, should be repainted, rather than stripped to raw wood and given a clear finish completely out of keeping with the original appearance of the piece. There are other reasons for painting. Most of the unfinished furniture around is made of wood woefully lacking in figure or grain. It is made of mixtures of wood, or of particleboard or plywood which must be painted over so the appearance of the material cannot detract from the lines of the piece. And then there is older furniture, so worn or ugly in its original finish that painting can do nothing but improve the appearance or make the piece look better in contemporary surroundings.

You can do a lot in the line of painting furniture besides laying on a solid color. You can put a glaze over the paint and wipe it to accentuate the mouldings (if any), or "antique" the finish in any of several ways. Colorful designs can be stenciled.

11-1 ENAMELED FINISH

Furniture can be painted a solid color and left that way, or the solid color can be the base for a more sophisticated opaque finish. The paint to use in any event is alkyd resin-base enamel. This type of enamel comes in flat, semigloss, and gloss, and in a complete spectrum of colors. Many paint stores today are pushing latex paints rather than alkyd resin and other oil paints, and some have stopped carrying these superior paints all together. You may have to search around for a source of alkyd resin paint; don't believe store clerks who tell you that oil paints are not being made anymore, or that latex paint will be just as good.

Latex paints are not recommended for any furniture work. First, most go on by necessity in heavier coats, destroying any moulding detail present. The heavier coats are in part necessary for an opaque finish as the paints do not have the same hiding power as oil paints in coats of the same thickness. Latex paints also cannot be sanded and rubbed down to as smooth and even a finish as oil paints, and there can be serious adhesion problems, particularly over old finishes.

Enamel is a varnish with enough pigment added to produce an opaque coating. An *undercoater* is different from an enamel in that it contains less resin which enables better penetration of the wood fibers and pores for adhesion to the surface.

Procedure

The surface to be painted must be clean and free of defects—unless you want to see them when you are done, as in a distressed finish. New wood must be sanded smooth, the finish on old surfaces must be either removed, sanded, or repaired smooth. If the wood is open grained and you do not want the grain showing through the enamel, you will have to fill the wood.

All surfaces must be free of wax or dust. Wipe down with silicone wash or paint thinner. Minor defects in the surface are sometimes easier to repair after the first coat has been applied—you can see them better and you can then determine what will and will not fill up in the course of additional coats.

The first coat should be an undercoat, which can be a prepared undercoat or enamel thinned slightly. Thinned enamel is often more practical when you are working in a rich color as prepared undercoats are white and cannot be tinted to any great extent.

After the undercoat is dry, sand it. You are not sanding only for adhesion, but to level out any ripples and brush marks. How long you have to wait for it to dry depends on the product you are using, room temperature, and humidity. Dust the surface, wipe with a tack rag, and apply the first coat of enamel. Brush on a thin coat, preferably with a foam polybrush and be sure you have eliminated all sags. Plan on at least one additional coat of enamel, or as many as it takes to produce the smooth blemish-free surface you want, with careful and thorough sanding between coats.

The final coat can be rubbed down with pumice and water to produce a fine soft polished surface. Alternately, the final coat can be

FIGURE
11-1

Glazed finish picture frame made of 3" cove moulding, trimmed with half-round rope moulding.

sanded, and a finish coat of varnish can be brushed on and then rubbed down. Varnish to be put over white or other light colors should be tested first because most varnishes will give a definite yellowish cast to the finish.

Enamel finishes can be applied by brush or spraying.

11-2 GLAZED FINISH

The application of a glaze over an enamel finish can do much to enhance the overall appearance, particularly if the piece includes mouldings and carvings (see Fig. 11–1). Glazing is particularly attractive on white-painted French Provincial furniture.

Glaze in this case is a thin coat of paint applied evenly over the base enamel coat and wiped so that the base color shows through the glaze coat except in depressions in carvings, mouldings, and other indented surface trim. The glaze is evenly wiped from broad surfaces without any texture or pattern being obtained from the wiping cloth itself. The residual film of the glaze usually imparts a coloration to the base color.

Glaze colors are usually burnt umber, raw umber, or burnt sienna, depending on the base coat enamel color, but you can make a glaze of any color.

224

FIGURE
11-2

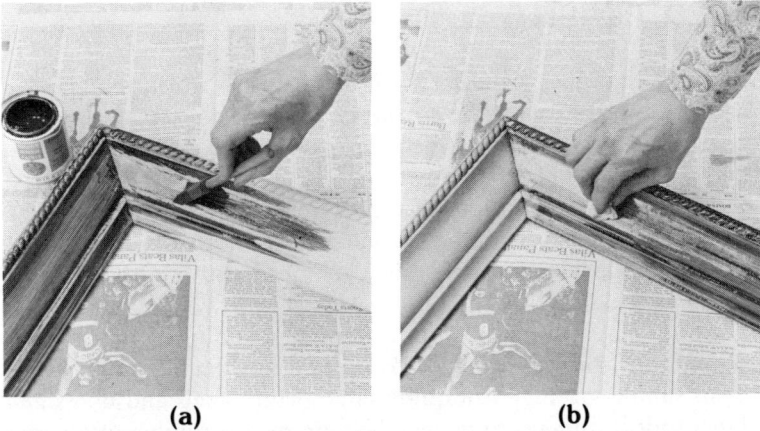

(a)   (b)

Glazing Procedure: (a) Glaze is applied over enamel undercoat. (b) Glaze is wiped off, leaving glaze in crevices and a glaze film on open surfaces. Glaze contributes shading to the end result, but no pattern of its own as in an antiqued finish.

For a glaze finish of this kind—one that is intended to accentuate mouldings, carvings, and so forth, it is very important that the surface be smooth and free of surface imperfections because every scratch and dent will be filled with glaze and accentuated. However, if the intent is a distressed finish, then this, of course, is desirable.

Procedure

The enamel base coat should be satin or semigloss, not gloss. It is not necessary to mix glazes yourself. The glazes used in antiquing kits can be separately purchased in 1/2 pint cans. The names of the colors on the cans may not be too informative as to the shade inside. You can also buy clear glaze liquid that you can tint any color you want with japan colors.

The glaze should be brushed on the work in a thin, but even, coat. (See Fig. 11-2.) Stretch the glaze as far as it will go. After a wait of about 15 minutes (read directions on the can), you can start wiping. Use lint-free cloths for wiping; do not use cheesecloth. Start wiping in the centers of areas you want glazed the least—areas that will be the lightest, such as the centers of panels. As you wipe, blend the glaze into an even coat without brush marks, shading from lightest in the center to dark near edges. Keep turning the cloth so you are wiping with a dry cloth. Leave glaze darkest in recesses in carvings and mouldings. Highlight the raised parts of carvings and mouldings by wiping harder. Wipe excess glaze from recesses and grooves with cotton swabs. Additional highlighting and shading can be done with grade 0000 steel wool after the glaze has dried.

The glazed surface should be given a protective varnish top coat.

Antiquing is a more elaborate form of glazing in which the glaze or glazes themselves contribute to the pattern of color on the surface. The pattern is controlled by the wiping technique and pad material. (See Fig. 11-3.)

The materials for antiqued finishes are packaged in kits consisting of an enamel base coat and one or more glazes, with a brush, and insufficient sandpaper and steel wool. You can also buy the enamels and glazes separately by the can.

Antiquing is easiest on furniture with mouldings, carvings, and grooves in the surface—the same kinds of pieces that lend themselves best to simple glazing. Antiquing large plain panels and doors and cabinet tops is difficult to do well because such antiquing often ends up just a color-streaky finish without particular charm. It is not easy to get a good woodgrain effect on large surfaces.

The dividing line between antiquing and woodgraining is more one of intent than anything. Really good woodgraining—the imitation of wood figure on a painted surface—requires special tools and techniques, and as a decorative art is seldom practised anymore. You can imitate wood grain in an antiqued finish effectively, but imitating the figure of a particular species is difficult.

**FIGURE
11-3**

Antiqued finish (particularly appropriate for French Louis XV and XVI furniture).

Procedure

Antiquing starts in exactly the same way as glazed finishing—enamel and brush out glaze, except that additional techniques are used in the wiping.

To simulate wood grain, drag a dry paper towel through the wet glaze, in the grain direction. Keep turning the towel over because it must be dragged dry. Rough in the grain pattern this way, then after the glaze is almost dry, start wiping with lint-free cloth. The pads must be dry. Start wiping lightly, then increase pressure as the glaze drys, blending the grain pattern.

Don't try to imitate the grain of any specific wood, but aim for a vague, subdued woodgrain effect. Have the grain run in directions appropriate to the construction of the piece. Don't do all the work from only one side because you will end up with a definite artificial direction in your wiping. Work from all sides.

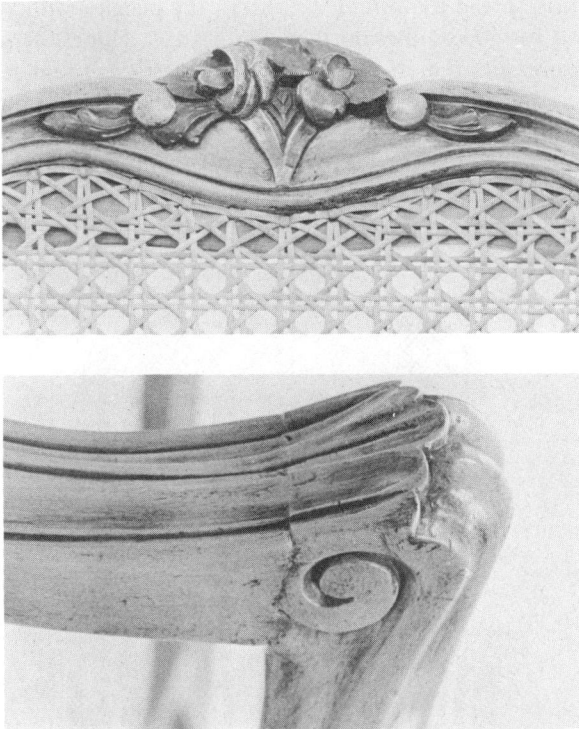

FIGURE 11-4

Details of Fig. 11-3. The base finish was an undercoat (two coats) of warm yellow flat oil-base enamel. Floral decorations were painted in bright colors. The whole chair was then glazed with thin burnt sienna japan color, and wiped. Japan color is hard to handle as a glaze, but produces excellent results. Chair was then given top coat of satin polyurethane varnish.

When the glaze is dry, repeat with the second glaze in the kit, if there is one. In woodgraining, the second glaze is usually more trouble than it is worth.

If, after the glaze is dry, you find it too dark, it can be lightened by careful working over with grade 0000 steel wool. This is difficult to do, however, without cutting through the glaze entirely and exposing bare base coat color.

Wipe with the same technique as used for padding lacquer. Never start the pad on the surface or lift it off the surface. Sweep on and sweep off.

A variety of texture patterns can be worked into the glazes. Grain lines can be emphasized by dry brushing. Pick up glaze on the tip of an otherwise dry brush and lightly brush the surface on the grain direction. Crumple aluminum foil or wrapping plastic; flatten it out and lay on wet glazes. Pounce the back side with your hand, keeping the pounced pattern random, then pick up the foil or plastic without dragging it across the surface. For a marbleized effect, crumple plastic as before and spread it on wet glaze. Twist the plastic around in spots. Press down for good adhesion in random areas. Hopefully you have trapped some air, too. Now pick up the plastic without dragging. Four hands are better for this step than two. You should have a fair semblance of marble.

Spatter glaze to distress the antiqued finish or enhance the marbling effect, but wait until the previous glazing is dry. You can also stipple a wet glaze finish, using a scrub brush or a piece of carpet.

FIGURE
11-5

Traditional chair stenciling in gold on black.

228

11-4 STENCILING

Stenciling is one of the easier ways to apply polychrome decoration to painted or clear finished furniture (see Fig. 11–5). Stenciling is appropriate if you have a repeating border design or must get the same design on several parts of the furniture; or if you can't draw a straight line free hand with a paintbrush.

You can make your own stencils, or you can buy stencil books containing patterns on stencil paper that you just have to cut out, or patterns on thinner paper that you must first transfer to stencil paper. (See Appendix.)

Materials and tools required for stenciling are shown in Figure 11–6.

Procedure

If you are making a stencil from your own design, the first step is to transfer the design to stencil paper, using carbon paper (see Fig. 11–7). Prepared stencil paper is oil-impregnated to make it tough and impervious to moisture. You can buy stencil paper at larger artist's supply stores or make you own from tan manila paper of the same weight as used in file folders. To make your own, brush both sides with a mixture of equal parts of boiled linseed oil and mineral spirits. After the paper is saturated, wipe off the excess and let the paper dry. Burn rags containing linseed oil immediately, store them under water or wash them out. Storing the oil-soaked rags any other way risks spontaneous combustion and a fire.

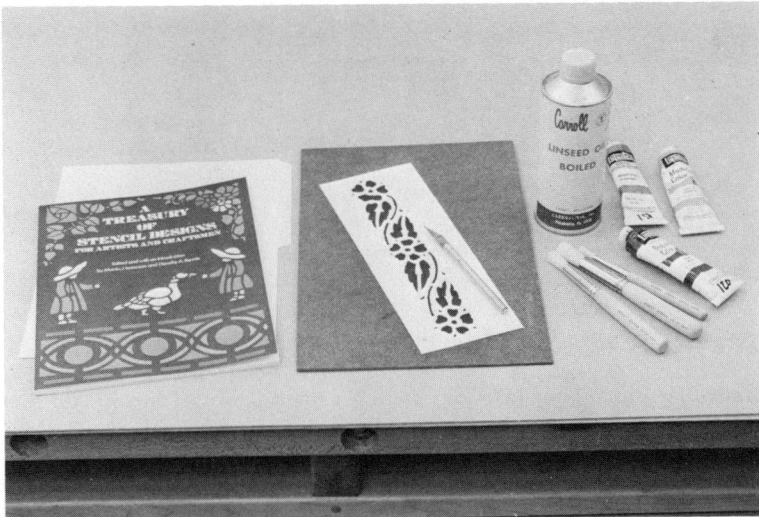

FIGURE 11-6

Stenciling tools and materials: Pattern book, manilla file folders for making stencils, hardboard cutting surface and sharp knife, linseed oil for treating stencil, paints and stencil brushes.

**FIGURE
11-7**

(a)   (b)

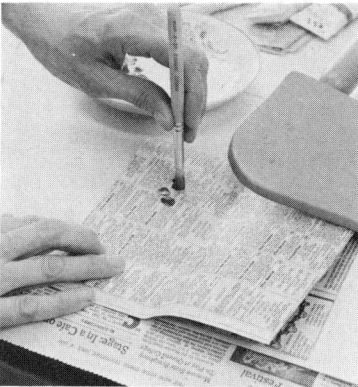

(c)   (d)

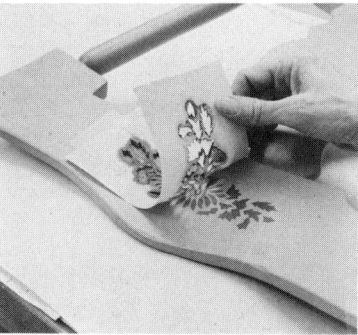

(e)   (f)

Stenciling procedure: (a) Coat stencil with mixture of linseed oil and
paint thinner to make the stencil impervious to moisture. (b) Cut out
stencil with sharp knife using tempered hardboard for backing. (c) Tape
stencil to piece. Take up paint on end of brush only, tap brush on paper
as shown to disperse paint evenly over entire end of stencil brush. (d)
Tap brush on work to apply paint. Paint must be quite dry to prevent
running under stencil. (e) Remove stencil as soon as possible. (f) Finished stencil decoration.

Stencils can be cut with a No. 11 X-acto knife or a stencil knife made for the purpose. It is important that the blade be kept sharp. Use the stone often. Any raggedness in the cutting will show up in the finished stencil work. Cut the stencil using tempered hardboard as a backing for a clean cut. Hardboard is better than glass (which is often recommended) because of improved blade life. Softwood, plywood, or newspaper is not firm enough. Take the small cuts out first, then the larger ones. Small circles are difficult to cut neatly. If you plan much stenciling, a set of leather-working drive punches might be a useful investment for making small round holes.

Paint used for stenciling should be relatively thick. For stenciling on furniture, alkyd enamels are recommended. Second choice would be acrylic water-based artists paint, for fast drying and ability to be mixed to a thick consistency.

The bristles of stencil brushes are held in a round ferrule and cut square across the ends, producing a flat circular working end. Brushes come in various sizes from 1/4'' up. If you are stenciling in more than one color, you will need a brush for each color.

Tape the stencil securely to the work. If more than one color is to be used, mask all cutouts except those to be printed in the first color with masking tape. Dip the flat end of the stencil brush in the paint just enough to pick up paint on the end of the brush *only*. Don't overload. Pounce the brush—tap the ends of the bristles—on newspaper to disperse the paint evenly throughout the end of the brush. When you can see that the paint is distributed evenly, stipple the openings in the stencil until they are completely covered. For additional colors, shift the masking tape over the just painted openings and stipple the next color, using a second brush, and so on. When the design is complete, remove the stencil, wipe off the excess paint and tape it down in the next location. When you are finished stenciling, clean out the brush and wipe the stencil clean for storage.

Appendix

Sources of finishing materials, veneer, hardwood, hardwood plywood, cabinet hardware, and upholstery supplies:

> Albert Constantine and Son, Inc.
> 2050 Eastchester Road
> Bronx, New York 10461
> Catalog 50¢

> Craftsman Wood Service Co.
> 2727 South Mary Street
> Chicago, Illinois 60608
> Catalog

> The Woodworkers Store
> 21801 Industrial Boulevard
> Rogers, Minnesota 55374
> Catalog

Source of professional finishing supplies and upholstery materials:

> Mohawk Finishing Products, Inc.
> Amsterdam, New York 12010
> Catalog, price list, full-color wall chart
> $4.00 ($2.00 refundable with order).

Sources of cabinet hardware:

> Ball and Ball
> 463 West Lincoln Highway
> Exton, Pennsylvania 19341
> > Catalog $4.00 (Reproduction American Hardware)
>
> Paxton Hardware Co.
> Upper Falls, Maryland 21156
> > Catalog $1.00 (Hardware, all periods, including Victorian)
>
> Smith Supply, Inc.
> 120 West Lancaster Avenue
> Ardmore, Pennsylvania 19003
> > Illustrated price lists $1.00 (refundable)
> > Cabinet Hardware, 50¢ (refundable) Wood Mouldings

Source of stencil patterns:

> Dover Publications, Inc.
> 180 Varick Street
> New York, New York 10014

Books on Furniture Periods, Styles and Construction:

Boger, Louise Ade, *Furniture Past & Present,* Garden City, N.Y.: Doubleday & Co., 1966.

Cescinsky, Herbert, and Hunter, George Leland, *English and American Furniture,* Garden City, N.Y.: Garden City Publishing Co., Inc., 1929.

Costantino, Ruth T., *How to Know French Antiques,* New York: Clarkson N. Potter, Inc., Publisher, 1961.

Gottshall, Franklin H., *Heirloom Furniture,* New York: Bonanza Books, 1957.

Gottshall, Franklin H., *Period Furniture Design and Construction,* New York: Bonanza Books, 1937.

Greenlaw, Barry A., *New England Furniture at Williamsburg,* Williamsburg, Va.: The Colonial Williamsburg Foundation, 1974.

Great Styles of Furniture, New York: The Viking Press, 1963.

Hinckley, F. Lewis, *A Directory of Antique Furniture,* New York: Bonanza Books, 1953.

Hinckley, F. Lewis, *Directory of the Historic Cabinet Woods,* New York: Crown Publishers, Inc., 1960.

Hummel, Charles F., *A Winterthur Guide to American Chippendale Furniture, Middle Atlantic and Southern Colonies,* New York: Crown Publishers, Inc., 1976.

Kates, George N., *Chinese Household Furniture,* New York: Dover Publications, Inc., 1948.

Koval, Ralph and Terry, *American Country Furniture 1780–1875,* New York: Crown Publishers, Inc., 1965.

Miller, Jr., Edgard G., *American Antique Furniture, A Book for Amateurs,* Vols. 1 & 2, New York: Dover Publications, Inc., 1966.

Montgomery, Charles F., *American Furniture: The Federal Period,* A Wintherthur Book, New York: The Viking Press, 1966.

Nutting, Wallace, *Furniture Treasury (Mostly of American Origin),* New York: The Macmillan Company, 1928.

Osburn, Burl, N., and Osburn, Bernice B., *Measured Drawings of Early American Furniture,* New York: Dover Publications, Inc., 1975.

Shea, John G., *The American Shakers and Their Furniture (with measured drawings of museum classics),* New York: Van Nostrand, 1971.

Shea, John G., *Antique Country Furniture of North America,* New York: Van Nostrand Reinhold Co., 1975.

Symonds, R. W., and Whineray, B. B., *Victorian Furniture,* London: Country Life Limited, 1962.

Index